# Ireland's Dream: A Romance Of The Future

Edmund David Lyon

# CONTENTS.

# IRELAND'S DREAM.

## PROLOGUE.

THE whole civilized world, after having calmly contemplated for years the unity of the British Isles, became suddenly horrified and amazed at the blackguard immorality of the Union, and at last, led by the great and glorious republic of America, who had only a few years before spent millions of almighty dollars and sacrificed thousands of precious lives to maintain her own union, cried, " Shame, shame!" and being moreover determined to make its voice heard, declared that an end must *at once* be put to so gross, so monstrous, so shameful an anomaly as forcing unhappy Ireland to remain an integral portion of the United Kingdom.  Then, by the universal acclamation of the whole of England, the Old Parliamentary Hand was placed at the helm, and the English people, satisfied that what the whole world said *must* be true, listened to the voice of the charmer, as Scotland and Wales had done years before. A general election took place. With scarcely a dissentient voice, members were returned pledged to support the Old Parliamentary Hand, who thus for the fifth time in his long life found himself at the head of a majority such as it has rarely been the luck of any minister even once to command.

Triumphant and radiant at thus being able to accomplish "his mission," the blackguard Act of Union was quickly torn up, two hundred and fifty millions of pounds sterling voted to buy out the Irish landlords, and, amid such ringing cheers as threatened to bring down the very roof, repeated again and again, the Old Parliamentary Hand announced to Parliament, and so to the whole civilized world, that *Ireland was at last free.*

One, two, three years passed. The Old Parliamentary Hand still commanded and steered the ship; but, alas! alas! what a change had come over the spirit of the dream! The noble vessel, which, when he first was called to the wheel, was flying before a fair wind, royals,

skysails, and stun'sails set, was now floundering
in a heavy sea, all her sails blown to ribbons,
her yards gone, two masts cut away and over
the side, the mainmast alone remaining. Still
the Old Parliamentary Hand stood at the helm,
smiling, contented, and perfectly happy, except
when any Randy or Smith dared to suggest
that the ship was going fast to the bottom.
Then his anger knew no bounds, and was
terrible to witness; nor could it be appeased
until, having chartered a train on some midland
line, he left London, having given orders to
stop at every station, when the people, forewarned of his intended visit, flocked to meet
him, and as he put his head out of the
carriage window, cheered him till they were
hoarse. Thus little by little his good-humour
was restored; and then having gone home, cut
down three or four tender young trees—typical,
no doubt, of his enemies whom he had defeated
—he would reappear once more in the House,
and announce, with a self-satisfied smile, that he
really could not permit himself to be badgered;
if members were not satisfied, they had only to
propose a vote of want of confidence, which, if
carried, would compel him to dissolve, as so

convinced was he of what the verdict of the country would be, that a general election, instead of having any terrors for him, was exactly what would give him the greatest pleasure.

Thus he remained in power, while every day the outlook for poor England abroad became worse and worse. France, who since the severance of the union of Great Britain had never ceased to press for the withdrawal of the English troops from Egypt, now insisted on the naming of a day for the complete evacuation of the country, while she herself was massing troops and transports at Toulon, and made no secret of her intention to seize the country and take possession of the canal as soon as the English were away.

Russia having lulled the English Government to sleep by numerous fair promises, lost no time in completing her railway to the borders of Afghanistan, and was literally pouring troops into that country, believing the moment had come when, by advancing two armies into India, she might drive the English into the sea. At the Cape of Good Hope the Boërs were openly defying the English, and made no secret of their intention of taking possession of the whole colony, and here also driving the unhappy English, should they attempt to interfere with them, into the sea. Such was the state of affairs abroad, while at home the horizon was not much brighter. At the time that Ireland had been declared free and independent, it had been arranged that in order to give the Irish Executive time to enrol a force of their own, for the first two years English troops should be lent to them, who should be available to keep the peace, protect life and property, and, if necessary, assist in the collection of the taxes which were to be paid to England as interest on the millions she had advanced to buy out the landlords. The Irish constabulary were to be disbanded at once, as also the coastguard, both being very expensive and no longer required.

The first year went by, but the Irish Government did not appear to be inclined to bestir themselves in organizing a force to keep order in the country, the fact being that the National League saw no need for such a body of men, and warned the Government that to enrol them would be a useless expense which would only lead to trouble and complications, the idea of which had therefore better be abandoned altogether. Thus a second year passed, and the time arrived for the withdrawal of the troops. Quite aware that no force existed in Ireland for any purpose whatever, the English Government made proposals to the Irish Executive as to the continuance of the troops in the country; but the latter, egged on by the National League, treated the proposal as a direct violation of the treaty, and demanded that the troops should be recalled immediately to England. A hint, however, having been thrown out that the interest on the two hundred and fifty millions was already in arrear, suggestions were made that the troops should remain, at any rate, until this was paid; but an insolent answer was returned, to the effect that if England was the first to show the example of setting aside the convention, the Government of that country could not blame the Irish Executive for doing the same, and, further, that no more interest would be paid until the terms of the convention were strictly adhered to. What the action of England might have been under ordinary circumstances it would be impossible to say; but the complications abroad were becoming so serious that every available regiment was wanted, and orders were therefore issued for the withdrawal of the troops as fast as transports could be taken up. There could be no doubt as to the sincerity of the English Government, but still excuse after excuse was made by Ireland, nor was any interest paid till only one regiment remained. Then the Old Parliamentary Hand came down to the House of Commons, and with a smiling face announced that he was happy to inform the House that the arrears of interest had been paid by Ireland to the very last farthing. He then launched into a long, rambling speech, of which no one exactly understood the purport, interlarded as it was with fulsome praise of the Irish people and nation, denouncing those who had ever for one moment dared to doubt their honour and trustworthiness. He went on to ask the House to show some consideration and pity for them, as they had had many difficulties to contend with, and could not be expected as a new Government to be able to manage matters as if they had always been an independent nation, and finishing up, as usual, by abuse of England, who alone, he declared, was responsible for all Ireland's shortcomings.

The House, as in duty bound, cheered the speech to the echo; but though by this time members ought to have been accustomed to the oratorical perorations of their pet minister, still there was a very large section who went home that night thoroughly dissatisfied at the speech to which they had listened; for, they argued, there must be something kept back, otherwise what was the necessity for all the excuses, unless to prepare the House and country for some revelation which was coming, and which would most certainly not be very palatable.

Their surmises turned out to be only too correct, for soon reports began to be circulated that the interest which had been paid by the Irish Government was only the arrears due up to the end of the second year, the fact being carefully kept back, that owing to the time occupied in negotiations, and then finding transports to move the troops, a third year was now nearly over; but the Irish Government had very coolly declared that as far as could be seen at present no money could be sent, as the peasant proprietors had one and all banded together and refused to pay a penny, and the Government was not in a position to oppose so powerful a combination, but hoped that in a short time the owners of the land would see the errors of their ways and listen to reason, when the interest should be at once forthcoming.

Questioned in Parliament as to the truth of these rumours, the Old Parliamentary Hand was forced to confess that substantially they were true, but implored the House to be reasonable and have patience, repeated the old arguments as to the English being really to blame, and so by a majority of forty on a division, it was decided to wait, and that no steps should at present be taken to enforce payment.

This was the state of affairs when the story opens.

# CHAPTER I.

## "MAYBE YOU'LL BE TOO LATE."

IT was a wild night. The moon, several days past the full, was high in the heavens, and large masses of cloud driven by the wind one moment obscured it, and the next being hurried on rapidly, allowed it again to shine forth. It was between one and two o'clock in the morning of May 1st, 18—, and the Irish mail steamer lay tumbling and rolling in the broken sea alongside the pier at Holyhead, waiting for the train already nearly an hour behind time. Presently the electric bell began to tinkle, and some one called out, "She's a-coming, Bill."

"The sooner the better," cried a surly voice from the steamer ; and in less than five minutes the bright light in front of the engine appeared in sight, as the engine itself, with three carriages behind it, winding round a sharp curve, ran down the pier, finally coming to a standstill exactly over the steamer.

Four passengers only alighted and hurried on board, three going below, while one remained on deck.   There were three mail-bags, half a dozen parcels, and about the same number of articles of passengers' luggage to put on board ; so that in less than five minutes from the arrival of the train, the hawsers had been cast off, and the steamer was on its way out of the harbour.

The passenger on deck, who remained standing beside the companion, seemed literally amazed at the whole proceeding, and involuntarily his thoughts went back to the last time— now nearly fifteen years ago—when he had crossed St. George's Channel, on which occasion there were, as he remembered, nearly a hundred passengers ; and notwithstanding the utmost exertions, nearly three-quarters of an hour were consumed in transferring the mails and luggage.

Presently a boy came along the deck and placed on a seat near him a filthy, dirty tin basin.   " Take that infernal thing away," cried the passenger, " or I'll pitch it overboard." The boy grinned, as, shrugging his shoulders, he again went forward.

They were entering the " race " now, and the steamer rolled terribly. She had been a good boat once, and done her sixteen or seventeen knots an hour, but was worn out now, as the skipper told the passenger, "and her boilers so shaky we daren't press her. However, we'll be there soon enough for the tide."

" Tide ! " echoed the passenger. " Surely you do not require to wait for the tide to get into Kingstown harbour ! "

" Kingstown ! " said the captain. " I thought every one knew by this time that no mail steamers are ever allowed to go there. Didn't Mr. Farrell get up in the Parliament and say that as the English steamers all go up the Thames to London, so the Irish steamers should go up the Liffey to Dublin ? and was he not cheered till the very roof shook over their heads, and the same day orders were given that no more steamers should either enter or leave Kingstown harbour ? They will find out their mistake some day ; that is, if the steamers don't give up running altogether, which seems likely enough." He walked away, and mounted the bridge, and the steamer creaked and groaned, rolled and tumbled, as she pursued her way.

They had a rough passage—a terrible and awful passage the poor sea-sick wretches below described it; but the passenger on deck had never known what it was to suffer at sea, and sat under shelter of the companion wondering, would daylight never come? for he longed for his first view of his native country as only those who have been absent for years from the land of their birth, and really love it, know how.

It came at last, that faint glimmer in the east; then the lifting as of a dark pall from off the steamer and surrounding sea. Soon every object became more and more distinctly visible on board, as well as the large crested waves rolling by; and there in the mist, on the port bow, was a long, low, grey line, unmistakably land, and equally certain to be the dear old country so truly loved by all her children, both sons and daughters.

As he stands with one hand holding on, in the other a pair of powerful binoculars, by the aid of which he was trying to make out more clearly the land in the fast-increasing light, let

us pause a moment to describe him.   His name
was John Cassidy, his age about thirty-five to
forty : a thick-set, powerful man about five feet
ten—not good-looking, but with an air of resolute determination about his face calculated to
command respect ; dark hair and eyes, a pleasant smile, showing a set of beautiful teeth.  He
was the youngest of ten children of a small
landed proprietor in the county Limerick.

Early in life he had fallen desperately in love
with a young girl named Norah Westropp, the
daughter of a tenant of a neighbouring estate—
a sweetly pretty girl of the true Irish type, but
without a penny in the world.  She was the
younger of the two by five years ; and when he
was twenty-three and she eighteen, it was generally supposed they were to be married ; but when
they met for their usual stroll on a never-to-be-
forgotten summer's evening, John Cassidy had
turned to his Norah and said, " We have loved
each other for some years, darling ; and that
any other girl will ever be to me what you have
been is no more likely than that any other man
will ever occupy my place in that warm heart
of yours.  That we are made for each other,
and must some day become man and wife, is as

sure as that there is a heaven above us. This
being so, we can afford to wait while I go forth
into the world and work to make some money
on which we can live, dearest; for to marry as
we are now would be simply madness." Norah
cried. She wound her pretty arms round his
neck, and whispered to him not to desert her,
but, wherever he went, to take her with him.
She tried all the sweet, persuasive ways that
Irish girls know so well how to employ, but
to no effect. John Cassidy was firm, and had
gone forth to win his wife before he would take
possession of her.

Fifteen years had passed since then, and
John Cassidy was now on his way home from
Australia, the land of his adoption, to claim his
bride and take her back with him to the New
Country. Fortune, the fickle dame, had smiled
on John Cassidy; and when at the end of the
previous year he had made up his accounts, he
had gone to bed that night with a bright, happy
smile on his face, for was he not the possessor of
a clear ten thousand pounds, and had he not a
right to go home and fetch his Norah?

As quickly as possible he arranged matters
for a six months' absence, and engaged a pas-

sage for England, one thing only marring the
delight he felt, namely, that though at first Norah
had sent him a letter occasionally, for nearly
two years now he had not received a line. He
had written to an old schoolfellow and friend
in Dublin asking for information, and in due
course had received a reply that his Norah was
said to be alive and well; nor had she, as far
as the friend could learn, as yet consoled herself in the arms of another husband. " But information is difficult to obtain now," he wrote;
"so the best thing you can do is to come home
yourself and marry her, and you'd better be
quick about it, or maybe you'll be too late."

# CHAPTER II.

## TOBY.

"KNOW the country, eh?" said a voice at Cassidy's elbow, as the latter was still standing, watching the land every minute becoming more distinct.

"Rather," replied Cassidy, as he took stock of the speaker, who was a queer little man in tight drab breeches and gaiters, cut-away coat, and grey waistcoat. He had a patch over one eye, but the other had a cunning look in it, and at times a merry twinkle which at once stamped the man as an oddity, but at the same time so cute that to hope to take in Toby, as he was always called, would necessitate getting up very early in the morning.

"Damned hole!" Toby next said; but seeing probably by Cassidy's face that he did not endorse this sentiment, he continued, "Don't agree, eh? Live here, I suppose?"

"Born here," said Cassidy, answering in the

same laconic style; " but been away for sixteen years."

" Where, eh ? " said Toby, cocking his one eye.

" Australia," was the reply.

" Fine country! splendid country! Often wish to go there myself; shall some day. Going back, of course ? "

" Yes," said Cassidy, smiling in spite of himself.

" The quicker the better," Toby went on. " Don't stay here. Damned hole! Going to the devil faster and faster every day. Married, I suppose ? every one is out there. Wife below, eh ? "

" No," said Cassidy, greatly amused at the man's odd manner. " I am a bachelor at present, but hope to take a wife back with me."

Toby gave a long, low whistle.

" The cat's out of the bag now," he cried. " Well, they are the only good things in this miserable country—the women and the horses. By God, sir! they are stunners both of them; but a man can only take one woman, and the difficulty is to choose where all are such clippers. A dozen times I have fancied I had found the cream of the cream, as Froggy says; but somehow I always discovered my mistake in time, and turned my attention to the horses, which are in every way more satisfactory. You see, you can buy a hundred of them if you like; and if one shows too much temper (I don't mind a little, you know), you can try gentle persuasion, and if that don't answer, send the four-legged beast off to auction, and let it go for what it will fetch; but you can't do either one or the other with the two-legged animal. I don't hold with beating a woman; and as to the auction, they have not got so far as that yet even here."

"Then it is to buy horses I conclude that you come to Ireland?" said Cassidy.

"That is about the truest thing you ever said in your life," replied Toby. "You have hit the right nail on the head this time, and no mistake."

"And you do a good business, I suppose," said Cassidy, "or you would never come to the 'damned hole,' which you seem to dislike so much?"

"As to the business," replied Toby—"ripping ;" and he winked his one eye, and made a peculiar movement of his right hand under the chin, which no doubt was very expressive to the initiated, but of whom, unfortunately, Cassidy was not one; " but as to disliking the country, there you are altogether wrong. I knew the old country many, many years ago, and got to love her then, and shall always continue to do so, even if she were the damnest hole in the universe ; and she is not that yet, though, unless things mend, she very soon will be."

" Is she so much altered, then, since I left ?" asked Cassidy, curious to see what the old fellow would say.

" Altered !" he exclaimed. " Is a man of ninety the same as he was at thirty-five ? Is a poor broken-down race-horse the same as he was at five years old, when he was in his prime? though Ireland has never been at her prime, and if allowed to continue to govern herself, never will be ; yet she could in proper hands become the finest country in the whole world, bar none."

The old fellow, when excited, dropped his queer, jerky manner of speaking, and the sub-

ject of Ireland was the one of all others which
he delighted to discuss.

"You have known the country a long time?"
said Cassidy, anxious to draw him out.

"Long before you were born, young man,"
was the reply. "I can remember the time
when 'dear, dirty Dublin,' as they used to call
it, was something like a city—when there used
to be people in the streets like London, and
shops, too, which were all open and full of
goods, lots of business doing, and there were
Pyms, and McSwineys, and Todd, and Burns,
just swarming like a hive of bees, and all the
grand houses in Merrion Square and Stephen's
Green full of the nobility and rich gentry.
Didn't I know them all? Haven't I sold them
horses again and again? Two hundred and
fifty and three hundred guineas they've given
me for a pair many and many a time; and
then there were the hotels all open, and full of
people too, doing a good business, and the balls
and the parties every night, and all the pretty
girls;" and again he winked his one eye and drew
his hand up under his chin as he continued,—

"There is nothing like the Irish beauties, the
darlings, in the whole wide world."

"And are they not the same now?" asked Cassidy; "but I suppose the gentry cannot afford to pay as much for the horses, that is what you mean."

Toby looked at Cassidy as if doubtful whether he were joking; and then, as he appeared to be in earnest, in a voice of commiseration, as if pitying his ignorance, he replied,—

"It would puzzle you to find the gentry—'the raal quality,' as you call them—there," jerking his head in the direction of Ireland. "There are the members of Parliament, of course," he continued, in a tone of contempt; "but they are not gentry, and as to money, they have hardly enough to buy themselves decent clothes in which to appear in the streets, let alone horses. No! I have not sold a horse in Dublin these three years—not since the repeal of the Union—and don't suppose I ever shall again."

"They buy cheap ones at Dycer's, I suppose," said Cassidy.

"What!" almost screamed Toby; and then calming down, he continued,—

"Young man, it is my opinion you are

chaffing me—taking a rise out of old Toby, eh ?"

" Upon my word I am not," replied Cassidy. " You forget it is sixteen years since I went away, and I am altogether ignorant of what has taken place since."

" Dycer has disappeared long ago. ' Toby,' he says to me the last time I saw him, ' Ireland is going to the devil fast, so I am off.' He had made his money years before, and only went on with the business because it brought him in with the lords and gentry; so when the quality departed, Dycer hooked it at once."

" But do you mean to tell me that there are no gentry left in Ireland at all ?" said Cassidy.

" Not one ! What would keep them in the country ?" asked Toby. " They got their money for their land, and so were not likely to stay where every one's hand was against them, where the very babies in arms, as soon as they could speak, were taught to curse them."

" And is it possible that all the millions which England paid to Ireland are gone out of the country ?" asked Cassidy.

" Of course it is," said Toby ; " not a penny

of it left.    Except in the North the country is
hopelessly bankrupt: no trade, no employment—
nothing.    The so-called Government make laws
and impose taxes; but people all laugh at them,
and well they may, for there is no one to enforce the one or collect the other.    The whole
thing from the very first was, and is, the greatest farce that ever was.    Imagine setting a lot
of bargees to drive a locomotive! well, it was
about the same as collecting the present Irish
Parliament together and expecting them to
govern this island, which perhaps of all places
on the face of the globe is the most difficult to
manage and keep straight.    No doubt they
mean well, and it is their misfortune rather
than their fault; but if the unhappy country
was to be governed by her own people, surely
it was the higher, the educated, and monied
classes who should have undertaken the task,
not the tag-rag and bob-tail of the population."

"Yes," said Cassidy, "that appears reasonable; but the people are, I suppose, contented,
and there seems little crime."

"Contented!" echoed Toby; "why, how
could they be otherwise?    They do exactly as
they like, pay neither rent nor taxes on the

land which they hold. Why, it is the very Eldorado for which they have all been sighing for so many years. But as to crime (at least, what I call crime, though I believe they do not), there is any amount of it, though it is kept out of the papers, because no one dare report it."

" I hardly understand you," said Cassidy. " Do you mean boycotting, which *you* call crime and they don't ? "

" Worse than that, though boycotting some-times is only another name for murder. No ! I allude first of all to the Land League, which at present is the only so-called authority in Ire-land, and which enforces instant obedience to its decrees by cruel assassination. No ques-tions are asked, no one is allowed to plead his cause : obey or die is the sole alternative given. Is that justice, liberty, freedom, about which you hear so many prate ? And this League exists throughout the whole length and breadth of the land, and the people allow it ; the Parlia-ment is afraid to meddle with it, and no won-der, when not a single minister even in Eng-land had the pluck to go to the root of the whole evil and stamp it out. And then the people themselves : I do not allude to the upper classes—they are gone—but the present inhabitants, the Irish of the present day. Now, don't get angry," observing Cassidy bristling up, "for, notwithstanding all their faults, I don't dislike the Irish—far from it, for there is a something about them that attracts me, even against my own better judgment ; but I cannot shut my eyes to the fact that they are, without exception, the laziest people in the world, utterly devoid of truth ; but that I can pardon them. I give them leave to take me in if they can, and always tell them so ; but what I can *never, never* forgive or tolerate, is their diabolical cruelty—the cool, systematic way in which they will proceed to torture a man's cattle because they may have a spite against the poor beast's owner. It makes my very blood boil to think of it, and the people were always the same too. I suppose you have read Froude ? No ! well, you should do so at once, and you will there see the barbarity that existed two hundred years ago, when, after having ravished the unhappy women, they stripped them stark naked, and turned them out into the cold to die ; and the men who did that called themselves Irish and human beings! Ah, bosh! But the worst of it is they are not a bit better now, but would do the same to-morrow if they only had the chance."

"How about the North?" inquired Cassidy. "Are they no better off there?"

"They are altogether a different race there, and if only let alone, would get on well enough; but, will you believe it? these asses are such infernal fools that they will never rest, now they have got rid of the English, till, as they suppose, they make the country too hot to hold the Orangemen, and they think that by this means they will be able to force the Orangemen to emigrate in a body. By God, sir, perhaps you never saw a poor benighted individual run his stick into a hornet's nest! Well, you can imagine, I dare say, what takes place, and that is precisely what will occur in the North; and I have warned them again and again, but they will not listen to me."

"You know the North well?" asked Cassidy.

"Not so well as I do the South," was the reply, "where I buy my horses. I used to bring the beasts up here, and embark them at once for Holyhead; but the last time I did this, they made me pay an export duty of ten per cent. on their value—not on what I pay for them, but on a fancy value of their own. Why, they pretended one animal I bought for ten pounds was worth fifty, and made me pay five pounds duty."

"But surely the export duties are the same everywhere! so what difference does it make whether you pay the duty there or here?"

Toby laughed, as with a wink of his one eye, he said,—

"Terence is an old friend of mine, and I go to him; he can generally manage to send my animals over for me, and what is still more extraordinary, he will not accept any remuneration. The last time, I asked him to accept a mare that was about as great a beauty as ever mortal set eyes on; but not a bit of it. He would buy her, he said, for he was rich and I was poor; so unless I would sell her, he would have nothing to say to her, though I could see his eyes sparkling as he looked at her. 'What is the price?' he asked; 'she's cheap at a hundred.' 'Forty pounds,' I replied. 'You are joking,' he said; 'you mean one hundred and forty, and I'll take her at that price.' 'No, you won't,' I answered; 'forty sovs is her price, and not a penny more will I accept.' 'Lead her away,' he said to the man who was holding her, though I could see it nearly broke his heart to say it. 'Let her be put on board with the others.' 'Look here, Mr. Terence,' says I, 'you may be a very rich man, and a very proud one, too; but for that very reason you ought to have some consideration for the pride of others. I should be glad if you would show me any reason why I should allow you to make me a present of a hundred pounds.' 'The mare is honestly worth the money,' he replied; 'and can you show me any reason why I should not give you her full value?' 'In London, yes,' I replied; 'here most unquestionably not; and she is a high-bred, fidgety beast, who might easily come to grief before she reaches London.' 'What did she cost you?' he next asked. 'Tell me the truth on your word of honour.' 'I will,' I replied. 'I paid twenty pounds for her, and say she cost me five pounds to bring her here, which she did not, surely fifteen pounds is a good profit.' 'And it is the plain truth you are telling me?' he continued. 'It is, indeed,'

I said. 'Then I'll take her,' he said, evidently much pleased."

While Toby had been speaking, Cassidy had been in deep thought, and now said,—

"Who is your friend Terence? What is his other name?"

"Terence O'Grady," was the reply. "Why, he is almost as well known as the Queen of England. You must have been out of the world if you have not heard of *him*."

Before Mr. Cassidy could say another word, he received a violent poke in the ribs from Toby, who at the same moment, with a mysterious wink of his one eye and a jerk of his head backwards, placed the forefinger of his right hand on his lips, as if to indicate silence.

Turning to see the cause of all these signs, Cassidy perceived that the other passengers from below had now appeared on deck—the sea being now comparatively smooth—and were standing so that they could overhear every word that was spoken. They were both of the male sex, but by no means prepossessing, nor, to judge from their dress, very flush of cash.

Searching in his breast-pocket, from among a multitude of other papers, Toby at last produced a card, saying almost in a whisper, as he handed it to Cassidy, —

"That is where I am to be found when in Dublin. Not half a bad billet. Come and look me up; always glad to see you; a hearty welcome and plenty of liquor—the raal stuff, you know. Not another word here; bad lot. Good-bye!" and with a hearty grip of Cassidy's hand, the funny little fellow walked away along the deck, never again noticing any one as long as they remained on board.

# CHAPTER III.

## MONSTROUS!

IT was past nine before the steamer was off the mouth of the Liffey. The day was fine, the sun, like the moon of the night before, going in and out by fits and starts. The ball, indicating that there was sufficient water over the bar, had just been hoisted, and so the skipper continued his course, but going at half-speed only.

There was only just enough water, their track being plainly marked by the mud stirred up by the screw. Their speed up the river was great, the tide carrying them along rapidly. A berth had been reserved for them just opposite the Custom House, and they hauled into it with little trouble. As they made fast fore and aft to the quay, a faint cheer attracted Cassidy's attention, and looking in the direction whence it proceeded, he observed a very fine steamer casting off from the shore, and the scarlet colour lining her deck showed that she was full of troops.

A couple of planks having been run out to the steamer, the four passengers were invited to land; and Cassidy, carrying in his hand a bundle of wraps, a hat-box, a small black bag, and his umbrella, followed the other three on shore; but though they at once walked up the quay townwards, Cassidy was led off to the Custom House, at the door of which the several articles he carried in his hand were taken from him.

He was now shown into a waiting-room, where, after about a quarter of an hour's detention, a side door was opened, and he entered a large hall, at one end of which, on a sort of shop-counter running the whole length of the building, were his two portmanteaus, tin trunk, lady's bonnet-box, and another good-sized box, marked "cabin," as well as the things taken from him at the door.

Cassidy had spent three whole days in London, which he had devoted to procuring for himself a new outfit. Two new suits of tweed, a frock-coat, and morning and evening dress-suit, had he bought from a fashionable tailor;

and then going to the stores, new underclothing had been chosen, and safely packed in a portmanteau, bought expressly for them.   Nor had he forgotten Norah, but was bringing her a present of several new silks for dresses, a couple of fashionable bonnets, a lace shawl, a couple of dozen pairs of gloves, besides other knick-knacks, suitable, as he said to himself, to the wife of a man with ten thousand pounds of his own.

As at the order of the official (there was only one) Cassidy unlocked his portmanteaus, etc., etc., the eyes of the man seemed literally to *gloat* over so rich a haul ; but Cassidy himself, remembering to have read somewhere that the police had now orders to examine all passengers' luggage for dynamite, concluded that such was the present object of the search, and cheerfully aided in emptying each case of its contents, and replacing them afterwards.   This having been done, he said to the officer,—

" Please call a porter to put these things on a car."

But the man, who was just then engaged in a long sum of compound addition, held up his hand, and a minute after said to Cassidy,—

"Twenty-two pounds eighteen shillings and twopence, please, sir."

Cassidy stared; he failed to understand the officer's meaning. It never entered his thoughts that there could be any duty on English goods which were being brought by a passenger into Ireland.

"Can I not go now?" inquired Cassidy.

"Certainly," replied the officer. "You will, I suppose, call later and clear your luggage. If you will name the hour, I will be here myself, which will save you much trouble."

"Can I not take my luggage with me now?" asked Cassidy.

"Certainly, if you will pay the duty."

"Duty!" exclaimed Cassidy; "duty on what? Every single thing, except that one box marked 'cabin,' did I buy in London only a couple of days ago."

The officer's attention thus called to the two portmanteaus, trunk, bonnet-box, etc., which he had previously overlooked, and perceiving they were all quite new, he took up his pen and made another entry in the paper he held in his hand.

"I beg your pardon, sir," he said, now offering the document to Cassidy. "I had over-looked the fact that the portmanteaus and other things were new. The amount now is twenty-five pounds three and sixpence."

"But the things are all English, I tell you," cried Cassidy, who, though as a rule very quiet and not given to many words, could on occasion get very angry and speak his mind as well as any man. "I can show you the bills of the several places where they were purchased."

"It is precisely because they *are* English that my instructions are to charge the full sum. Had they been French or German, then I could have allowed you a reduction of twenty per cent."

"I never heard of anything so monstrous," exclaimed Cassidy. Then, after a moment's consideration, he went on : "I shall only be in Ireland a fortnight or three weeks, so I will leave all these things here, and only take this one portmanteau with me."

The officer shook his head as he replied,—

"It is too late to do that now, sir. Had you delivered any of the cases into bond at first, it would, of course, have been easy to have left them here ; but now, as they are entered in our books, you can only clear them all or none."

Grumbling to himself at such extortion, as he called it, Mr. Cassidy paid the money, handing to the officer twenty-six sovereigns, and receiving as change some of the dirtiest paper notes imaginable. A porter being called, the luggage was put on to a car, and Cassidy himself was about to mount, when, perceiving how dirty and greasy were the cushions, he spread his own rug on them for fear they would spoil his clothes. He told the driver to take him to the Shelborne Hotel in Stephen's Green; but when the poor, miserable horse had reached the spot where O'Connell's Bridge spans the river, the beast obstinately refused to cross, and so Cassidy, telling the man to drive him to " The Imperial," the animal's head was turned up Sackville Street, and at a pace considerably slower than a man's walk, they proceeded towards their destination.

The state of the street itself was a curiosity, —for as the car proceeded, it soon became evident that what appeared to be a smooth, level road was in reality nothing but an immense pool or puddle of liquid slush, reaching up to the horse's fetlocks, which made it quite impossible to see the many holes and ruts with which the roadway was interspersed, and into which first one wheel, then the other, of the unhappy car kept plunging, until it seemed marvellous how any springs could stand it.

# CHAPTER IV.

## THE PARLIAMENT IN COLLEGE GREEN.

NOTWITHSTANDING the discomfort and jolting he was undergoing, Cassidy noticed, as the car crawled along, that the streets were almost empty of people; and even the few who occasionally appeared seemed to have nothing to do but stop and talk with every second person they met. This struck him the more after London, where he had passed the three previous days, and where, though the streets were crowded, every one seemed in far too great a hurry to stop to exchange a single word, a quick nod in passing being apparently deemed sufficient. But in the shops there was an even more remarkable difference between the two cities,—in London every shop being open, and the windows dressed, thus imparting to the street a gay and lively appearance; while in Sackville Street quite two-thirds of the shops had their shutters up, and those which had not were so dingy and dirty as to give them the appearance of not having had their windows touched for months.

Arrived at last opposite the hotel, a porter appeared, who proceeded to carry the luggage upstairs, while Cassidy, taking a shilling out of his pocket, handed it to the driver, who, after examining it as if he had never seen such a thing before, handed it back with a shake of his dirty head. Supposing he wanted more, Cassidy now offered a florin, but with a like result, when the hotel porter explained that it was paper money which the man wanted, silver having long ceased to be current in Dublin.

Telling the porter to settle with him, Cassidy went upstairs and asked for a room, when, the landlord coming forward, took him into the bureau, and, producing a printed paper, informed him that it must be filled up and sent to the Strangers' Office before he dare receive him into his hotel.

Since he had been swindled out of his money at the Custom House, nothing seemed to surprise Cassidy, and so he consented to fill up this most inquisitorial return, in which he not only gave his name, age, place of birth, and how long he had been absent from Ireland, but also his object in returning, whither he was bound, and for how many days he requested permission to remain in Dublin.

While this paper was being despatched to the office, and the answer awaited, Cassidy was shown into the coffee-room, which was crowded with gentlemen, all eagerly engaged in discussing some momentous question, though what it was Cassidy neither knew nor cared. It being already past one o'clock, he ordered some food to be served at once, and stood drumming on the panes, while he looked out of the window into the street, watching the few miserable vehicles crawling through the slush. Never, perhaps, in the whole of his life had John Cassidy felt so utterly wretched as at that moment, and resolutely was he forced to keep his thoughts fixed on his darling Norah, whom he had come so far to fetch, to prevent him starting off back again to England by the very first steamer.

Tired of inspecting the dreary street, Cassidy

sat down at the table which had been prepared for his meal, and calling the waiter, told him to bring a Bradshaw. Not understanding what was wanted, the man laid a newspaper on the table; and a few minutes after, the soup being brought, Cassidy, who was very hungry, was engaged in partaking of it, when he observed a gentleman, who had entered the coffee-room a moment before, coming straight towards him with outstretched hand. Cassidy rose from his seat, and, as their hands met, the two gentlemen stood contemplating each other, noting the changes that fifteen years had wrought in each.

That they were both glad to meet again there could be no doubt, for with the impulsiveness of their country they could not hide their feelings; but of the two, Cassidy was far the most changed, and of this he was fully aware. Even in their very demeanour this was apparent; for while Cassidy was quiet, grave, and even sad, his friend was loud, boisterous, and gushing, apparently in the very height of spirits and delight.

"Sure, it's a sight for sore eyes you are, John," said the new-comer, as, unclasping their hands, both seated themselves. "When did you arrive?"

"This morning only; and somehow I seem to have come to the wrong place. It is not like the ould country at all."

"True for you!" replied his friend. "Never perhaps in this world has any country improved so much in so short a time, not even excepting Australia."

Cassidy smiled as he thought to himself if his friend only knew Australia, and had ever been there, he would not have made such a remark.

"Shaugh! Shaugh! come here a minute; we want you," was now called out from a table near; and Cassidy's friend, rising, answered the summons.

His real name was O'Shaughnessy, but it had been abbreviated to Shaugh by every one to such an extent that even notes were often addressed to him by the shorter name. He was a man of about the same age as his friend Cassidy, but in every other respect totally un-like him,—very tall and thin, a long neck, supporting a fine head covered with curly hair, a very bright and intelligent face, always laughing, gay, and *insouciant*—a thorough Irishman, living for and enjoying the present, without a thought for the morrow. He had been called to the bar, and was said to have now a large practice,—in fact, was considered one of the most rising men of his day, being an universal favourite with every one. He had, at the last election, put himself up as a candidate for the county Dublin, and having been elected by a large majority, it was to his parliamentary life that he now chiefly devoted himself, work in the law courts being by no means brisk at present.

Such was the man who, a few minutes after, again seated himself at Cassidy's table, saying as he did so,—

"You must come and dine with us at six sharp, and I'll take you down to the House afterwards. There will be a great debate to-night."

"What about?" asked Cassidy. "I hardly got a wink of sleep last night, so shall be pretty tired after dinner."

"Go and lie down for an hour or two now," replied his friend. "The Prime Minister is to close the debate on the land question. It will be the finest speech that you have ever heard, or are ever likely to hear, in your life, John, and something to talk about when you go back to those foreign parts. It would never do to miss it."

Very little more passed between them. Shaugh was again called away to another table, and Cassidy having finished his lunch, took his friend's advice, and, on being shown to his room, lay down on the bed, and slept soundly for several hours.

Punctual to the minute, Cassidy ascended the stairs of Mr. O'Shaughnessy's house in Dame Street, and, on being shown into the drawing-room, was welcomed by that gentleman and introduced to his two sisters, who kept house for him, the younger of whom was justly considered the belle of Dublin, and a more lovely or more aristocratic-looking girl it would be difficult to find in all Europe ; while the elder, nearly ten years her senior, was a fine, handsome woman, fit to adorn any man's table as its mistress; and why she had remained so long single was a puzzle to every one.

Dinner was announced almost immediately.

There were no other guests, and they sat down at once—a very pleasant, cosy party, fully determined to do justice to a most excellent dinner, though the attendance was very bad, the fact being, as Mr. O'Shaughnessy told his friend, that it seemed impossible to get a servant in all Dublin who knew how to wait at table. Where they had all gone, no one knew; but it was certain there were none to be had for love or money.

The conversation turned chiefly on Australia, the ladies being most anxious to hear all particulars connected with that vast country, while Mr. O'Shaughnessy did nothing but draw comparisons between it and Ireland, which somehow or other he always twisted so as to be greatly in favour of the latter. This for awhile amused Cassidy much; but after a short time he turned to his friend, saying, in the quietest and gravest manner,—

"When you left Melbourne, Shaugh, had they finished that new street leading to the landing-place?"

"Very nearly," was the reply. "They expected to open it in about another month, they told me."

"Do you remember what name they had given it?"

"No. They wanted to call it after me— O'Shaughnessy Street—but I begged them not; and, after some trouble, I persuaded them to give up the idea, which, considering I had little or nothing to say to the place, was really too absurd."

Both ladies stared at their brother as if they could hardly believe their ears; then catching the merry twinkle in his eye, they went off into a fit of laughter.

"Don't mind him, Mr. Cassidy," they cried; "it's fooling you he is. Sure he never set foot out of Ireland in his life. What made you suppose he'd been in Australia?"

"Isn't he after telling you he saw me there?" cried Shaugh, before Cassidy could reply.

It was the turn of the latter to stare now. "I said I saw you in Australia, Shaugh? I appeal to Miss Grace if I ever made such an extraordinary assertion."

"Well, if you did not say it, you inferred it, which is the same thing. The words you used were, 'When you left Melbourne.' Now for me to have left Melbourne, I most certainly must

have been there ; and what's more, you must
have known that I had been there, and how
else could you do that but by seeing me there
yourself?   Now that's what we lawyers call
a *sequitur;* so that point being satisfactorily
settled, let us be off."

They rose, and Cassidy having shaken hands
with the ladies and wished them good-night,
the two friends strolled arm-in-arm down Dame
Street towards College Green.   There was a
great crowd assembled outside " the House";
but as the members were recognised, a path
was made for them after some trouble, and
thus at last Shaugh and his friend reached the
building, and entered the large hall where the
Parliament sat.   It was early yet, and so Shaugh
was lucky enough to find a seat under one of
the galleries for Cassidy, who would thus be
able to see and hear all that passed.   But he
had more than an hour to wait—it was not yet
eight o'clock, and as the Prime Minister and
other members of the Government were din-
ing at a grand banquet given by the Lord
Mayor, it was not expected that business
would commence much before nine.

Still feeling very tired, and having had an

excellent dinner, Cassidy, left to himself, dozed gradually off to sleep, and never woke till a wild noise, half-yell half-roar, outside the building, made him spring from his seat. For a moment he could not remember where he was; but as he rubbed his eyes and saw a continuous stream of human beings pouring into the hall, he realized the situation, and doubted not that the great man and his myrmidons had come, and would soon take their places. Looking round, Cassidy now observed how full the whole room seemed to be, and yet still a struggling, swearing, pushing, but nevertheless laughing mass kept pouring in and found places somewhere.

At last it ceased; every bench was full; the ministers were all in their allotted places, and Opposition also; the mace on the table; the Speaker, clerks, etc., etc., all there. One seat remained empty, and every one waited in breathless expectation for him who was to fill it. Presently a door opened behind the Speaker's chair, and a small, active, wiry man entered. Every eye was fixed on him; the whole House was waiting to give him a most enthusiastic reception, but paused wonderingly and astonished, for their idol was dressed in his usual black evening suit and waistcoat, *but had no coat on.*

What could it mean ? Was it possible that the Lord Mayor's champagne had proved too irresistible and too strong ? Hardly likely, for the great man was known to be particularly abstemious. In a silence so intense that a lady's dress in one of the galleries could be heard to rustle, he came forward till he reached the place reserved for him to the left of the Speaker's chair. Here he stood still while he calmly surveyed the House from end to end, and then, raising his eyes, inspected the galleries also. He evidently knew that every eye was fixed on him, and smiled complacently, as if much pleased that it should be so.

At last his clear, sonorous voice broke the silence which was fast becoming oppressive.

" Mr. Speaker," he said, " it is many, very many years ago now when we sat in another House in a foreign land, that members were fond of throwing in my teeth a remark I once made that I had taken off my coat and did not intend to put it on again till Ireland, our loved country, was free. It is my proud privilege to announce to you to-night that such is now the case, for did not the last, the very last, of the foreign troops leave our shores this morning? The whole object and aim of my hard work being thus accomplished, therefore I put on my coat."

And suiting the action to the word, he took his coat, which, unperceived, had been lying beside his seat, and in the presence of them all, put in first one arm, then the other, and as soon as it was really in its place, sat down.

The scene which now ensued defies all description. There was first a roar of laughter, then a wild shout of triumphant delight as every member rose and began to demonstrate his joy. Hats were thrown into the air, while cheer after cheer ringing through the building were taken up by those outside, and thence by those in the streets, who cheered because others did so, but without the least knowing why. Great big stalwart men hugged and embraced each other like a lot of school-girls; while others, sticking their arms akimbo, began to foot a jig on the floor of the House.

Both Speaker and Prime Minister evidently enjoyed the scene, for they both laughed heartily, till suddenly there was a rush of members towards the latter, who, despite his protestations, was seized, hoisted aloft on their shoulders, and thus borne round the House, the cheering being renewed again and again.

From sheer exhaustion of all concerned, the turmoil ended at last, and the Speaker was enabled to restore order so that business might begin; and when silence was once more established, he called on the member for Tyrone, who was first on the list, to put his question.

He rose at once, and asked whether, having had due notice, the Home Secretary was in a position to give him any information about a dastardly outrage which had been committed on a cousin of his, a Mr. Mullany, at a place called Balla in County Mayo?

"From inquiries made," the Home Secretary replied, "it appears that this Mr. Mullany is a Protestant, who inherited through his wife the property on which he now resides. Having thought proper to import several Protestant servants, as well as farm-labourers, into the district, he duly received warning that such was contrary to the unwritten law of the land, and could not be permitted; he was therefore given sufficient time—a month, I believe—to send the strangers about their business, and provide himself with servants and labourers from the neighbourhood; but he thought proper to disregard the notice, and retained the strangers in his employ.

"In due course he was informed that it was considered desirable that he should quit the district, as not only had he acted as already stated, but had on a certain occasion insulted the parish priest, who, being in a hurry, was urging his horse rather fast over a portion of the road which had been newly repaired, when Mr. Mullany had shouted out, 'Easy over the stones,' thereby causing several persons present to laugh, thus turning his reverence into ridicule.

"The property of Mr. Mullany being an exceedingly good one, there had been no difficulty in finding a purchaser, who, having taken a fancy to the place, was kind enough to offer several pounds more than the land was worth at its present valuation; but Mr. Mullany altogether declined to listen to reason, and declared he had no intention of selling his property.

"Thus it became necessary to resort to extreme measures, and a party of four men had entered his house in the middle of the night, and having made Mr. Mullany get out of his bed, had forced him to go down on his knees and swear to clear out of the farm in fifteen days. The conduct of these men had been most exemplary, as their mission being accomplished, they had retired without touching or damaging anything in the house.

"It was true Mrs. Mullany had received a shock from fright, from which she was still suffering; but had she wisely persuaded her husband to be reasonable and give up his farm when requested to do so, there would have been no cause for interference. She had, therefore, clearly no one but herself to blame in the matter."

Hardly had the Home Secretary finished speaking than the member for Tyrone began an indignant protest, but he was instantly called to order.

The second question was also addressed to the Home Secretary, and was put by the member for Londonderry. It had reference to a report which had been circulating as to the

murder of a farmer, his wife, and three small
children, in County Galway, and information
was now asked as to its truth. In reply, the
minister said,—

" This miserable affair arose out of a family
quarrel, which always have and always must
occur in every community, and which are unquestionably much better settled without any
interference from the Government. I will, in
as few words as possible, state to the House all
we know on the subject. An old man named
Tierney had two sons, the elder, Mick, being
unmarried ; but the younger, Tim, having
married, had with his three children, since
the death of the old woman their mother,
resided with and kept house for their father,
the elder, a cattle-drover, living chiefly in
this city. Three months ago the father died,
leaving a document described as an informal
will, under which Tim claimed the house and
property ; and possession being already his,
held it against all comers. Mick, however,
waited his opportunity, and having bribed three
or four resolute boys to assist him, watched his
brother one Sunday morning ride off to chapel,
and then hurried up to the house to seize it.

They never counted, however, on Tim's wife,
who, seeing them coming, and being a determined woman, barricaded the door and
positively declined to open it.

" Not wishing to make a noise on Sunday,
one of the party proposed to smoke her out,
and accordingly they made up a devil, composed of wet gunpowder, saltpetre, and other
ingredients, which, having lighted, they introduced into the room.   They still failed to get
admittance, and ultimately made off, intending
to return the following Sunday.

" On Tim's arrival from chapel he found the
house still barricaded, and was obliged to force
an entrance, when he found his wife and
children quite dead from suffocation.  Suspect-
ing the truth, he started in pursuit, and being
on horseback, soon overtook his brother, who
was on foot.  A fair fight ensued, when Mick,
who is represented as a very powerful man,
easily conquered his brother, and the property
is now in the possession of its rightful owner."

The member for Londonderry asked whether
the Government intended to take any further
action in the matter, but was called to order,
and informed that the question was answered,

and if any further information was needed, he must move a resolution.

The next question had reference to boycotting, which the member for Westmeath declared to be alarmingly on the increase, and must be put down, when the Home Secretary, in reply, said,—

"There are no less than fourteen questions on the paper relative to this subject, and one answer will be probably sufficient as a reply to all; but as there may be individual cases alluded to in the other questions, I propose, with the permission of the House, to defer my reply for the present."

Then a Major O'Flaherty—a very stout, large man—rose, and, evidently in a most excited state, began,—

"This, sir, is the fourth time I have been obliged to allude to the subject of Mrs. Kelly; and if the Government delay any longer to take action in this matter, I am damned if I don't do it myself (cries of Order, order—Hear, hear). The case has been so recently brought before the House that it is not necessary I should go into particulars, so will merely state——" Here the honourable member was interrupted by the Speaker, and reminded that he was not called on to make a statement, but as briefly as possible to put his question ; when the Major exclaimed sulkily, "What are the Government going to do in this matter?" But the Speaker again interfered, to point out that it was necessary to describe the matter in which the Government were asked to take action.

For a moment the Major seemed inclined to walk out of the House; but, recovering himself, began in the strongest brogue—" For the fourth time, as I said before, I rise to bring the case of that accursed she-devil, Mrs. Kelly, to the notice of this House. For the fourth time I state that this damned old woman, having been boycotted as she richly deserved, set to work to fortify her house, and build round it a high wall, loopholed for shooting. This she did by means of a band of accursed Orangemen, who came by train and marched over from the station in the middle of the night.

" When the wall was up, which was completed in a wonderfully short space of time, the neighbours came to consult me as to what was to be done. I was informed there were supposed to be altogether between forty and fifty of the damned heretics, and as they had brought very little with them, it was clear there could be only food for a short time in the house, so I advised that the place should be rigorously watched, and care taken that no food was surreptitiously carried in. It was about a week later that I heard that the damned old hag had sallied out at the head of her people, had attacked the mill, and using the miller's own horses and carts, had conveyed a quantity of flour to their own house; she had also seized about forty cattle belonging to a farmer in the adjoining parish. This state of things has now gone on for four months, and the Government allows the people to be thus openly defied and robbed by an old devil of a woman who, mounted like a man on horseback, rides forth at the head of her rabble, and has succeeded in terrifying the poor, quiet, harmless people to such an extent that they fly to hide themselves the moment they hear she is coming. It is too scandalous that such a state of things should be allowed to exist for a moment, and for the fourth time I ask the Government when it is to be put down." There was great applause from the Opposition at the end of this speech; and when this had subsided, the Prime Minister himself replied, —

"The Government are quite aware of the state of things referred to by the gallant Major, the member for Tipperary, and are even now taking steps to deal with this Mrs. Kelly; but there is one point which the gallant Major has strangely overlooked in the very clear and interesting statement he has just made to the House, and that is, he has forgotten to inform the House that Mrs. Kelly was a quiet, inoffensive lady till the people, for some reason best known to themselves, thought proper to boycott her; they have therefore, to a great measure, brought her treatment of them on themselves. At the same time it is the intention of the Government to put down such open defiance of the law, and a special envoy will be sent down to Mrs. Kelly to-morrow to inform her of the fact."

Again the Major sprang to his feet, declaring he would not allow it to be said that Mrs. Kelly was "a quiet and inoffensive lady"; and though called to order again and again by the

Speaker, he would not resume his seat ; but, drawing a revolver from his pocket, swore he would shoot the first man who dared to interfere with him and his liberty of speech and action. As the Major was well known to be a man who invariably kept his word, it was thought more prudent to move the adjournment of the House, which was done by the Prime Minister, the whole of his followers, to the number of one hundred and fifty, rising instantly in their places. But by this time several of those who had questions on the paper had got round the Major and persuaded him to listen to reason ; so a compromise was effected, the motion for adjournment withdrawn by the Prime Minister, also the epithets " quiet and inoffensive " as applied to Mrs. Kelly; and the Major having been permitted to state that Mrs. Kelly's cruel treatment of the poor was the cause of her being boycotted, the business of the House was resumed.

The member for Limerick county, a Mr. Joseph Gilly, next rose. He stated that he had drawn a considerable income, sometimes over five hundred a year, from the salmon-fishing at Castle Connell, which belonged to him; but that last season gangs of roughs from Limerick had come out and poached the water, netting it by day and spearing the fish by night; and though repeatedly requested to desist, had declined to do so, but in the most impudent and determined manner continued their lawless occupation before the very eyes of his own caretaker and the river conservators, the consequence being that no one would rent the fishing. The property was heavily taxed, and he wished to ask the Home Secretary how it was possible to pay this money when the source from which he drew the income was cut off, nor was it fair to expect taxes to be paid unless, in return, protection were afforded to the property.

In reply, the Home Secretary spoke as follows :—

"From inquiries which the Government had caused to be made, it appeared that Mr. Gilly only kept one old man to look after the whole of the Castle Connell water; and though, as he had himself informed the House, he often drew as much as five hundred a year from the fishing, not one penny of this money was spent in giving employment to the people.

Until the honourable member was prepared to take proper measures for the protection of his own property, he need expect no assistance from the Government."

The next question was put by Mr. Sealy, the member for South Cork, who asked whether the attention of the Government had been directed to the very heavy drain on the country caused by emigration? and that, unfortunately, it was precisely the very best class—he might say the very backbone of the country—who were realizing their property and crossing the water, as was evidenced by the fact that every mail steamer was crowded with people, so that it was hardly possible to get standing room on board. The honourable member further asked whether it was true that it was proposed to start a second daily mail steamer from Dublin to Holyhead for the accommodation of the crowd of passengers.

In reply, the Prime Minister said,—

"It is true that a proposition has been made to us to allow a second mail steamer to be despatched daily from our shores, to which we gave at once a most emphatic refusal. It is a source of great pain and astonishment to the

Government to observe the tide of emigration setting steadily outwards; and as the Government have done all in their power to give full liberty to all persons, both collectively and individually, and to govern the country in the freest and best manner according to the most advanced Liberal opinions, the Cabinet are driven to the conclusion that foreign agents are being employed to persuade the people to leave their homes, and are even paying them large sums of money to do so. As the only means to effectually stop this, a bill will be introduced to-morrow, for which urgency will be asked, to establish henceforth a system of passports, by means of which it is confidently believed that a check will be put on the emigration of our people." There was continuous cheering from all parts of the House as the Minister sat down.

The next question was put by the hon. member for Dublin, Mr. Murphy, who said,—

"I wish to ask the Prime Minister how far the reports which are being circulated in the city are true relative to our compatriots in America, who, it is alleged, have sent in a claim for the fabulous sum of five millions of pounds

sterling, which they allege that they advanced to
the Irish Nationalist leaders, in order to enable
them to carry on the fight for their indepen-
dence which has now been so gloriously accomplished ; and further, that therefore the money
so advanced, which, with compound interest,
they assert amounts to the above-named absurd
sum, must be repaid to them forthwith, or they
will cross the water and take the government
of the country into their own hands, and hold
it till they have recouped themselves both for
the advances as well as for their expenses."

"As is usual in these cases," the Prime
Minister began, "there is a certain element of
truth mixed up with any amount of exaggeration
in the report just alluded to; but as negotiations
are now going on with America at this present
time, it would not be compatible with the public
service that I should do more than state that,
with the proper patriotic feeling which animates
both sides, there can be little doubt that a
satisfactory arrangement will be arrived at, and
that our countrymen will at once see that
should they wish to participate in the government of this great country, they can only do
so after being duly elected members of this

House by some of the constituencies whose
suffrages they are of course at liberty to solicit
at the next General Election; but that no
amount of money, either lent or given as the
case may be, could be held to constitute the
slightest claim to become members of the
legislature. More than this at the present
moment I cannot state, but hope to be in a
position in a week or ten days to lay the whole
correspondence on the table of the House, and
make a further statement."

The next on the list was a Mr. Ormsby,
member for the city of Limerick, who asked
leave to call the attention of the Government
to several cases of boycotting, among which
was one more than usually cruel in its application.

"There was," Mr. Ormsby said, "a poor
struggling tenant-farmer, an old man, residing
about five miles from Limerick, whose name
was William Westropp. He had had several
children, but all had left home except the
youngest daughter, named Norah, who not
only took care of her old father, but managed
the farm, which she did so well that it was acknowledged that there was not another within

twenty miles in any way to be compared to it ;
and the young woman was also noted for her
kindness to the poor, not one of whom was
ever sent away unaided from her door.  About
two years ago a young man named Michael
Conway, who had been left a small independent
fortune by his father, which he had squandered,
and now lived by his wits, made Miss Westropp's acquaintance, and had not ceased since
to persecute her to be his wife.  This, however, she would not consent to become—first,
because she was already engaged, as she told
him; and secondly, because as long as her
father lived, she would marry no one.  Finding
fair means of no avail, this Conway determined
to try foul.  By a little artful manœuvring, he
made out that she had bought a horse and cart
belonging to a Protestant landlord who had
been expelled from the district, and whom
Miss Westropp had pitied, declaring openly
that it was a shame to rob a man of his
property and turn him out of his house, just
because he happened to be of a different religion.

"Being questioned as to whether she had
ever so expressed herself, she denied in the

most emphatic manner the allegation; but being
further asked whether she thought the landlord had been properly served, she declined at
first to answer, but when at last forced to give
her opinion, she unhesitatingly said the way
in which he had been treated was shameful.
From that moment her fate was sealed. Her
servants were all ordered to leave her immediately; her two horses were butchered; her
cows—for she had a dairy farm—were one after
the other mutilated, till they died before the
poor girl's eyes in the most terrible agonies;
and her poor father, who had been ailing for
some time, now took to his bed apparently
dying. Day after day every means was used
to make her consent to marry Conway, even
the priest calling and assuring her that if by
such a promise she would thus show herself
to be a good and true Catholic, then all further
molestation should instantly cease; but still to
no effect; and though now the order had been
issued that no shop should supply her with
anything she might require, and though the
doctor, whom her poor father was ceaselessly
asking to see, dared not go near the house, at
four o'clock that afternoon—the hour of the

latest telegram—she still held firm in her refusal, and showed no signs of yielding.   I ask
the Home Secretary to take immediate steps
to rescue this brave girl, and have her and her
poor old father brought up to Dublin, where
I am sure there would be no difficulty in finding
her a safe asylum."   As Mr. Ormsby resumed
his seat, a whispered colloquy took place between the Home Secretary and Prime Minister,
during which a gentleman was observed to
rise from his seat under one of the galleries,
and before turning to depart, he exclaimed in
a loud voice,—

"As sure as there is a God above us, every
soul who has had any part in the hounding
down of this poor girl shall yet pay dearly for
it."

Needless to remark, the speaker was John
Cassidy, who at once left "the House," and
having hailed a cab, was conveyed to his hotel.
Mechanically he mounted the stairs, entered
his own room, locked the door, and placing
a chair beside the table, sat down to endeavour
to realize the fact that he was really awake and
not asleep.

"So this," he said to himself, "was the

country of which in Australia we had heard
such wonderful accounts—which, having at
last been granted a Parliament of its own by
England, had little by little struggled to get
altogether emancipated from the foreign yoke,
and, having succeeded, was to show the world
the glorious spectacle of a country governed
according to the 'most advanced Liberal
opinions,' as the Prime Minister had himself
expressed it. Was it really the case that he
was then in Ireland—the pattern which Canada,
Australia, and New Zealand would do well to
imitate ; THE one spot on earth where the
people were to enjoy a greater amount of
freedom than had hitherto been found possible
under any known form of government, and
at the same time to be not only happy and
contented, but prosperous beyond the wildest
conception ? And after all this high-flown talk
which had been rammed down their throats
at the Antipodes, what was the real truth as
revealed to him that night in their own Parliament ?—the simple fact that the country was
not governed at all ; that though the taxes
were heavy, there was no security for life or
property ; and as to the so-called Government,

it was the most absurd farce that had ever been imagined in the brain of the wildest madman." Then, as his thoughts reverted to Norah and the state of extreme peril in which his true-hearted love was now placed, Cassidy rose from his chair and began, not only to walk up and down the room, but in his fury to stamp on the floor, to the no small disgust, not only of the unhappy native who slept in the room beneath him, but also of those adjoining, one of whom soon called out, " If No. 49 cannot sleep himself, he is requested to remember that there are others in the hotel who can, and who insist on being allowed to do so."

Thus reminded where he was, Cassidy sat down and began to write a long letter to Australia, in which he attempted to give some idea of the true state of affairs in that most ill-fated Ireland ; but he found it impossible to remain long quiet. Do what he would, he could not forget for many minutes at a time the terrible sufferings of his poor Norah ; and even though as yet he did not quite see what he alone, and an utter stranger, could do, nevertheless he was determined to rescue her.

His sole chance lay in his friend and in his own command of money, which he rightly judged must always ensure a certain amount of power in a country where it was so scarce.

# CHAPTER V.

## "A MAGNIFICENT SPEECH."

AFTER a miserable, sleepless night, soon after seven on the following morning, Cassidy rang the bell at the door of Mr. O'Shaughnessy's house in Dame Street. The barrister, he was informed, was still in bed; but as Cassidy would take no denial, he was at last admitted into his friend's bedroom, whose first exclamation on seeing him was,—

"What a magnificent speech! was it not? You won't hear the likes of that in Australia, eh, John? Worth coming all this way to listen to, eh? Of course the bill passed by nearly two to one."

But Cassidy, whose thoughts were far away from speech or bill, instead of replying, took a chair, which he brought to his friend's bed-side, and having seated himself, said,—

"We are old friends, Shaugh, and you were always one of the best-hearted fellows that ever walked; I feel sure, therefore, you will help me if you can." This was said in so grave and serious a tone, that the careless, light-hearted barrister instantly sat up in bed, and seizing his friend's hand, gave it a squeeze as he said,—

"What! got into a scrape already! Never mind; tell me all about it, and you may trust me to see you through it."

"You have, I dare say, often wondered," Cassidy now said, "what has brought me all the way from the Antipodes back to the old country. I have come, Shaugh, to redeem my word, given fifteen years ago to the only girl I ever loved, that as soon as I was in a position so to do, I would return and claim her as my wife. This is the reason why I am here to-day, and——" He paused for a moment, when Mr. O'Shaughnessy interrupted him, saying,—

"You find on your arrival that the lovely creature of your choice, tired of waiting (for fifteen years is a long time, John), has found consolation in the arms of some other husband."

"On the contrary, Shaugh," continued Cassidy, " my own loved one has been true to me as the magnetic needle is to the pole, and is even now being hounded to death because she refuses to break her plight to me and marry another."

" Explain yourself, John, and be assured I will help you if I can. Do you want me to act as best man, or shall I give the bride away, or is there a sister whom you want me to take off your hands ? I may be a devilish good fellow, John, and for auld lang syne willing to oblige a friend to a certain point; but you must draw the line somewhere, you know, and I really *must* see the young woman before I commit myself, as I suppose nothing less than matrimony would answer the purpose."

" The woman I am engaged to marry is Norah Westropp," said Cassidy solemnly, utterly ignoring what Mr. O'Shaughnessy had just been saying; then, as he perceived by his friend's face he had altogether failed to realize the situation, he continued : " Do you not remember the cruel case relative to this poor girl, and the application made in her behalf by Mr. Ormsby, the member for Limerick, and how she was being persecuted by a blackguard named Conway to marry him?"

Mr. O'Shaughnessy gave a long, low whistle ere he said, "So that's the young lady, is it? I heard something of it, but to tell you the truth I did not pay much attention, as the matter in no way concerned me. Did Ormsby say whether the neighbours took any interest in the affair?"

"He said the priest was urging the girl to marry Conway."

Again Mr. O'Shaughnessy whistled as he seemed to be considering the best course to pursue.

"I much doubt," he said presently, "whether I have sufficient influence with the Government to induce them to depart from the course of action laid down by the Home Secretary last night. I will see the Prime Minister if you like, but I know he will say that it would be establishing a precedent which would lead them into endless complications and trouble; and yet though I feel sure it will fail, there really seems no other course open to us."

Cassidy rose from his chair. "In that case," he said, "as my last, my only hope, has failed me, it is useless to waste time here. I must go myself to Limerick, and see what can be done. As this Conway is such a thundering blackguard, I may be able to buy him off."

"Wait a moment!" exclaimed Mr. O'Shaughnessy. "Sooner than throw away money in that manner, there is just a chance of a more satisfactory mode of settling the business; but it will cost more money probably than to bribe Conway."

"How much do you suppose?" asked Cassidy.

"From two to three hundred pounds probably. I wish to God I had the money by me —I'd lend it to you with the greatest pleasure, John; but somehow, under our present Government, people do not take so kindly to law as they used to do, and consequently we lawyers are not so flush of ready cash."

"Luckily I have brought plenty with me," replied Cassidy. "I would give double and treble that to rescue poor Norah from her present danger, so tell me, please, what plan you propose."

For all reply, Mr. O'Shaughnessy slipped out of bed, put his feet into his slippers, threw a dressing-gown over his shoulders, and sat down at a writing-table. He wrote two lines only, which he read aloud : " To introduce my old friend and school-fellow, John Cassidy," and having signed it, he folded and placed the half-sheet of note-paper in an envelope, which he directed to John French, Esq., Slane Cottage ; and as he handed it to Cassidy, he said, " If you hurry, you will catch the train for the North ; but stop this side of Drogheda—any one will tell you where. French is the only man in Ireland who *can* help you. Whether he will or not is another matter. You can but try ; but whatever you do, don't let any one know *I* sent you to him. Good-bye ! you have no time to lose. I wish you luck with all my heart."

Half an hour later, John Cassidy was seated in a second-class carriage which formed part of the train timed to leave Dublin for the North at nine o'clock on that same morning. He had bought and held in his hand one of the morning newspapers, but his thoughts were too far away to enable him to concentrate his attention on its contents ; so before they had started a quarter of an hour, he folded it up and deposited it in his pocket.

# CHAPTER VI.

### "YOURSELF, OF COURSE."

SITUATED on the rising ground just above, and in full view of the river Boyne, only a few miles before that noble river flows into the sea at Drogheda, was a very pretty cottage which had lately been purchased by a gentleman named John French, who, after making several alterations and refurnishing all the rooms, had taken up his abode there. He was a man between forty and fifty years of age, small, not more than five foot five in height, very thin, but of an iron constitution, and possessing to an extraordinary degree that undefinable something which is best described as born to command and to be obeyed. He lived a very retired life as far as the neighbours were concerned, apparently not caring to know any of them, his only visitors being persons who came by train, stayed a few hours, during which they were engaged in close conversation with the owner of the cottage, and then again returned to the railway. These persons it was supposed brought him the few supplies he needed, for as yet he had never spent a shilling in any of the village shops close by. He kept two servants, a man and his wife, both old and very ugly, but, to judge by the state of the cottage, rare treasures both of them in their several capacities—the man as butler and valet, whom Mr. French had nick-named Beelzebub; the woman as cook and housemaid, whom her master called Jezebel. Where they had come from, no one knew, nor had any one cared to inquire. The three lived entirely to themselves, troubled no one, and had, on one or two occasions, shown very clearly they would allow no one to trouble them.

As the clock in the hall struck eleven on the same morning on which John Cassidy was travelling northwards, Mr. French came out of his library, where he had been writing letters, and walking to the hall door, opened it and looked out. "Beelzebub," he shouted, which may be safely said to be his usual habit, "if any one comes, I am gone down to the river to fish." There was a curious noise, something between a grunt and a groan in reply, but it quite satisfied Mr. French, who thereupon took from a corner of the hall a heavy rod in three pieces, a gaff on a long pole, a tin box, and a hat, round which several casting lines of gut were twisted.

As he emerged from the house and descended the path towards the river, he again surveyed the weather, remarking to himself, " Simply perfect—just enough wind to make a nice curl, clouds to obscure the sun, and so soft and mild that the fish *ought* to rise. Whether they will or not remains to be seen."

He sat down on the bank and began leisurely to splice together the two joints of his rod, which, being completed, he proceeded to prove, by taking the butt end in his hands and giving it two or three quick jerks.

" A fine rod, a beautiful rod ! but a trifle heavy," he soliloquized, " for a man of my size." He next began to unwind the line from the reel and pass it through the rings on the rod ; then he attached the casting line to the silk one, and having chosen a fly, it was soon made fast, and he was ready to begin.

From the direction of the wind he determined to fish down stream, so walked up nearly a quarter of a mile before he wet his line; but from that spot he fished every inch of his water the whole way back to the place where he had put his rod together. He had risen two fish only, but had not touched either of them, and now his arms were beginning to ache terribly, for a twenty-two foot rod is too long for a man only five foot five, as he found to his cost. Once more he brought the point of his rod up, sent the fly well behind him, and then with his whole force spun it right across towards the opposite bank.

He was pondering what he should do—go home, get a mouthful to eat, and, having rested, try again later, or should he go back up stream and see if he could coax one of the two fish who had already risen to give him another chance. He was in the act of looking at his watch, when his rod, which he was holding very loosely, was nearly pulled out of his hands. To tighten his grip, and with a firm jerk to send the hook home, was the work of an instant; but the fish, who had taken the fly deep under water, no sooner felt the prick than

he started off down stream at a terrific pace.
The click of the reel was distinctly audible to
John Cassidy, who, under Beelzebub's guidance, was just leaving the cottage on his way
to find Mr. French; and as they came into view
of the river, they observed Mr. French himself
literally running along the bank, hoping thereby
to ease the speed with which the line was
being dragged out.

"O Lord, have mercy upon us!" cried out
Beelzebub; "but he's got hold of a fish, and
a big one too, and it's help he'll be wanting,
that's sartain.  Run, man, run, though it is not
much use you'll be, anyhow; but it would be
a pity to lose the baste, so it would."

At a pace which soon left Beelzebub far
behind, John Cassidy started off down the hill
towards the river.  As he approached, he
observed that Mr. French was either a very
inexpert fisherman or very tired, as the way
he was handling the fish was by no means such
as an old Castle Connell man could approve.
He longed to give advice, but thought it better
to hold his tongue—he might give offence instead; and as his object in coming there was
to conciliate the man before him, not offend

him, he kept a little back from the stream and watched the fight. In a few minutes the fish started off up stream at, if possible, a greater speed than he had just before come down, and again the little man attempted to run after him. It was now that he appeared to see Cassidy for the first time, and he instantly called out, " I'm bate! I'm bate entirely! Take hould of the rod, for the love of God, or he'll be gone! I tell ye he'll be gone!"

Cassidy required no second telling. Slipping off his coat, he seized the rod; but instead of letting the fish have it all his own way, he gradually raised the point of the rod and pushed the butt against the fish, who, though still taking line, moderated his pace considerably. Suddenly the fish stopped and the line slacked, an opportunity which Cassidy instantly took advantage of to wind on the reel as fast as he could, for he guessed there could not be less than one hundred yards out, and there might be more. Again the fish started; he literally raced towards the opposite bank, where he sprang high into the air three times in succession, thus showing himself for the first time, and a noble fish he was. " A grand

baste entirely!" as Beelzebub, who had now
come down to the river, termed him. "Sure
he'll be weighing near on a hundred pounds!
but we'll never know, for we have only the
manes to weigh fifty-six pounds," he soliloquized. "But we ain't got him yet, and not
likely to, I fear, now the master's bate."

Meanwhile the excitement of Mr. French
himself was a sight to see. No sooner had he
let Cassidy take the rod than he instantly
began to give directions as to what was to be
done. "Run, run!" he cried; "don't attempt
to stop the baste; you'll lose him, I tell you."
Then, as he saw Cassidy raise his rod, which
bent nearly double right down to the reel, Mr.
French shouted,—

"Tear and 'ounds, you'll break me rod. Do
you hear what I say, man? Don't do that! It's
a good rod that I got all the way from Castle
Connell, and a lot of money it cost me, too; but
I'd sooner lose the fish than have it broke."

Cassidy made no reply to any of the remarks
and advice so freely bestowed on him. His
thoughts went back to the old days on the
Shannon, where in his youth he had hooked,
played, and landed many a noble salmon; and

though he carefully refrained from saying so, he fancied he knew better than Mr. French what was to be done. Both, however, were well aware that a most critical moment had come when the fish, with the large quantity of heavy wet line in the water, sprang into the air. Cassidy dropped the point of his rod till it was nearly in the water, and waited patiently ready for the next manœuvre, while Mr. French danced with excitement as he called out to Beelzebub, "Hould your blasted old tongue, will ye, you damned old fool!"

The fish now came straight towards Cassidy, diving to the bottom of the deep river, and the line hung slack from the top of the rod. "We've lost him," cried Mr. French; "he's broke the cast, I guess." But Cassidy, though he said nothing, was of a contrary opinion, and wound at the reel with all his power. Soon, however, he began to fear Mr. French was right, for the winch was getting very full, and as yet it was not possible to get any strain on the line. Mr. French now advanced and stood close beside Cassidy, ready to take the rod out of his hand, when Cassidy, who by this time had wound up all the line except about twenty yards, again felt he had hold of something, and that the end of the line was fast close under their feet.

" The fly's fast in the weeds at the bottom ! " shouted Mr. French. " Don't pull too hard, or you'll break it," he said to Cassidy, who, first up stream, then down stream, was straining the line to try and ascertain what held it. " Bring me the gaff, old cock," Mr. French shouted to Beelzebub ; and as soon as he had possession of it, he proceeded to unscrew from the end the bright steel hook and replace it with a sharp curved knife he took from a case in his pocket.

" Is the fish gone, sir ? " asked Beelzebub.

" Yes," said his master, "and my fly, too, I fear, unless you will go in and get it out for me. I'll try this affair first ; but if it doesn't answer, I am damned if we don't lower you down to clear it."

Beelzebub, who had been standing close to the water's edge, retreated rapidly ten or twelve yards, and would, in all probability, have gone straight back to the cottage, only his master shouted to him, " Not so fast, my cockie ; just stay where you are, till I know whether you'll be wanted."

Mr. French now took the line in one hand, and holding it taut, tried to follow it down with the long pole he held in his other hand. He had already about seven feet of the pole in the water, when the line was jerked suddenly from him, and with a mighty rush the "grand baste" went off into the centre of the river.

And now began a steady fight between Mr. Cassidy and the fish, which lasted for half an hour. Three times that gentleman brought him up near the bank, but before the gaff was in the water he was off again, and so his arms aching and wet through and through with perspiration, Cassidy called to Mr. French to take the rod once more, which that gentleman at once did, anxious to have the honour of landing the fish. Cassidy now took the gaff, and kneeling down about fifteen yards below where Mr. French stood, he immersed the ten-feet pole in the river, and waited. The fish was coming up the centre of the river, while Mr. French, winding up the line, gradually drew him nearer to the bank. Presently he lay wagging his tail gently about three feet from the bank, and the same distance under water, evidently watching Mr. French. He was not

a very long fish, but his immense girth was
remarkable, and fully accounted for his indomi-
table pluck, for, even now, Mr. French could
not fail to remark he was only resting, and
very far removed indeed from allowing himself
to be landed.

What could not be effected by force, however,
might, as so often happens, be managed by
stratagem; and before either Mr. French or
the fish had the least idea of his intention,
Cassidy, creeping up stream, brought his gaff
up with a powerful sweep, and the fish was
struck below the shoulder. To lift so heavy
a weight on to the bank was impossible; but he
could hold him where he was, and the fish, in
his frantic efforts to get away, with his powerful
tail sent the water in volumes over Mr. Cassidy, saturating him to the skin, and knocking
a new hat, which he had bought in Dublin, into
the river.

Throwing down the rod, Mr. French ran to
his assistance, and together they hoisted the
monster on to the bank and away from the
river, where he lay gasping for breath, while
the three watched his dying agonies.

" Beelzebub, you old ass! what are you

standing grinning there for?" shouted Mr. French. "Carry the fish up to the house, and tell Jezebel to boil a piece of the tail for dinner, sharp." Then turning to Cassidy, and having coolly surveyed him from head to foot, he cried out, "I'm damned if I know you. Who are you, and what do you want here?" Then observing Cassidy shiver, as the wind pierced his wet clothes, he continued, " Never mind ; come and change, or you'll get your death of cold. It will never do to lose you ; there's not many can handle a rod like you." And he strode up the hill towards the cottage at a pace which made Cassidy nearly run to keep up with. Arrived at the door, he observed Cassidy's car waiting there, and on it a portmanteau, when he shouted out, " Come to stay, eh ? Brought your portmanteau ? Damned if I know you, all the same. Here, Jezebel, take this portmanteau to the spare room, and show the gentleman the way." Then observing Cassidy apparently about to speak, he shouted, " Off with you ! follow the old hag, and when you're dressed, come to me in the dining-room."

It was about ten to fifteen minutes later, that, when Mr. Cassidy descended the stairs, he found Beelzebub waiting for him in the hall, and he at once conducted him to the dining-room, where Mr. French was seated at the table reading a newspaper.

"So they've passed the bill, the idiots!" was Mr. French's first exclamation. "What do you think of the speech?"

"What speech?" asked Cassidy.

"Man alive! Why, this is your own newspaper, which I found you had left on your car, and you mean to tell me you have not read the Prime Minister's speech!"

"No," was the reply. "I left the House last night before he began, and so do not even know what it is all about."

Mr. French looked at him for a moment, as if he could not believe his ears; then he cried out, "Well, I am damned if I know what to make of you. If any one else had told me he had been lucky enough to obtain a seat in the House last night, and had then gone away before hearing our Irish Prime Minister" (these last three words were spoken with a contemptuous sneer impossible to render) "deliver himself of his great speech, I would have told him to his face he was a liar; and yet, damme, you appear to be speaking the truth.   Perhaps you won't mind telling me when you left, and why?   Were you ill?"

"No; I was perfectly well, but terribly upset at hearing that a young woman named Norah Westropp was being hounded to death because she would not marry a blackguard named Conway, when her word was already given to another."

"That other being yourself, of course," coolly remarked Mr. French.

Cassidy nodded.

"Then why the devil did you not go straight off to Limerick, give your rival a good thrashing, and marry the girl off-hand?   You fought the *fish* well, but perhaps you are afraid to fight *a man*," Mr. French added, with a sneer.

It was a sore temptation to John Cassidy to show the man to whom he was talking that he was not afraid to tackle *him;* but he restrained himself, and having with a great effort kept down his rising temper, he answered, "If we were only alone, I'd soon teach him a lesson; but he has the whole country backing him, and what can one man do against several hundred?"

"Are you sure of that?" asked Mr. French.

Then after a pause he continued, " How long
is it since you saw the girl ? "

" Fifteen years," replied Cassidy quietly.

" Fifteen what ? " literally yelled the little
man. "And what the devil have you been
doing with yourself all that time ? "

" Been in Australia, and only just come back."

" Is it possible ? " cried Mr. French, springing from his seat. "And what the devil made
you leave the finest country in the whole world,
bar none, to return to this God-forsaken hole ? "

" To redeem my word. I promised Norah
Westropp I would come back when I had
made money enough to keep a wife and marry
her, and here I am."

" And she has waited for you all this time ? "

" Did you not read in the paper the description of how she has been persecuted to marry
this scoundrel Conway ? " asked Mr. Cassidy.

" Wonderful ! " exclaimed Mr. French.
" Damned if I can hardly believe it now. A
man and woman waited fifteen years for each
other ! Damn it, sir, it's grand ! upon my soul
it is ! There ! shake hands ; proud to make
your acquaintance, Mr. ——. Damned if I
even know your name."

"John Cassidy," put in that gentleman ; but Mr. French went on without heeding.

"I've seen *you*, now I must see *her ;* so remember the *first* visit you pay after you are married must be to this house—the very first ; do you hear ?"

"We are not married yet," began Mr. Cassidy ; "and I fear——"

Mr. French interrupted him, saying,—

"Not married ! no ; but you are going to be. Did not I tell you so ? God damn it, man, to wait for fifteen years, and then lose the wench after all, would never do. What I say I mean. Before forty-eight hours have passed, if the girl is willing, she shall be your wife. You see if she is not ! Here comes old Beelzebub with the fish. Wait five minutes while I wash my hands, and then we'll feed." So saying, Mr. French hurried away, leaving John Cassidy not a little elated at his own diplomacy in having gained over so powerful an ally, who, after what his friend Mr. O'Shaughnessy had told him, he had little doubt had both the power and the will to keep his word as to the marriage.

# CHAPTER VII.

## "DRINK FAIR, AND NO HEEL-TAPS."

FULLY ten minutes passed before Mr. French returned, when both gentlemen at once sat down to table, and the cover being removed, they proceeded to prove the super-excellence of the Boyne salmon, as is too well known to need any comment. The weight of the fish had been forty pounds, Beelzebub informed his master, inquiring at the same time what was to be done with the remainder, a very small portion only having been required for the meal.

"Cut it in half," said Mr. French, "and pack the head and shoulder end in a basket to be sent by train this afternoon."

A beefsteak done on the gridiron to a turn, with some deliciously fried potatoes, followed the salmon, and with some bread, butter, and cheese, completed the repast, when the table being cleared, and Beelzebub having disappeared, Mr. French produced a bottle of port wine, which, notwithstanding Cassidy's remonstrances, he insisted on opening, remarking that they had, he knew, nothing like it in Australia, and after his hard work and thorough drenching, a drop of generous wine would do his visitor no harm, more especially as it was probable he would travel all night.

Mr. French now brought his chair from the head of the table and placed it close to Cassidy's, with the bottle between them, remarking, with a smile, " Drink fair, mind, and no heel-taps."  Cassidy started, looked hard at his companion, but said nothing; he believed it was with reference to his marriage with Norah that they were about to talk, and waited impatiently for his host to begin.

" Your name ? " began Mr. French curtly.

" John Cassidy," was the equally sharp reply.

" Your occupation in Australia ? "

" Partner in the business of Butterworth & Sons, one of the oldest firms in Melbourne."

" Lucky, were you not, to get so good a berth ? " asked Mr. French.

" Undoubtedly!  I went out with Mr. Butterworth's eldest son, who took a fancy to me, and insisted on my coming to his father's house on landing. The old gentleman took me into his counting-house, and two years ago made me junior partner."

"Both Mr. Butterworth and his son are members of the Parliament or Legislative Council, and the old man has been, if not still is, in the ministry. Am I not right?"

"Quite so," replied Mr. Cassidy.

"And the junior partner comes to this country on his own private affairs, but at the same time is charged with a message from Sir John Squire, the Prime Minister of Victoria, to Terence O'Grady. Am I not again right?" Mr. French's quick eye had detected Cassidy's sudden start, so he smiled as he continued, "I see I am, and in the interview you had with Sir John just before starting, you were instructed to deliver your message to Terence O'Grady; but on your very properly suggesting that to prevent mistakes some mode should be devised by which you should be sure as to O'Grady's identity, you were told that he to whom the message was to be given would say to you, as I have already done, 'Drink fair, and no heel-taps.' So now for the message."

John Cassidy stared. It seemed to him little short of miraculous that all this should be known to the man before him, the full and true particulars of an interview between himself and the Prime Minister of Victoria, which took place only a few hours before he sailed. The instructions he had received had, however, been fulfilled; and though told that he should most likely find Terence O'Grady at Belfast, the password on which he was to rely had been correctly given, and John Cassidy, after looking carefully round, was in the act of whispering something into Mr. French's ear, when a bell rang in the next room. Mr. French, however, simply saying, "Don't mind that; go on," listened attentively to every word Cassidy had to say to him. No sooner, however, had he finished, than rising from the table, and remarking, "I will be with you again in five minutes," he left the room.

When he returned, he laid a printed paper on the table, which Cassidy read as follows:—
"N. W. consented to marry M. C. to-morrow morning at 11 o'clock."

"Good God!" cried Cassidy, "and I sitting so quietly here leaving the poor girl to her fate!

Let me order my car and be off at once, please, Mr. French."

" I took the liberty of dismissing your car long ago, the truth being, I do not like these carmen about the house : they are half of them spies. I myself am going to catch the six p.m. up-train, and will drive you to the station. You will be in plenty of time for the night train to Limerick, which is the only one you could catch now. Meantime, do not make yourself uneasy about your Norah. As she has consented to marry, the boycotting is at an end, and both she and her father will be no longer molested, the doctor even having already been to visit the old man."

Again for the second time John Cassidy stared at his companion.

"Who are *you*," he cried, "who knows so wonderfully what passes, not only here, but even at the Antipodes, and who, I find, are known here as Mr. French, while in Australia they call you Terence O'Grady ? "

" Before answering your question, let us go and sit outside," Mr. French now said ; "it is a lovely afternoon, and it seems a pity to remain indoors."

Each man carrying his glass, Mr. French the bottle, they left the cottage and seated themselves on a rustic bench outside, in full view of the river, with lovely Slane Castle and its grounds lining the banks.

"My real name," continued Mr. French, "was Terence O'Grady, and by it I am still known in most parts of Ireland. I took the name of French when I inherited a fortune from my mother's brother, and so am called sometimes by one name, sometimes by the other."

"I understand now what certainly was a puzzle to me before. Perhaps you would also kindly explain to me what this wonderful speech was about. I remember now Mr. O'Shaughnessy alluded to it also; but the truth is, I was so upset about Norah, that I never thought of the speech till you again mentioned it."

"So you know Shaugh, do you?" replied Mr. French,—"as good a fellow as ever lived, and a very old friend of mine, though now of course we see little of each other—our politics are so different."

"Yes," replied Cassidy; "he gave me a note

to introduce me, but I must have left it in my other coat."

"Never mind," said Mr. French; "the fish did that better than he could. Of course he praised the speech."

"He did, said it was worth coming all the way from Australia to listen to."

"Ah! ah! ah!" laughed Mr. French, "that is a good 'un, at any rate; but, joking apart, you are, I really believe, the only man in all Ireland who is not aware of the great importance of the Prime Minister's speech last night, terminating as it did the most momentous debate in the House since the G. O. M. gave us repeal of the Union and a Parliament of our own. Even though it was of course directed against us, I should like much to have heard it. The result of the vote was known to me ten minutes after it was given."

"Does it affect you then so vitally?" asked Mr. Cassidy.

"As you come to me as an accredited agent of our friends, I do not mind telling you in confidence that it seals their own fate," said Mr. French; then, observing that Mr. Cassidy

was as far as ever from understanding him, he
went on,—

"It is now over three years since this country
was handed over by the greatest traitor that
ever lived in times past, present,—and I trust
for the sake of future generations I may say,
to come,—to the mercies of as great a set of
cut-throats as the world could produce, who,
having been allowed to form themselves into
a so-called 'National League,' began little by
little to acquire such power over the miserable
uneducated masses, that they were virtually
masters of the situation, and no one was strong
enough to withstand them.  I need hardly say
that no really respectable individual of any
position or family would have anything to say
to them, so that, in order to find representatives
whom they could elect and send to Parliament,
they were forced to take schoolmasters, poteen
shop-keepers,—any one, in fact, who could sign
his name, and would consent to hand himself over, body and soul, to the control and
orders of the League.  Now, in order that
such a body should continue to exist, it was
absolutely necessary that they should have
money, and it was very soon found that the

miserable driblets which could be wrung from their dupes here in Ireland were mere drops in the ocean towards the thousands and tens of thousands needed. They were forced then to appeal to America, and O'Donovan Rossa and his crew, instantly seeing the chance thus offered to them, never hesitated for a moment to forward any amount of money. Thus the League, while ruling Ireland with an iron hand, were in their turn subject to the velvet glove of the money-lenders, who, very cleverly and judiciously playing the never-failing waiting game, have, like a cat lying before a fire purring, watched, while their prey, carrying out their suggestions, paved the way for their own seizure of the country and assumption of power, holding it nominally only till the capital advanced and interest thereon were repaid,—in other words, for ever.

"They knew that as long as English, or, as they called them, foreign troops were in the country, the Americans could not hope to be allowed peaceable possession. Well, the English troops have been got rid of. They further believe that as long as the Orangemen exist in the North, the O'Donovan crew will not be happy in the South, East, and West, and so the edict went forth that the Orangemen must follow the soldiers, and to bring this about a bill was introduced, which passed last night by an overwhelming majority.

"And what have they done? and what do they hope and believe will be the result? In the first place, under the pretence of protecting Irish manufactures, they have put a prohibitive duty on all linen goods, which makes any export of such quite out of the question; they also insist that mill-owners shall take out a license, according to the number of hands they employ, the impost being so iniquitous that some of our larger firms will be mulcted to the amount of more than one thousand pounds a year; and lastly, they have fixed the rate of wages we are to pay our mill hands at so exorbitant a figure, that to continue to work under such conditions would mean ruin in two months.

"This is the price we are to pay for the honour of being governed according to the most advanced Liberal opinions, as is so often stated in the House,—in other words, not governed at all, but robbed,—for, look where you will, the Government exists only in name. Any clever blackguard who has the gift of the gab can stir up his neighbours to help him in committing any piece of villainy on which he has set his heart, for which there is no punishment, for the simple reason that there is no law, and even if there were, there is no one to put it in force. The police, the finest body of men in the world, where are they, you will perhaps ask? Gone! left the country *en masse*, disgusted at the miserable pittance they were offered as pay, and when they indignantly refused it, were coolly told police were not a necessity under an advanced Liberal Government.

" Need I say that the one sole object they have in view is to get rid of *us*, to force *us* to leave Ireland, and, will you believe it? they have been kind enough to allow us to carry off the whole of our machinery out of the country, free of duty. Is not that a tempting offer? All our manufactured goods and raw material we must leave behind us, or pay the duty on its exportation, which is pretty nearly equal to the sum it is at present worth in the foreign market. The land which we own the Government will buy of us at a valuation which they term 'prairie value,' and then we, our wives, and little ones, are driven forth from our houses in the country, in which we have been born and bred, and which we have been taught all our lives to consider as our own."

As he ceased speaking, he rose from the bench and began walking up and down the narrow path in front of them. For several minutes not a word was said, then Cassidy remarked,—

" I have always said the same, and will maintain it to my dying day, that of all the mean, cruel, cowardly acts ever committed by a great, rich, and powerful country towards a small and weak one, nothing ever could come near the treatment Ulster has experienced at England's hands. Without even so much as saying, With your leave, or By your leave, what right had England to hand over thousands of quiet, peaceful, and loyal people, who were contented and happy, and whose sole wish was to be let alone, to the mercies of a Government composed of the scum of the earth, the vilest refuse of a miserable population, who do not know what content means ? Too idle and lazy to work, they never knew when they

were well off under the freest and finest
Government in the world, and who now, when
left to themselves, cannot be quiet, but must
be everlastingly 'schaming' to cheat and rob
each other.

"They are as unfit to govern themselves as
a lot of babies of a year old, the great and
only difference being that the latter are harmless if helpless, whereas the former are equally
helpless, but of all nations under the sun the
most cruel, dissatisfied, cunning, and tyrannical
—not by nature, but made so by the education
they have received from the so-called National
League. This is the view we take of the
matter in Australia, and the lookers-on generally see the play, and are far better able to
judge of the result than those who are actually
the chief actors."

"Yes," replied Mr. French, "you are right,
there cannot be a doubt of it; and you understand, then, the message you brought me, and
endorse every word of it?

"I!" said Cassidy; "of course I do. The
message has only one fault, it is too mild, and
so I ventured to tell Sir John."

"It answers the purpose," said Mr. French,

with a smile. "Once married to the lovely Norah, what say you to joining us ? We want such men as yourself terribly."

"If my partners can spare me, I am with you heart and soul ; but I undertook to be back in six months at latest, so, until I hear from them, can only promise conditionally."

"Leave that to me," said Mr. French. "Shake hands on the bargain ; and now, as they are putting the horse in the car, we must get ready for a start."

Warmly the two men wrung each other's hands, and entering the house, were soon ready and standing at the hall door as the car came round. They caught the train without any difficulty, and arrived safely in Dublin, where, as Mr. French stepped on to the platform, three men came up to him, one of whom exclaimed, "Drink fair, mate ;" to which Mr. French replied, "And no heel-taps. Is that you, Peter?" And then turning to Cassidy, he went on, "We part here. Peter will go with you, and explain how matters have been arranged. You have no time to lose to catch your train. Take your wife straight to the cottage, and whether I am there or not, make

yourself thoroughly at home. Beelzebub and
Jezebel have their orders. Good-bye, and may
luck attend you!"

"I thank you," said Cassidy very quietly.
"I am a man of very few words; but deeds,
not words, shall prove my gratitude."

"I believe you," replied Mr. French, and
then, after another hand-shake, they finally
separated, Peter going with Cassidy, and the
other two men with Mr. French. The latter
mounted a car, and were driven away in the
direction of Westland Row, which being passed,
they took the Blackrock road, but stopped
about three miles from the city, where, the three
men alighting, ordered the car to wait while
they proceeded on foot.

Five minutes later they left the high-road,
descended a small lane, opened a wooden
swing gate, which having passed through, they
crossed what in the darkness seemed like a
glass plat, and stopped before the portico of a
low house. One of the men now produced a
key with which he opened the door, and they
entered. On a shelf close by was a candle and
some matches, and a light having been thus
procured, they found themselves in a small

but well-furnished hall, through which Mr. French passed on rapidly into a morning-room, against the wall of which was hanging a telephone.

Instantly connecting the instrument, and unhooking the two handles, one from each side, he applied them to his ears, as he said in a low but clear voice, "Lucy! Lucy!"

For a moment there was no reply, then he heard some one say, "You are very late."

"Is he coming?" asked Mr. French.

"Hush! he is here! shut up!" was the quick reply, as at the same moment he could hear a door shut and a sound which was not very clear in the telephone, but which Mr. French believed to be kissing.

"Whom have you got here?" asked a man's voice.

"No one!" was the reply, in the clear tones of a young girl.

"Lucy, you are deceiving me. I distinctly heard the words 'shut up' as I came in. To whom did you say that? I insist on knowing."

"You were dreaming," Lucy replied. "I never made use of such an expression."

"I am going to search the room, Lucy."

"Search my bedroom! What an idea!" and the young girl laughed.

"Do you object, Lucy?" asked the man.

"Why should I object? I tell you there is no one there; but of course you won't believe me, so the only way is to look for yourself."

For a minute not a word was said, then in Lucy's pretty voice, "Well! where is he? for of course you found him. What have you done with him? why did you not bring him to supper? Do you mean to say you never discovered any one? You could not have half hunted. Did you look *under* the bed and IN the bed?" and then there was a loud, merry laugh.

"Oh, you dear darling, but very silly George," she went on, "why are you so jealous, and never will believe me? You only make yourself ridiculous. Now give me a kiss and let us go to supper; it is quite ready."

For several minutes nothing was said, then the man asked, "You didn't expect me last night, Lucy?"

"No," she replied; "only a little. I guessed you would be too tired after your great speech. I read it, George, every word of it, from beginning to end.   It was fine, very fine.   I should like to have been there."

"Why did you not say so?" he asked.   "I dare say it could have been managed."

"George," she went on after a short pause, "I want to understand all about it.   The bill has passed, and the newspaper declares there is now a heavy duty on linen fabrics; does that mean that I shall have to pay a great deal more for my handkerchiefs and other linen things which we won't name?"

"No, you silly little puss, just the contrary. The duty is only on goods which are sent *out* of the country, not on those which are sold in it; and as the manufacturers will not be able to pay the duty and then sell at a profit in England, it stands to reason the linen must be sold here for whatever it will fetch."

"And is this what you call protecting the home industries?" asked Lucy.

"Well, not exactly, though it is a step in that direction; but our first object must be to get the home industries into our own hands."

"I do not understand.   Whose hands are they in at present, if not your own people's?"

"How many more times must I beg, Lucy,

that you will *not* call the Northerners our own people? They are even more foreigners to us than the English—aliens in race, religion, and disposition, an idle, worthless, good-for-nothing set, whose one idea is to get all Ireland under their thumb, and who must be got rid of at any price."

"And is it with this object you have put a duty on the linen?" asked Lucy.

"In the hope that when they see that all chance of continuing their present business is at an end, they will get disgusted and be off elsewhere."

"Of course you know best," said Lucy.

"Which means that you do not agree with me."

"It seems to me," Lucy continued, "that you will find it very hard to stop smuggling. Just look at the long line of coast you will have to watch, to prevent the linen being smuggled out of the country. Why, there will be steamers upon steamers engaged in the trade."

"I think not," was the quiet rejoinder.

"Have you the means to stop it?"

"We intend to try. We are drafting the old coastguardsmen up from all parts of Ireland;

they will constitute a fine force of over five hundred men; and as we shall not interfere with them, but simply let them keep for themselves whatever they can seize, I fancy the coast is sure to be well watched."

"Your men are strangers, the others are bred and born on the spot. If you want to be sure of success, you must, by bribery or other means, persuade some of the local fishermen to help you; but even then I doubt if you will drive many of the manufacturers to decamp. You must remember that I was brought up in the North of Ireland, and no one knows better than I do the wonderful love the people have for their homes, which I have heard many of them say they would rather part with their life than desert."

"They may be called on to make the choice sooner than they think for. But there! let us talk of something else, Lucy darling. I did not come here to discuss politics, but to be amused and enjoy myself."

"One question more. What about those horrid Americans; they are not really coming, are they?"

"I fear so," was the reply, "nor am I at all

sure that it would not be better that they should. They would bring over two or three thousand men who would act as police, and make the people understand that taxes *must* be paid, for they really seem at present to have an idea that now the English loan is repudiated, no more money is required, the consequence being, the Treasury is bankrupt; and though we have managed to contract a loan for present expenses, when that is gone I do not know what we shall do."

"And what do the English say about the interest of their loan?"

"They were inclined to be nasty at first, but the G. O. M. soon got them in hand. As long as he lives, they will give us no trouble. How the country allows that man to lead them by the nose beats me altogether! It is lucky for us he is so stanch a friend, or it would be all up with us entirely; and as for when he is gone, I dare not even think, much less speak of it!"

"'Sufficient unto the day,' you know; and now, as supper is over, let us——"

With a grave face Mr. French hung the two wooden handles which had been pressed against his ears, and by means of which he had heard every word of what had passed, on their hooks, one on each side of the telephone ; and rousing the two men who had dropped asleep, the three quitted the house, re-locked the door, and started off to where they had left the car.

# CHAPTER VIII.

## "WELL DONE! WELL DONE!"

THE driver was now directed to return to
the city, and, crossing O'Connell's Bridge,
to keep to the left, and to follow the quay beside
the Liffey till they arrived at the last turning but
one before reaching the Royal Barracks.   Here
they dismissed the car, and, turning to the right
on foot, went on up Queen Street towards
Stoney Batter.   In less than five minutes they
crossed a small court and entered a house,
ascended a dark stair, where they were chal-
lenged by a man standing sentry on top.
" Drink fair, mate," he said ; but it was a mere
form, as, without waiting for the answer, he
opened a door on his left, and Mr. French
entered.   There were about a dozen men
present, all of whom rose to salute the new-
comer, who at once said,—

" I fear I am very late, and must have kept

you waiting; but it was unavoidable, as you will hear directly. Now to business! What reports have been received?"

"Several," was the reply, "from different parts of the country—all representing that matters are going from bad to worse. Law has become a dead letter, there being no one to enforce it. It exists only in name. Every one does exactly as he likes. To obtain money is impossible; even the taxes are not paid, the collectors being only laughed at when they apply for them."

"Anything from Mrs. Kelly?" asked Mr. French.

"Yes! One of her men is here now, waiting to see you."

"Call him at once," said Mr. French; and on his being summoned, he proceeded, in obedience to orders, to inform his hearers that a Government agent, who had been sent down to see them, had told Mrs. Kelly that Parliament had decided to put an end to "such lawless proceedings," and therefore gave her fair notice that unless she discharged her men, and behaved herself as others did, she must take the consequences. She replied that she had paid her taxes (exorbitantly high though they were) regularly, and that in return she expected Government would protect her; but as they had failed to do this, so she had been compelled to adopt measures for her own safety. These had proved very costly, and she would therefore most willingly return to her old mode of living if the Government would only show her they were able to ensure her freedom from molestation. As to the seizure of food, she had sent a written order for its delivery, and had been prepared to pay for it; but after waiting two days, and finding it did not come, she went and took it.

Her man then said—" Two nights ago, hearing that a well-to-do farmer had been proscribed by the League, Mrs. Kelly started off with a dozen of us to his house. It was between ten and eleven o'clock when we arrived. We found the hall door of the house open, but no one was visible either upstairs or down. Fearing the man and his wife had been made away with, Mrs. Kelly was about to search more closely, when one of the men called her and led the way to the shed where the farmer kept about a dozen very fine and very handsome cows, of which he was passionately fond and very proud. As we approached, we could see a light, distinctly hear voices, and also the low, sad moan of some animal in great pain. Mrs. Kelly approached cautiously and looked in, as, never for an instant supposing there could be any interference, no sort of precautions had been taken. The farmer, bound hand and foot, was seated close to the door on a corn-bin, his wife beside him. The face of the latter was stern and determined, but tears were streaming down the man's cheeks.

"'Will ye swear?' asked one of the ruffians beside him.

"'No!' replied the wife; 'never! while I have life to prevent it.'

"The man who had asked the question made a sign, and one of the poor cows was detached from its stall and led up close to her owner, within the radius of the light hung from the roof. The poor creature was of a dun colour, and looked so mild and inoffensive that the man must be a brute indeed who could harm it.

"'Is this beast to be served like the rest?' asked the same speaker as before.

"There was no reply, and after waiting a

moment, he approached the animal. As he did so, the farmer's whole form shook with convulsive sobs, while he literally writhed on his seat; but his wife's face was hard as iron.

"Drawing her knife, Mrs. Kelly in an instant cut the cords which bound the farmer. For a moment the poor man seemed dazed with astonishment, and hardly able to realize the fact that he was free; but, following the direction in which Mrs. Kelly was pointing, and observing the ruffian seize his cow by one of her horns, he hesitated no longer, but with one bound caught his victim by the throat and bore him to the ground.

"'Seize them all!' rang out the clear, commanding tones of Mrs. Kelly. 'Don't let one of them escape!' and the other five villains, too much astonished to make any resistance, were at once overpowered and bound.

"Two of Mrs. Kelly's men now advanced towards the farmer, who held his man still pinned to the ground; but she ordered them back, saying, 'Leave them alone; he cannot get more than he deserves.'

"'Bedad, it's kilt he is entirely,' one of our men remarked, as, stooping, he observed the ruffian's lips were black and frothy, while blood was issuing from his mouth and nose. Mrs. Kelly, however, paid no attention; but, approaching the farmer's wife, offered her her hand, saying, 'Will you not come to the house?'

"She rose, and as she turned to leave the shed with Mrs. Kelly, said, 'Oh, madam, if you could only discover what they have done with my poor little ones!'

"'Bring those men on to the house,' called out Mrs. Kelly; and at the same moment the farmer got up from the ground, and came towards Mrs. Kelly and his wife.

"Two of our men who had been at the far end of the shed now approached and said, 'Several of the poor bastes seem terribly hurt; it would be a mercy to kill them.'

"'Oh! no, no! don't, please don't,' cried the farmer, who seemed on the point of going to see them; but Mrs. Kelly caught him by the arm, saying,—

"'You will only distress yourself, and can do no good.   Come on with us to the house.'

"'I always told him he cared more for the bastes than his own childer,' cried his wife.

" Mrs. Kelly delayed a moment to whisper the order that the bastes should be destroyed at once, and then went on to the house with the farmer and his wife. She entered the kitchen and seated herself while they lighted a lamp. The farmer stood on one side of her, and his wife sat on the other. 'Bring in one of the men,' she said; and a great hulking fellow was led forward. He looked around in a careless, defiant sort of way, and then put his tongue in his cheek, as if to show his contempt.

" 'Your name?' said Mrs. Kelly, as she eyed him narrowly.

" 'Pater!' was the reply.

" 'Pater what?' asked Mrs. Kelly sharply, for I saw while standing beside the man the old woman was getting angry; but faix, *he* saw nothing, so, shaking his head, he replied with a broad grin,—

" 'No! not Pater what, but Pater—jist that and no more.'

" She raised herself slightly from her seat, and before the man, who was still grinning, had a notion of her intention, she struck him with her riding whip across the face a single blow. It did not appear to be a heavy one, but it broke the skin, and the blood poured out, while the howls of the man could have been heard a mile off.

"Mrs. Kelly signed to me to stop his noise, which I did at once; while the farmer's wife, clapping her hands, exclaimed, 'Well done! well done!'

"'Bring in the others,' Mrs. Kelly next said; and as they appeared, it was evident they knew pretty well what had happened, for there was no appearance of impudence, but rather of fear.

"'Listen!' said the old woman; 'if you want to leave this room alive, answer my questions, and speak the truth. I've warned you, so you have only yourselves to blame if you get into trouble. Who are you, and where do you come from? I never saw one of you before.'

"'It's near upon tin miles we've come,' was the reply.

"'Who sent you?' asked Mrs. Kelly. There was no reply.

"'Ye may as well tell me first as last,' Mrs. Kelly went on; 'for I will know.'

"'Sure it was Tim Hoolahan that told us that orders had been received from Dublin, and that we were to come here with him to-night.'

" ' And didn't he tell you why ? '

" ' He did ; but sure the master there knows better than us, for has he not had the notices ? '

" ' I did receive several letters threatening that if I did not dismiss an old cowkeeper who has been with me all my life that I should be turned out of my own farm and ruined.'

" ' And did they give no reason for his dismissal ? '

" ' It is said his son has turned Protestant,' answered the farmer.

" ' Now about the children,' Mrs. Kelly went on, turning to the farmer's wife. ' How many have you ? ' but before she could reply, two boys and a girl appeared, accompanied by their maid, who at once stated that she had been downstairs when the men arrived, and being frightened, had roused the children, dressed them, and they had then gone off together to the stable, where, mounting to the hay-loft, they had concealed themselves, and had only now just come down, as, all being so quiet, they supposed the men had left the farm.

" ' And now,' said Mrs. Kelly, turning to the

farmer, 'what do you propose to do—remain here, or return with us?'

" ' If I go with you, what will become of the farm, my horses, cows—in fact, everything I possess ?'

" ' And if you remain here, what will become of your life?' asked his wife.   It was therefore at once settled that the wife and children should accompany Mrs. Kelly, and accordingly orders were given to harness a horse to a light cart, and the children were put into it, with their mother to drive them.   Then came the question as to what was to be done with the farmer, who positively refused to leave his cows, and yet to remain behind must mean certain death in the morning; so, most unwillingly, Mrs. Kelly consented to drive the seven cows with us.   We had a long and most fatiguing march, but luckily arrived just before daylight.   Two of the cows, however, were so tired and footsore, they had to be slaughtered forthwith; and such a bother and hullabaloo as we had with the farmer in consequence, who declared he would kill the first man who laid a finger on any of his animals.   Of course he had to be overpowered and shut up; but the mistress hardly knows what to do with him, and thinks perhaps he had better be sent up here."

"What would be the good of that?" asked Mr. French. "These are not times to be worried with a fool of that sort. Tell your mistress to turn him out if he gives her any more trouble. What else?" Mr. French continued, observing the man evidently had more to say.

"Could your honour spare us a few more men? The mistress says she'll take every care of them; but if there is an attack again, she ought to have a hundred men at least. She has plenty of arms, but wants ammunition."

"Very well," said Mr. French. "She has done, and is doing, us good service; she shall have what she wants. Some of them shall go down to-morrow night—the rest the night after."

The man was now dismissed, and Mr. French proceeded to inform those who had assembled there to meet him of the conversation he had overheard, and also that the Prime Minister had stated deliberately that the time was not far distant when the Orangemen would have to choose between death and desertion of their country.

"Such is the state to which things have come," Mr. French said in conclusion. "Forewarned is forearmed. We know now that to pay the heavy duties and licenses with which they have saddled us would be money thrown away; confiscation of everything that we possess, and a peremptory order to quit Ireland immediately is surely coming, and for this we have to prepare. Will you submit tamely to be so treated?"

A loud burst of "No! no! Never! never!" broke from the lips of those present.

"You will fight, then," muttered Mr. French in a low voice.

"To the death," they all exclaimed, slowly, but solemnly.

"To do so successfully will require money," said Mr. French. "Without it we can do nothing; and you must also name one leader in whom you can trust, and to whom you will render implicit and unquestioning obedience."

"You are surely not going to desert us at such a moment!" they all cried as one man.

"I!" said Mr. French, rising from his chair;

"I desert you! You *must* be mad to suppose for one moment that Terence O'Grady could be a traitor. Explain yourselves, gentlemen. I *must* know what this means."

"Did not you yourself call on us to name a leader? So long as you are with us, what want we with any one else? Where could we hope to find another in whom all have such implicit confidence, and under whom every soul will be so proud to serve? Do not refuse us, Terence, in our need; but in the name of our wretched, miserable country—in the name of our poor wives and children—in the name of our religion—in the name of the Almighty Himself, we implore of you to be our leader, director, and guide. Can you, dare you, refuse us?"

"I have no wish to decline the position you offer me," said Mr. French, seating himself again at the table. "I most willingly give both my fortune and my services to the good cause; but, gentlemen, let us look at the matter calmly and dispassionately. We, a mere handful of men, are about to set ourselves in opposition to the Government of our country, backed up by ten times as many men as we can possibly hope to get together. Nevertheless, that we shall, that we *must*, ultimately win the day, is as certain as that I am now sitting here; but, gentlemen, we have a long and very arduous task before us, and if victory is to be ours, it can only be by union amongst ourselves. I do not mean a simple obedience to orders, but a cheerful, ungrudging, unquestioning acceptance of the tasks I may have to impose on any of you, all working together cordially and pleasantly, with the one end in view; namely, the preservation of our homes and hearths from spoliation and robbery; and if, gentlemen, you find me, as I feel is only too probable, a hard, a very hard taskmaster, you will have only at any moment to name my successor. I will— believe me—work just as cheerfully under another leader, and be only too glad to be quit of the heavy load of responsibility which, till that time arrives, will never be for one moment off my shoulders. I promise to do my best, gentle- men; no one can do more."

All rose, leaving Mr. French alone seated. "Terence," they cried, "you, and you only, shall be our leader. Among the thousands, the tens of thousands, the hundreds of thousands whom we shall, when the proper moment comes, most cheerfully place at your disposal, there is not one who does not trust you and love you, and who would not be only too proud to be given the chance, as we have to-night, to shake you by the hand."

Mr. French stood up, as one by one those present advanced and wrung his hand, each man saying as he did so, "Thank you, and God bless you."

"What about the money?" asked Mr. French, as he observed the others preparing to depart.

"How much will you require?" was the reply; and then observing Mr. French hesitate, the same speaker continued, "Will one hundred thousand be enough?"

"I should think so, indeed. I was nervous about asking for the fifth part of it."

"The money shall be paid to-morrow," exclaimed several voices. "Good-night!"

"Good-night to you all!" replied Mr. French, who a moment after was alone.

Opening a door behind where he had been sitting, he now entered a small inner room, and, tired and worn out both in body and mind, took off his coat and shoes, and having extinguished the light, threw himself, dressed as he was, on a small truckle-bed in the far corner.

Those, in the meantime, who had just left him, descended into the street below, where they separated into small parties of twos and threes, and in their shabby corbeens and long frieze coats, reaching to their ankles, looked like Irish labourers seeking work, rather than the masters of Orange lodges in the North—men who had counted their "hands" by thousands, and collectively were worth millions sterling, and who, for the good of the cause, now handed over one hundred thousand pounds as coolly as if it was a matter of a few shillings only. Separated, but within easy call of each other, they made their way through the back streets to Sackville Street, which they crossed, and entered a house about twenty yards from it on the opposite side.

# CHAPTER IX.

## " THIS IS LUCK INDEED ! "

TIRED though he was, Mr. French wooed sleep in vain that night. The position which he had been so unanimously chosen to fill showed that his own people had so much greater an amount of confidence in him than he had any idea of, that he lay awake thinking of the future, and the chance that was now being given to him of making himself a name in history, and a world-wide reputation of which any one might well be proud. He felt the power in him to achieve success, and if he were only seconded, had no doubt whatever that he would one day enter Dublin at the head of an army which would, should he so order it, in a short time place all Ireland under his control, and sweep the whole of its present miserable population into the sea.

While these thoughts were passing through his mind, he heard a board creak over his head, and he fancied he could distinguish the sound of a light footstep above him. Fearing treachery, and well aware of the danger which, had any one been listening to what had passed that night, threatened not only himself, but also the others who had so lately left him, Mr. French instantly rose, and, creeping to the door, placed his ear against it, and listened attentively. For several minutes he heard nothing, but then his quick ear detected a whispered colloquy, as if two persons were talking together outside. Soon the creak of the stair told Mr. French that one of the two had left the house, while the other remained to watch. Returning to his bed, he seated himself upon it, and began to moan and groan as if in the most fearful pain. Soon he heard the door of the outer room open, and the man who was on watch come creeping along the floor towards him.

"Is that you, Mike?" called out Mr. French.

"It is, your honour. Were you wanting anything?"

In reply came a succession of the most terrible groans imaginable, and then, between them, Mr. French, apparently with great difficulty, said, "A light, Mike; have you a match?"

Immediately after a candle was lighted, and then Mr. French could be seen seated on his bed, doubled up, with both hands pressing his abdomen, rocking himself to and fro, as if suffering the agonies of the damned; while the perspiration was pouring down his forehead and cheeks.

" Is your honour ill ? " asked Mike.

" I am, and what's more, getting worse every minute. Run for a doctor, Mike, and look sharp."

" I will, your honour; I will," replied the man, as, hurriedly making his way to the door, he descended the stairs two steps at a time, saying to himself as he did so, " Bedad, it's in luck we are! Ill as he is, he'll be taken at once. I've half a mind to do it myself."

Quick as he had been in his movements, Mr. French had put on his coat and shoes, and was down at the door in time to observe the direction which the man Mike had taken; and as he himself went off in the opposite one, he smiled as he soliloquized, " A narrow shave! though they will be bothered to find the Prime Minister to-night, and there is no one else to attempt a thing of the sort; but wait—

unless I am mistaken, *he* was to be in Dublin to-night;" and then, taking a piece of paper from his pocket, he stopped under a lamp to glance at its contents. "Yes," he continued, "I am right. The one man in all Ireland who is likely to give us any trouble—the only one who has a head on his shoulders—is here, sure enough; and the sooner, therefore, I and all belonging to me are out of this, the better." Hailing a cab, he was driven to Sackville Street, where, alighting, he lost no time in making his way to the house whither his late companions had preceded him. Having roused them, he warned them not to lose a minute in leaving Dublin; and having offered three of them a seat on his own car, they drove off, taking the road to the North, determined to be guided by circumstances as to where they would dismiss their vehicle and take the train.

In the meantime, the man whom Mr. French had so luckily for himself heard descending the stairs in the house at Stoney Batter, ran as fast as his legs would carry him to the quay, where being lucky enough to find a car, he was driven to a house in Dawson Street, at the bell of which he pulled vigorously. The door was opened almost immediately; but on the man's application to see the "Master," he was informed it was impossible, as he was not at home, but he had better call again in the morning.

Not believing this to be true, he insisted, stating that his business was most important and urgent, requiring immediate action; in the morning it would be too late ; but again and again the servant assured him that the master was really not at home.

"But is there no one I can see?" the man asked, almost at his wits' end with annoyance. The servant whispered something, as if afraid to pronounce the name aloud, when the man started violently, exclaiming, "Is it possible? When did he arrive ?"

"About two hours ago," was the reply.

The man hesitated for an instant, as if undecided ; then having apparently made up his mind, he said to the servant, "All right ; many thanks !" and instantly ran down the street into Nassau Street. Stopping at a house a few doors round the corner, he rang the bell, and when it was opened, asked anxiously, "Is *he* here ?" A nod was the reply, when the man exclaimed, "Tell him Pat Coolahan is here, and is wanting to speak to him immediately. Tell him it is important."

The servant shut the door and departed on his mission, returning, however, in less than a minute, and signing to Pat to enter. Not a word passed as the door was secured, and Pat, following the servant, mounted the stairs, and was shown into a room on the first floor, at a table in the centre of which a gentleman sat writing. Two powerful gas-lamps, covered with opaque green shades, were pouring the whole volume of their light upon him, and leaving the rest of the room in comparative obscurity. He looked up as the door opened, and observing some one had not only entered, but remained in the room, he asked,—

"Is that you, Pat?"

"It is, your honour."

"You are the very man I wanted to see, and was wondering where I'd find you. I have work for you, Pat—work which shall be well paid, too. Come over here. Why are you standing at the door, as if afraid of me?"

Pat, thus addressed, came forward into the radius of the light; but he seemed far from being at his ease. He stood first on one leg, then changed on to the other, while he kept twisting his hat round and round in his hands.

"Any one, to look at you, would say you *were* afraid, Pat," said the gentleman, with a laugh. He waited, expecting a disclaimer on Pat's part; but the only effect of the remark seemed to be to increase the man's nervousness; so the gentleman continued,—

"What brought you here to-night, Pat?"

"Sure, your honour, it was to tell the master how some money could be made; but as he is not here, I'm afeard it will be too late."

"Tell *me*, can't you, Pat?" said his companion.

Now this was precisely what Pat did not wish to do. A sort of intuitive perception seemed to tell him that "the work for him to do, which would be well paid," would be found to be connected with the same business which had brought him there, only with a very different result, as far as he was concerned. However, there was no help for it now, so he replied,—

"Mr. French—your honour knows who I

mean—is now lying asleep in a house in Stoney Batter. He is alone, and could be easily taken prisoner, and kept till a heavy ransom is paid for him."

"Mr. French!" exclaimed the gentleman. "Is it possible that he has been such a fool as to put himself into our power? This is luck, indeed! Pat, Mr. French must never see another sunrise. You can name your own price; and the sooner it is done, the better."

Pat still continued twisting his hat; but his face, as he heard his companion's remark, turned perfectly livid, and his legs shook to such an extent that it seemed doubtful whether they would support him.

"What are you standing there staring at?" cried the gentleman. "Do you not hear what I say? Waste no more time, or it may be too late."

The man dropped his hat on the floor, and stood looking at it. It seemed as if he dare not stoop to pick it up. He knew if he did, he would not be able to raise himself. He was struggling hard to speak, but for the moment words were not at his command. To save his life, he could not have uttered a single syllable.

His companion watched him like a cat would a mouse, smiling as if amused at his pitiable condition.

"I—I—I can't. It—is—no—use—to—pretend—I—can," he stammered ; then with a violent effort he went on : "Oh! *you* do not know what I have suffered since that last time. You saw me strike him as he was getting into the car. The blade was sharp, and I drove it well home. You stood by, and urged me on. He fell, and as he did so, he turned round and gave me one look. Oh! oh! oh! Shall I ever forget it? Will it ever leave me? There! I see it now. Look! look! on the floor; there it is, just as it appears to me the first thing in the morning when I wake, and the last thing at night before I go to sleep. Oh, the horrors of it! The only wonder is I am not in a madhouse long ago. And now you are urging me again to do another ; but I can't. I have suffered more than enough already ; so it's no use to ask me. If it must be done, you must get some one else, for *I* won't; I tell you once for all, *I won't;*" and he turned away, covering his face with his hands and sobbing like a child.

It was still the case of the cat and the mouse,

and a more cruel, pitiless, relentless cat the whole world could not produce than he who, leaning back in his chair, now caught Pat by his arm, and swinging him round, forced him to look full into his face, as he said,—

"You tell me, Pat, you know the house in which Mr. French is now lying fast asleep. Look at that clock; it is half-past two. I give you one hour, and if by half-past three you are not back here and the deed done——" He stood up and whispered a few words in the man's ear; then taking a long case-knife which lay on the table, he led the man to the door, put the weapon into his hand, and uttering the one word "Remember," watched him while he descended the stairs, and never moved till the hall door had been opened and shut by Pat from the outside.

The man walked along the street like one in a dream. He did not know where he was going or what he was doing. Intuitively he grasped the weapon which had been put into his hand, and when he arrived at the river, crossed the bridge, and turning to the left, followed the quay. The errand on which he was bent was murder—cold-blooded and deliberate—for which, if caught, he ought to be hung; though it is doubtful how far he was a free agent, and really responsible for his actions. He had distinctly and decidedly declined to commit the deed, but had been overawed, and a stronger will than his own imposed on him, which, holding him in a grip of iron, gave him no choice but to obey orders, whatever they might be. Like a machine wound up, on, on he went straight to the house where he had left Mr. French asleep, as he supposed. He crossed the court, opened the door, ascended the stairs, and then, at the entrance to the room where the meeting had been held, he stooped down and took off his boots. Leaving them on the landing, he went forward, and, as noiselessly as a mouse, made his way to the little inner room, and stood beside the truckle bed. He listened for the sleeper's breathing, in order to know how his head was placed, but could hear nothing. He stooped down, so as to be able to bring the line of the mattress against the faint light of the window, and could then see there was a blanket tossed carelessly on the bed, but no human form was there. For a time he could not believe his own eyes. Hold-

ing the weapon in his right hand, ready for use
if required, he very cautiously drew his left
hand across the surface of the mattress.  There
was no longer any room for doubt—the bed
was empty; and as Pat at last realized this
fact, the power of the spell gave way.  A
sensation of relief greater than words can
describe, or the wildest imagination picture,
came over him, as, uttering a loud cry of joy,
he sank himself on to the bed.  It was but for
a moment, however.  His quick ear caught the
sound of a step ascending the stair.  In an
instant all his previous horrible sensations returned, increased and intensified tenfold by the
exquisite feeling of relief in which he had just
revelled.  Springing from the bed, he placed
himself behind the door, ready for his victim
as soon as he should appear.  He had not long
to wait, for the individual whose step had been
heard entered the conference chamber.  He
came no farther, however, but called in a low
voice,—

"Pat!  Pat!   Is it there ye are?   Is it
a-calling of me yez were?"

For the second time that delicious feeling of
being freed from a hateful thraldom was ex-

perienced by Pat, though not to the same extent as before. Again he approached the bed and sat down, as he replied,—

" Is it yourself, Tim ?"

At the sound of Pat's voice, Tim came forward to the door and looked in.

" Is it alone ye are ?"

" It is."

Pat's eyes were on the ground. He seemed to be enjoying his rest and ease of mind, and little inclined to talk. So Tim went on,—

" Ye'd hardly gone when I heard him as was lying there," indicating the bed with a motion of his head, "amoaning and agroaning terrible. ' Are you ill, your honour?' I inquired, putting my head in at the door. ' I am,' he replied; 'took bad all of a sudden, and getting worse every minute. Run for a doctor, will ye ?' So, congratulating meself on our luck, believing he'd never be able to move, and so could be took quite aisy, I ran to Dr. Milligan, whom I found just getting out of his gig, and who came on at once with me here; but the place was empty when we reached it. Divil a soul to be seen at all, at all, anywhere. So the doctor, he was inclined to be angry at first.

' Is it a fool you've been making of me, Tim ?'
he cried, ' keeping me out of me warm bed just
for nothing at all ; and who's to pay me fee ?
Ten shillings it is at night, and divil a hap'orth
less.'	I had walked over to the bed while he
was speaking.	' It was here, in this very spot,'
I replied.	' I left him amoaning and groaning
fearful, and by the same token here's his over-
coat, which he has left behind in his hurry,' and
stooping, I lifted it from the side of the bed.
He came over and took it from me, carrying it
to the window to examine it.	' I'll kape it,' he
said a minute after ; ' sure it'll be safer with me
than here ; and if the gentleman sends for it, ye
can tell him Dr. Milligan has it, and that his
fee is ten shillings.	Good-night to you, Tim,
or	rather	Good-morning,	for	it's	daylight
already.'	And so the doctor goes home with
the coat on his arm.	I did not tell him who
the gentleman was, Pat, as I thought maybe
't would be better not."

While Tim had been speaking, Pat remained
seated on the bed, tapping the floor with the
forepart of one foot, as if the narration worried
him.	As Tim ceased, Pat still kept silence,
and it was Tim who, after a pause, continued,—

"Sure it would be aisy to take him yet," he said. " It will be two hours and more before a train will be laveing the city, and four or five of us to watch each station, he could never get away. But it is not by sitting there ye can do it, Pat. Get up, man, quick, and be off and see the master. There's time enough to do it yet, but none to spare."

Thus urged, Pat rose and went down the stairs into the street. He retraced his steps along the quay, and in due course arrived at the door of the house in Nassau Street. His hand was on the bell-handle to pull it, when it suddenly seemed to strike him that he had no proof of the truth of his statement that the bird had flown before his own return to its nest, whereas the undoubted fact remained, that he had received a positive order from the man he was about to interview, which had *not* been obeyed ; and he, Pat, knew only too well that the one fault which was never forgiven was disobedience, and which, according to the laws of the brotherhood, was punishable by death.

His hand let go the bell and fell to his side ; for the second time that night his whole body shook from head to foot. Miserable as he had

described his life to have been, he was too
great a coward to himself face the death which
he had meted out to others.   Like a whipped
hound he slunk away towards the purlieus of
the city, hoping to find some hole or corner
where he could hide himself.   Whether he
would have been wiser to have seen the man
whose orders he had done his best to obey,
and told him the plain truth, no one will ever
know.

Patiently that individual continued his
writing, glancing occasionally at the clock till
half-past three.   " I will give him half an
hour's law," he said to himself, which he did,
and another quarter of an hour added to that,
but longer than that he would not wait.   Without leaving the room in which he was sitting,
he telephoned orders that every railway station
in Dublin should be rigorously watched that
morning, and any one bearing the slightest
resemblance to Mr. French be at once seized,
and if found to be he, accounted for in the
usual way.   He also notified that Pat Coolahan
had been guilty of gross disobedience of orders,
and must be found and punished.

With regard to the first portion of the order,

though every possible effort was made, Mr. French, as already related, was far too knowing to be trapped so easily; but as to the second, the poor wretch was easily traced to a stable in Dundrum, where, among the straw in an empty stall, he was found fast asleep. Needless to say, from that sleep he never woke, and his body was buried in a ditch close by, thus showing that the organization which had so long virtually ruled Ireland, and with which England, with all her boasted strength, had been either unable or afraid to grapple, still held undisputed sway over the unhappy land.

# CHAPTER X.

### "IT IS YOU I WANT."

IT will now be necessary to go back a few hours to the evening previous to the events just described in the last chapter, and shift the scene to the neighbourhood of Limerick. It will doubtless be remembered that Mr. French had informed John Cassidy that " N. W. consented to marry M. C. to-morrow morning at eleven o'clock;" and it was for the purpose of making the final arrangements that Michael Conway drove to the door of the farmhouse between five and six o'clock in the evening.

Alighting from his cart, he entered the house as if already one of the family, and making his way upstairs, opened the door of a good-sized room on the first floor. On a bed at the end furthest from the door lay the old man, Westropp, apparently asleep—at any rate, his eyes were closed—while beside him sat a young woman, who, though undoubtedly she had once been handsome, now bore such evident traces of sorrow and trouble stamped on her wan features that not a remnant of good looks remained. She rose when she saw who was her visitor, but did not leave the old man, her father's, side, one of whose hands she held in her own. Michael Conway came straight up to her, and putting his arms round her neck, kissed her cheek. She shuddered as he did so, but if he noticed it, he said nothing; while her father opened his eyes and looked at her, mumbling something which was quite unintelligible.

"Norah, darling," Michael Conway said; "I have made all the arrangements exactly as you wished. Your uncle and aunt, Pat Westropp and his wife, have agreed to come out here to-morrow morning, and stay for two days with the old man. I have hired a carriage to convey them, which, after leaving them here, will bring you on to the chapel, where his Rivirence will be waiting. You will be ready by ten o'clock, darling?"

Norah looked up at him with her swollen red eyes, and there was a mute appeal in them which few could have resisted.

"I must be going, now," Conway continued; "it is getting late, and I do not care to be out after dark."

A contemptuous sneer curled Norah's lip for a moment, but the next instant it was gone, and letting go her father's hand, she placed herself between Conway and the door.

" Michael," she said, placing her two hands on his arm as he approached, " is there nothing I can say or do that will move you? Can you not see that my heart is breaking? that if I fulfil my promise, and you force me to be your wife, you will make me hate you— loathe the very sight of you! What prospect of happiness can there be for us under such circumstances as that, Michael? What is it that you want? Is it the farm? the house? Take them! everything! Leave me only the old man, for whom I will work as long as he lives, and then——"

" Enough! enough, Norah!" Conway interrupted, "how many more times am I to tell you the same thing? It is *you* I want—*you* and *you* only; I care for nought else. Mine you have promised to be, and mine you *shall* be ere another sun has set; for I love you, my dearest one—ay, love you as man never loved woman before!" and he folded her in his arms, holding her in a close embrace while he covered her

whole face with his impassioned kisses. A
minute after he was gone, and Norah, who by
the failure of her last appeal seemed turned to
stone, went back to her father, with whom
she spent the whole night—the last, something
told her, she would ever be with him.

At seven she gave him his breakfast. He
was very weak, and required to be fed like a
baby, and Norah could not shut her eyes to the
fact that he was sinking fast—in all probability
would not live through the day; nor could she
resist the feeling that it was better so; for in the
new life which was before her, married as she
was about to be to such a man, what suffering
and misery might not be in store for them?
As far as she herself was concerned, she cared
not; but to see the poor old man neglected,
illtreated, perhaps even starved, she neither
could nor would, and if such were attempted,
there would be terrible quarrels which might
end in fights, for Norah had been proud of her
strength, and if Michael Conway struck her,
she had quite decided to show him she could
defend herself; and if he were the cowardly cur
she believed him to be, he would get a thrashing he would never forget.

At eight o'clock she left her father, and entered her own room. She went to a cupboard and took from it her desk : it had been a present in years gone by from John Cassidy, and contained the letters he had from time to time written to her, a ring, a brooch, and a few other trinkets he had given her. As she looked at these things for the last time, the poor girl's courage broke down, and, throwing herself face downwards on her bed, she gave way to a paroxysm of tears, crying as if her heart would break.

Rising while the tears were still pouring down her cheeks, she set to work to break up the desk, and then, having built up the pieces with the letters and all the ornaments into a funeral pile on the hearth, she applied a match to the dry paper, and sat down on the ground to watch it burn. Brightly it blazed for a few minutes, and then, as it burnt lower and lower, Norah clasped her hands over her heart as she murmured,—

"Oh, John, John ! my own, my only loved one ! To have waited all these years, and then to lose you at last, is too, too cruel ! ! ! I would have stood out for ever, my John. They might have beaten me, starved me, tortured me even to death—I cared not; no one but you should ever have been my husband; but it was the old man who made me give in. It broke my heart to see him suffer. Oh, were they not fiends to starve a poor help- less creature like him! His cries for food by day were terrible, and at night, as I used to lie awake and listen to his moans, you, my loved one, will never know, can never even imagine, what I suffered; I must have been more than human to have borne it. And when the last night I rose, and standing over my poor old father actually asked myself whether it would not be better to put an end to such sufferings at once and for ever, then I knew that I was on the verge of madness, and—and —I yielded. Oh! John, John, to ask you to forgive me, I dare not; but you will, you *must* pity your poor wretched Norah, who, you know only too well, in her heart has been, and ever will be, true to *you* and *you* only, and so will remain to the bitter, bitter end!"

She sat there till the fire had completely burnt itself out, never taking her eyes off it; then she rose and proceeded to collect together the few articles she required to take with her, which she placed in a bag. She then dressed, and had barely finished when she heard the sound of horses trotting, and wheels.

She knew at once that the hour had come, and ran down to meet her uncle and aunt, who were getting out of the carriage. They wanted to congratulate her, but she implored them not; and when they observed how wretchedly ill and heart-broken Norah looked, they said no more. She took them upstairs to her father, who was fast asleep, gave them a few necessary instructions concerning him, and then, kissing him lightly so as not to wake him, took her bag, wished her uncle and aunt good-bye, and, descending the stairs, got into the carriage and was driven away.

The farm-house was situated about three hundred yards from the road, up a small boreen or lane, which, not having been lately attended to, was much out of repair, and, consequently, great caution was necessary in piloting the carriage over it. It was an old-fashioned post-chaise, with a postilion and pair of grey horses, which had been sent, and the man had got himself up extensively in an old scarlet hunting-coat, velvet cap, breeches and top-boots, with a white rosette at his button-hole. It took him nearly fifteen minutes before he reached the high road, which for the next three-quarters of a mile was as straight as an arrow.

There was not a living soul visible anywhere along it, but about a quarter of a mile from where the boreen joined it, the post-boy noticed two carts of turf, each drawn by a donkey, which he had passed before on his way to the farm.

It was about a quarter-past eight that same morning, and the priest—or his Rivirence, as he was called by the people—who was engaged to perform the ceremony which would unite Norah Westropp to Michael Conway, was sitting at breakfast, when his servant informed him that a man was waiting to speak to him, who, though told by her that his Rivirence was engaged, would take no denial, declaring that he was in no hurry, and would wait, as see his Rivirence he must.

"Let him come in," said the priest. "Do you know who he is, or what he wants?"

"No," was the reply in a sulky tone; for Nancy, the servant, prided herself that there was not a living soul within twenty miles whose name she did not know, and being also endowed with any amount of curiosity, was always terribly "put out" when any visitor to his Rivirence would not first impart to her his business, as, to her intense disgust, had been the case now.

Not daring, however, to disobey instructions, Nancy at once ushered the man into the priest's presence, and closing the door, placed her ear against it, hoping to hear what passed.

"Your name?" said the priest, surveying the man all over with a quick glance. "You are a stranger to these parts, or I must have known your face."

"Peter Maguire, and I came from Dublin this morning, plase your Rivirence;" and the same Peter who, it will be remembered, had accompanied Cassidy from Dublin the previous night, came forward and stood at the foot of the table opposite the priest, who again looked at him with his quick glance.

"Well," said the priest, "tell me what you want. If it's masses, I'll say them for you, and chape too; for money, bedad, is hard to get these times. There's little of it in the country, I'm thinking."

Peter shook his head as he replied,—

"It's sorry I am to hear your Rivirence say that, for it's fearing I am that I have had my trouble for nothing in coming to see your Rivirence about the five-acre field opposite."

But the priest put his finger to his lips in token of silence, and, rising suddenly from his chair, strode to the door, which he opened quickly and suddenly, thus precipitating into the room the servant who was leaning against it, listening. He caught her by the arm to prevent her falling, which she must otherwise have done. Laughing heartily at thus detecting her, he gave her a commission to execute, and, waiting till he had seen her put on her shawl and leave the house, he pushed the bolt in the door to prevent her slipping back unknown to him, and then returned to Peter. He was a large, coarse man, with a red, bloated face, but a quick, piercing eye. He did his duty as a priest, so that no fault could possibly be found with him ; but the god that he worshipped was money, and in order to gain that, it is probable there was nothing that he would not stoop to do, provided always there was no fear of detection. He had, when he first took charge of the parish, bought a small plot of land, on which he had built himself a cottage, which was the one he now occupied. Little by little he had

picked up one piece of land after another, till
he owned nearly forty acres round his dwelling;
but there was one field of five acres which, as
it happened, was exactly opposite his front door,
of which he had never been able to get possession. It was let, and the rent was paid to a
solicitor in Dublin, whose answer to all applica-
tions as to purchasing was to the effect that the
field was not for sale. Who the owner was, or
where he resided, had thus always remained
a mystery.

The inward delight of the priest at thus hearing that the one ungratified desire of his whole
life might now be about to be accomplished,
may be easier imagined than described, and it
was with the greatest difficulty that he could
command himself to say, with assumed indiffer-
ence,—

"And is it to you it belongs?"

"They told me your Rivirence had been
offering two hundred pounds for it; and as
money is scarce, I thought I'd just come and
tell your Rivirence that I'd let you have it."

The priest burst out laughing. He had been
heard to say over and over again he would give
two hundred and fifty for the field, but he

thought he had an omadhawn to deal with in Peter, and so said,—

" If it was to tell me that you took the trouble to come all the way from Dublin, it is back again you may go by the next train. Where would I get two hundred pounds to throw away just for five acres of land, which would be dear at fifty, so it would."

"I beg your Rivirence's pardon," replied Peter, backing towards the door. " I'm thinking I'll be after following your advice, and go back again by the first train."

" Don't be in such a hurry, man," cried the priest. " You are wanting to sell, that's evident, or you would not be here ; and I—well, I don't mind telling you, that sooner than anybody else should have the field, I'd give one hundred pounds, which is double its value, as you know as well as I do. What do you say ? Is it a bargain ? "

And the priest held up his hand in the air as if to strike Peter's to clench the agreement.

The latter, however, shook his head, and again began to back towards the door, as he said,—

" It's taking up your Rivirence's time I am, just for nothing at all."

But the priest caught him by the arm, and, forcing him into a chair, said,—

"Come, Peter, be reasonable; suppose we split the difference, and say one hundred and fifty?"

Peter hesitated, which the priest observing, exclaimed,—

"It's a bargain; shake hands on it."

"It is," replied Peter, extending his hand; "but only on one condition."

"And that is ——?" asked the priest.

"That the money is paid and the matter settled by twelve o'clock to-day, so that I may be off by the train, and back in Dublin to-night with the money."

"It is nearly ten now, and I have a couple to marry at eleven. Will it not do if you leave by the mail train, and are in Dublin to-morrow morning?" asked the priest.

Peter, however, was firm, and as the priest would not lose his chance of securing the field for twenty marriages, he and Peter started for Limerick, where they arrived at eleven o'clock —the same hour at which his Rivirence had promised to marry Conway to Norah Westropp, at his own chapel five miles away.

# CHAPTER XI.

## "NEVER! NEVER!"

NORAH arrived at the chapel at five minutes to eleven, and was met at the door by Michael Conway, who was waiting for her. She took no notice of him, however, but passed at once into the sacred building, where, in a dark corner, as much out of sight as possible, she knelt down and remained wrapt in prayer and lost to all external influences. Conway left her undisturbed, preferring to wait till the knot was tied, and she was really in his power, before taking any steps to convince her that he would not stand such treatment from any one.

Meanwhile time was going by : eleven o'clock had struck, and another five and even ten minutes passed, and still no sign of his Rivirence. Conway began to fume and fuss, and wonder what it could mean; and yet the

priest kept his flock in such wholesome awe
of him that Conway as yet could not make up
his mind to stir in the matter. At the quarter-
past eleven, however, he asked one of "the
boys" to go as far as the priest's house, and
remind him they were waiting, as "maybe he
has forgotten all about it." It was a ten
minutes' walk, but by "hoorrying," as he was
told to do, he might be back in fifteen; and
sure enough at half-past eleven he appeared,
hot and out of breath, and informed Conway
that his Rivirence was not there at all, at all,
nor Nancy either; at least, he could make no
one hear, though he had knocked at the door
loud enough to wake the dead; he had also
gone round to the back of the house, but no
one was visible.

What was to be done? Conway's first idea
was to go himself to the priest's house; but if
his Rivirence should arrive and find him (Conway) absent, he might take huff at being kept
waiting, and go away again at once. At twenty
minutes to twelve, however, he could stand it
no longer, but started off at a run for the cottage; but his mission was as barren of any
result as his friend's. He found Nancy, it is

true, but she was walking round and round the house, unable to get in.

" Sure he sent me hisself to Pat Duigenan's," she exclaimed, in answer to Conway's inquiry, " and told me to be quick back, for he had to be at the chapel at eleven for a wedding ; and sorra a one of me has set eyes on him since, nor knows what's become of him. He's locked up the house and taken the key in his pocket, bad cess to him ; and what will I do at all, at all ? Divil a one of me knows," cried the indignant Nancy.

" And it's meself that would like to be told what to do," cried Conway. " Sure we have been waiting this half-hour and more at the chapel beyant, and didn't he promise to be there at eleven and never been near the place at all ? "

" Waiting ! what for ? " asked Nancy.

" To be married, to be sure—what else? If it was any one else but his Rivirence, I would say it was making a fool of me he was ; but sure it is not himself who would do that same."

" You'll have to wait till to-morrow now," cried Nancy with a grin ; " it must be past the hour by now. And, after all, sure it doesn't signify whether it is to-day or to-morrow—a few hours more or less; you'll have enough of her and to spare before long, and by this time next month will wish you had never seen her; but to keep a lone woman out of her house and home, and it going to rain too, it's cruel **and** wicked, that's what it is. Ochone, Ochone," and sitting down by the side of the road, she began to wail and moan, as if some dreadful calamity had befallen her.

If ever a man found himself in a fix, it was Michael Conway at that moment. What to do he knew not. To return to the chapel would be to make himself the laughing-stock of about a hundred of "the boys," who would by this time have certainly assembled there for no other purpose.

And if there was a man on earth who hated ridicule, it was Michael Conway.

"Look here, Nancy," he said, going up to her, " it is going to rain hard, and ye can't sit there; so go to the chapel; ye'll be safe enough inside, and, Nancy, ye can tell 'em I am gone home, and to come to-morrow. Do ye mind, Nancy? to-morrow at eleven o'clock," he called out as the old woman hobbled away towards the chapel, where, having delivered her message, she knelt down, and in a few minutes was muttering her prayers as if her very life depended on it.

The chapel in the meantime was nearly deserted, as the boys, not to be baulked of their fun, started off as soon as they heard Nancy's message to find Michael Conway. So good an opportunity for a laugh was not to be lost on any account. It was at this moment that a man whom no one seemed to know, and who had been observed several times hanging about the chapel, stealthily entered, and having glanced round, went over to where Norah was still kneeling, and placing himself on his knees beside her, muttered her name in a low voice. At this moment the heavy shower which had been threatening for some time began to come down, and the noise made by the rain on the roof was so great as to drown all other sounds. Norah, who had not heard her name, drew away from the stranger and continued her devotions.

" Damn the rain," muttered Cassidy—for he it was—between his clenched teeth ; " it is impossible to hear a word that is said, and yet she must be told somehow." His meditations were cut short by a woman's arms being thrown round his neck, and a kiss being imprinted on his cheek, as a voice cried,—

"John ! John Cassidy ! is it yourself, me darling ?  Sure did I not know you at anst, though it's sixteen years and more since I set eyes on your handsome face, and it's glad Nancy is to see you looking so strong and so well, more power to you."  While engaged in muttering her prayers, the old woman's eyes had been roving round the chapel, and she had consequently observed some one enter.  She instantly, as she thought, recognised him ; but though the next moment she discarded the idea as absurd, she rose nevertheless, and made her way unobserved over to where he had knelt down, and now not only caught a good view of his face, but heard him say " Norah."  All doubt was therefore at an end, and she greeted him as related above.

Notwithstanding the noise caused by the rain, Norah's quick ear had caught the name uttered by Nancy, and she looked up.  It was the first time Cassidy had seen her poor wan careworn face, and it cut him to the very heart ; but while tears almost came into his eyes, he observed a

change—such a change!—pass over her countenance, which, a moment before so sad and
miserable, now suddenly seemed to light up, her
eyes to brighten, and a beautiful smile to play
over her mouth as, stretching out her two arms,
she exclaimed,—

"Oh, John, *my* John, are you come at last!"

Taking one of her hands in his, he placed
his other hand on her lips as he said,—

"Hush, Norah darling—hush! for God's sake
keep quiet, or we are lost," and he looked
cautiously round to see if they were watched;
but the old woman, Nancy, had placed herself
between them and the door, so as to screen them
from the one or two persons getting shelter from
the rain.

"Give her a kiss, honey," she whispered;
"the poor crittur been true to you all these long
years, it's meself that is telling it to you."

Perceiving that, thanks to Nancy, there was
no chance of their being observed, Cassidy drew
Norah to him, and their lips met in a silent but
long and loving kiss. "And now one for me,"
cried Nancy as she lowered her head, and
Cassidy kissed her too, for she had been a very
old servant of his family's, and one of the

first to take him in her arms when he was born.

"Oh, John, John!" cried poor Norah, hugging Cassidy's hand and covering it with kisses, "you'll NEVER leave me again now you've come back at last; swear it, John, swear it."

"Have I not come all these thousands of miles to fetch you, my darling? Why would I go away without you; but you must marry me, dearest, and be off *at once*—we cannot stay here."

"Marry you, John? what else have I been waiting for these fifteen long years? and why would I delay now? But if we leave at once, what will become of the old man, who has no one but meself to care for him?"

"He's gone, Norah, about half an hour after you left—passed away in his sleep without a struggle."

Norah covered her face in her hands and cried.

"It is a sad moment, I know," Cassidy continued, "for a wedding, but there's no help for it; as soon as the priest comes it *must be done*, as it is many miles we'll be from here before the sun sets." Norah made no answer—she was too happy for words. They were alone now, she

and her John, the old woman Nancy having gone
to the door to look out, and Norah, creeping to
Cassidy's side, nestled up to him and laid her
head on his shoulder, just as she had pictured
to herself during all these long weary years
she would do, but under what different circumstances! in her own house, by her own fireside,
the meeting was to be; she had planned and
arranged it all again and again, but never in
her wildest imagination could she have con-
ceived anything like the reality. "No matter,"
she said to herself half aloud. "I am once
more in my darling's arms, and though of course
they may separate us when dead, as long as I
live I will *never* leave him—never! never!" and
Cassidy, who had heard what she said, echoed
the word "*never!*"

To return to Peter and his Rivirence. As
they entered the suburbs of the city, the priest,
turning to Peter, asked where they were going,
to which Peter replied, "To Joel's"; but as
his Rivirence declared he could not be seen
entering such a place, they drove to an hotel
where, in a private room upstairs, the priest
installed himself and Peter left him. He re-

turned, however, in about ten minutes, and from one of the pockets in the long skirt of his frieze coat, produced a bottle which he showed to his Rivirence, assuring him it was "the raal thing—not a headache in a gallon of it." Concealing the bottle again, they rang for a noggin of whisky and some cold water, and then, as Peter declared, for luck's sake having tasted the "raal thing," he again left the hotel.

The man Joel, whither he was bound, was ostensibly the proprietor of a small cigar shop, in which customers were served by two exceedingly pretty girls, who called themselves the old man's daughters, and who, if report spoke true, were about as fast a pair as could be found in Ireland ; but as they brought grist to the mill, the old man never interfered ; so long as money flowed in, what cared he for aught else ?

Joel himself was invariably to be found in a room upstairs, where he carried on the business of an attorney openly but secretly of a money-lender, and many of those who came to waste their time flirting in the shop, finished by paying a visit upstairs, where, if they had any security to offer, they were accommodated with a loan at "shent per shent." No one probably was more thoroughly conversant with the business of the neighbours for many miles round than Joel, and it was to him Peter had gone on first arriving at Limerick, and having told him plainly the facts of the case, asked for his assistance, when, after a moment's consideration, Joel replied,—

"It's meself that would help you if I could, Pater, for it is old friends that we are. Sure, were we not boys together forty years ago ; but it is yourself that knows I am a poor man and without money. What could I do at all, at all ?"

Peter, who understood the man thoroughly, replied instantly,—

"I have two or three hundred pounds of savings that I brought with me, thinking maybe they might be wanted."

Peter, who was watching the man closely, could see his eyes sparkle, but he only shook his head as he answered in a low voice, "It is five hundred he wants, and divil a shilling less."

At Peter's solicitations, however, he told him about the field, and how anxious the priest was to get it, but it belonged to Joel's brother, who lived in Dublin, and who was determined the priest should not have it; but as a great favour he'd let Peter have it for five hundred pounds.

"Five acres you said?" Peter remarked quietly; "in other words, one hundred pounds an acre. It's much obleeged to you I am;" and Peter, who had been fumbling in his pocket, now drew out three notes, each for one hundred pounds, and spread them out on the table. They were quite new and crisp, and as Peter contemplated them, he soliloquized,—

"It is weary work saving money it is; sometimes a shilling, but more often only sixpence at a time was I able to put by, till it's just three hundred pounds I have altogether; and if I offer it you for the five-acre field, sure it's not yourself, Joel, who'll refuse me."

But though Joel had lifted the notes from the table, and was examining them, he again shook his head as he said,—

"The field is not mine to sell, Pater, or you should have it and welcome; but it was just five hundred my brother said, and how could I sell it for three?"

Peter stretched out his hand for the notes, but like a true Hebrew, as Peter guessed, Joel

having once fingered the money, could not
bring himself to let it go again; but after some
more cavilling, at last agreed to draw up a deed
of sale from himself to Peter, as also a second
deed in blank, both on stamped paper, and he
promised they should be ready by half-past
eleven.

True to his word, Peter found both documents prepared, and returned at once with them
to the priest. As he entered the room, a
glance at the table showed him that the bottle
of whisky was three-parts empty, and Peter
guessed at once that as far as any examination
of the legal documents went, his Rivirence
would give little trouble, and in this respect he
was correct; but when the deed was filled in
and duly executed before witnesses, and all that
remained was to pay the money, then the bother
began. Producing an old leather pocket-book,
his Rivirence slowly and with the most evident
reluctance counted out one hundred pounds,
and then closing the case, replaced it in the
breast-pocket of his coat. He tried hard to
get hold of the documents which would give
him possession of the field, but Peter was not
so easily taken in, and insisted that the other

fifty pounds must be paid first. The liquor which the priest had imbibed made him both quarrelsome and obstinate, and, as it certainly did not suit Peter to have any misunderstanding with his Rivirence, he returned to Joel, who quickly drew up a proper promissory note for fifty pounds, armed with which Peter returned to the hotel. By this time the remainder of the whisky had disappeared, and his Rivirence, who was drowsy and stupid, consented with little difficulty to sign the note; and when this had been accomplished, Peter handed him the deed of sale and other documents, and then gave his Rivirence an arm to escort him downstairs to the car waiting to take him home. As they left the hotel, the clocks of the town were striking twelve. The fresh air and the shaking of the car roused the priest at once, and instead of being drowsy, he became hilarious and boisterous. Slapping Peter on the back, he declared he was a broth of a boy entirely; and then suddenly remembering the wedding, he insisted on the driver making the horse gallop, or he would be too late. It was half-past twelve when the car arrived at the chapel, and the priest, aided by Peter, got down,

and taking Peter's arm, was led by him inside the building. Cassidy and Norah were
waiting, and his Rivirence, who, after his rapid
drive through the open air, was now very far
gone indeed, asked no questions, but having put
on the surplice given him by Peter, instantly
began the service. He knew he had a couple
to marry : it was enough for him that a man and
woman were there, and he proceeded to tie the
knot.

It did not take long, and both parties had
just signed the register when there was a noise
at the door of the chapel, and Conway entered,
accompanied by about half a dozen of his
friends. He had been told that his Rivirence
had arrived, and had run to the chapel, hoping
to persuade the priest to at once perform the
ceremony. He never for one moment suspected
anything could have happened ; he had not the
slightest idea that there was any one else there
who would care to marry Norah, and now that
he had obtained her consent, felt not a shadow
of a doubt that, if not that day, most certainly
on the morrow, Norah would be his wife.

As he passed through the chapel towards the
vestry where the priest was disrobing, he

observed Norah (whose back being towards him, did not see him) talking to a stranger, but went on, without stopping, to his Rivirence. Nancy, however, who had been delighted at the wedding, now rushed up to the newly-married pair exclaiming,—

"Be off with you! Sure you have not a moment to lose if ye'd get away alive. He'll raise the whole country agin you."

Peter now joined them, and the three hurried to the car which had brought the priest from Limerick. The horse was grazing beside the road, the driver was nowhere to be seen, but Peter seized the reins, and Cassidy, having helped Norah to mount, took his place beside her, and they started, while in the vestry of the chapel the priest was still seated dazed and utterly bewildered, with Conway on one side, forgetting whom he was addressing in his fury at learning that Norah had been actually married to some one else, while on the other side of him was Nancy, who, to make a "divarsion," as she called it, was shaking her fist at him, and abusing him at the top of her voice for having taken the key and kept her out of the house.

# CHAPTER XII.

## "HOULD YOUR TONGUE!"

AS the car and its occupants left the chapel
farther and farther behind them, Norah,
who now at last began to realize the truth,
became so excited and wild with joy that
Cassidy was obliged to take her in his arms
and soothe her, for she really hardly knew what
she was saying or doing; but when, wrapt in
that strong embrace, she became calmer, then
Cassidy was able to explain to her how he
had learnt in Dublin of the terrible straits to
which she had been reduced—how he had been
lucky enough to meet with powerful friends, by
whose aid the marriage with Conway had been
delayed and their own brought about.

There was no need to say much—Norah was
too happy, and contented to find rest, peace,
and comfort in the arms of him whom she had
so long and truly loved, and whom, only a few

minutes before, she believed lost to her for ever, while Cassidy could not take his eyes off that long-loved face, and registered many an oath that if ever he had the chance, he would call those to a bitter account who had so cruelly treated his darling as to destroy all her beauty, and condemn her to endure the suffering of which her face gave such too-evident proof.

At the pace at which Peter was urging his horse, it did not take long to reach Limerick, and they drove straight to the same hotel at which his Rivirence had stopped. Here Peter left them, but returned in about fifteen minutes, and as he entered the room which they had engaged, Cassidy was instantly struck at the stern, anxious look on his face, so different from his usual joyous expression. He beckoned them to follow him from the hotel, and then, through some of the most odoriferous alleys of that dirtiest of towns, he led the way at so brisk a pace that it taxed Norah to keep up with him.

Soon he pushed open a door, and, ascending a filthy stair, entered a miserable garret of a place containing a table, three chairs, and a large painted press in a corner. Closing the door, he took from his pocket a telegram, which he handed to Cassidy, who, on opening it, read as follows :

" The cat is there, let mice beware."

With a smile, Cassidy looked up at Peter, saying,—

" What does this mean ?" but the latter shook his head as he replied,—

" I thought you knew. It is no laughing matter, I can tell you : it means that the man who is generally known as No. 1 has come back from America; that, thanks to that powerful organization, the so-called League, which he, to give the devil his due, so ably directs, nothing of any importance takes place in all Ireland of which he is not instantly, as if by magic, informed; and secondly, that every order which he, in consequence, may give, is obeyed to the letter. There can scarcely be a doubt that ere this he knows of this young woman's being carried off, and orders have been already issued that the trains are to be watched. At every station as far as the junction there will be persons on the look-out, to escape all of whom would be impossible ; and no sooner have they accomplished your destruction, than your wife, or widow rather, will be sent back here, and married to Conway within twenty-four hours."

"Good God!" exclaimed Cassidy. "Is it possible? But surely there must be some hope for us. Could we not go by car? they cannot watch all the roads."

"To attempt to hire a car would be hopeless; and besides, I have little or no money," Peter replied.

"I have still nearly three hundred pounds with me," exclaimed Cassidy; "but it is all in gold."

"How unfortunate that you did not change it all in Dublin!" said Peter. "The very fact of possessing gold here would at once excite suspicion. I must go again to Joel," he went on after a pause, "who might take it; but of course the old villain will rob us heavily."

"What matter," replied Cassidy, "so long as we get away out of this?"

"Give me another hundred pounds," said Peter, "and I will see what can be done; and in the meantime you must change your clothes and dress as a car-driver of the poorest class. You will find everything you require here, and when ready wait for me at the door below."

He opened the large painted press and then hurriedly left the house.

It was upwards of two hours before he returned, when he was so altered that Cassidy at first did not recognise him. He had shaved off his beard, moustache, and whiskers, as well as a round spot on top of his head as a tonsure, and was dressed in a seedy black suit and shabby tall hat, such as is worn by many of the priests all over Ireland. He was seated on a car evidently quite new, and was driving one of those thoroughbred, skinny, vicious mares so peculiar to that country. He signed to Cassidy, whose get-up was excellent, to mount the box, and to Norah, who had also changed her dress to be more in keeping with a car-driver's wife, to get up on the other side. They started as soon as ever Cassidy had hold of the reins, the mare laying back her ears and making her heels sound loudly against the bottom of the car as they did so. Not a word was spoken except the directions Peter from time to time gave Cassidy as to their route.

It taxed Cassidy's capabilities to the utmost to guide the mare; not only did she shy at everything she actually saw, but also often, as a Pat would say, out of mere divilment, besides which she had a habit of turning corners so sharp that three or four times it was a wonder they were not upset. At last they were clear of the purlieus of the town, and Cassidy, touching the mare with the whip, spun her along at a good ten miles an hour.

This, however, did not last long, but the baste soon settled down into her long swinging pace of between six and seven miles an hour, and then Peter told Cassidy how he had persuaded the Jew to buy both car and horse, for which, with harness, the old man had asked seventy pounds, but Peter had offered him ten pounds and the priest's acceptance for fifty, which, after much trouble, he had agreed to accept; but when he saw the gold, he had tried to go back of his bargain, so Peter had to give him five pounds extra as a bonus, and a second five to change forty more sovereigns into paper.

"I felt sorely tempted to throttle the ould blackguard," Peter said, "when he kept on pretending the sovereigns were only worth fifteen shillings each, when, by the newspaper which I asked him to show me, but which of course he declined to do, the real exchange is, for each sovereign twenty-five shillings in paper, as I saw afterwards."

Peter then went on to explain that they had forty-five miles to drive to a place which he knew, where they would halt for a rest, and probably spend the next day, partly on the mare's account, but more particularly to ascertain whether or not they were being pursued.

It was past twelve at night when they arrived. It was a weird place—an old deserted farm-house and buildings fast tumbling down, situated about a hundred yards from the high road on the top of a small hill, which rose alone in the otherwise flat country, and which thus gave them a commanding view on all sides, and so made it impossible that any one could approach them without being perceived some time previously.

Having fed the mare, they all slept till day-light, and then it was agreed that they should take it in turns to watch two hours at a time.

Slowly hour after hour passed ; they were to start after dark, and the sun was already on the horizon, when Norah, whose turn it was to watch, suddenly cried out that there was a car coming from the direction of Dublin, on which were seated four men besides the driver, one of whom she was certain was Michael Conway. Peter at once congratulated himself on the tactics he had adopted; for, as he remarked to Cassidy, had they continued their journey, they must have met Conway and his party face to face in the open road, and the contest between five men on one side and two encumbered with a woman on the other could hardly be doubtful.

"Now," he continued, "we have a chance at any rate, but there must be no half-measures; in the same manner as they will most certainly serve you and me if they can, so must we do to them. If one of those men lives to tell the tale, we are ourselves hopelessly doomed."

The three now descended the hill on the far side, so as to be unobserved from the approaching car, still **over a mile distant**, and concealed themselves among some scrubby bushes just at the spot where the boreen left the main road to ascend the hill to the ruined farm. They were armed with three revolvers, one belonging to Cassidy, one to Peter, and another Peter had bought in Limerick, and which was given to Norah to hold in readiness if wanted. Both men looked at her as she took the weapon, and both remarked, with satisfaction, that her hand was as steady, if not more so, than their own, and that though her face was pale, there was a look of stern determination on it which said, as she looked with a smile at her husband, if you die, I will not survive you.

It was decided that Peter, who was to the right, should take the man nearest the driver, and with his next barrel should shoot the horse, while Cassidy should settle the other man on their own side, and if he fell forward out of the way, his second shot should be for one of the men on the other side of the car, who would thus be exposed to view ; but no shot was to be fired till Peter gave the signal.

" Your man is Michael Conway," whispered Norah.

" Wait till they are right opposite, and then shoot them in the face," said Peter.

The car was now close by. It was coming very slowly, and a discussion seemed to be going on as to whether they should stop at the ruined farm on the hill or not.

" There is some one there, bedad," cried one of the men. " Didn't I see smoke coming from the chimney ? "

"If it's that ould blackguard Peter that's with them, as they say it is, shure he knows the place well; shure his father lived and died there."

"Let's go there then," said Conway, "and oh, Norah darling, if it's there you are, it's mine you'll be this blessed night. I gave you the chance, fool that I was, of his Rivirence's blessing, but as you declined it, I'll just take you without it, and it's sweeter, maybe, you'll be, my honey," and he opened his arms as if to clasp her in them, while he gave a hideous laugh, in which the others joined.

The car was exactly opposite to the three now; but it is probable that Peter had decided, as he heard they were about to visit the ruined farm, to wait till the car was in the act of turning before giving the signal, as it would then be more or less stationary.

Michael Conway's coarse jest and laugh, however, was more than Norah could bear. The very idea of falling into his clutches in the manner at which he had more than hinted, gave her a strength and courage which she herself little believed she possessed. With an inward resolve that if she could prevent it, never, never should he lay a finger on *her*, she forgot all Peter's instructions, and raising the pistol she had been instructed to hold, she pointed it straight at Conway's grinning mouth, and pulled the trigger. At the short distance the man was from her, it was almost impossible she could miss her mark, and as Conway fell forward shot dead, Norah, horrified when she saw what she had done, sank also on the ground beside her husband. Never was surprise more complete, and before those on the car had recovered from it, the man who sat on the same side as Conway, as well as he whose back became exposed when Conway fell, were shot down.

The horse, at which Peter fired his second shot, was not killed, but in his mad plungings upset the car, thus throwing off it both the driver and the last man. The former was struck by the horse's hoofs almost before he reached the ground, and thus rendered senseless; but the latter, falling unhurt, was in the act of rising when Peter rushed up to him. He was, to all appearances, unarmed, for though he had both knife and revolver with him, he had not had time to grasp either.

"Be me sowl!" he cried, as, while still on his knees, he saw Peter, and instantly recognised him, "if it is not Pater himself, and it's glad I am to see you, and that is the truth," and then, observing that Peter raised his revolver, he cried out, "Arrah, be aisy now! Don't ye know me, Pater? And would you be after shooting an innocent man as ye would a dog?"

"Is it know you! Faith, and I do; who better? It is many a long day since we met, Larry, but it's no fault of mine, for I've hunted for you from one end of the country to the other."

"Is that true?" Larry exclaimed, with an admirably assumed air of innocence; "and to think that I never knew it!"

He was kneeling on his coat in such a manner that it was impossible to get at the pocket where his pistol was lying; but Peter, who never took his eye off him for a moment, observed how he was trying to change his position, so as to release the weapon. He was a large and very powerful man in the prime of life, and Peter, who was small and thin, and past sixty years of age, knew well that in a hand-to-hand encounter he would not have a shadow of a chance, and so took care to keep several yards distance between them.

As if in attempting to rise to his feet he had overbalanced himself, Larry rolled back on to the ground, and instantly his right hand, sliding to the bottom of his pocket, grasped his pistol, and was in the act of cocking it as he drew it out, when there was a loud report, and his right arm fell helpless to his side,—Peter, to save his own life, had shot him with his revolver just below the shoulder, and broken his arm.

There was a howl as of a wounded wild beast, while the oaths and imprecations which he showered on Peter were awful to listen to.

"Hush! hush!" cried the latter; "hould your noise, can't ye? I've one or two questions to ask ye, if for onst ye can spake the truth."

"And if I do, will ye let me go?" asked the man.

Peter shook his head, as he replied,—

"It is now near twenty years ago since with your palavering ways ye persuaded Biddy— do you mind *my* Biddy?—to leave her father's house, and when under a solemn oath to marry her she trusted you. Did you keep your word? Is she your wife now? Was she ever your wife? If so, tell me what has become of her?"

"She is dead," he murmured.

"Dead, did you say?" Peter continued. "How do you know that? Yes; she died in these arms, of want, starvation, with just strength enough left to tell me how you had illtreated her, and how, weary of being beaten nearly to death, as you, cowardly baste as you are, were always doing to the poor crittur, she ran away and left you. It was then, as I closed her eyes, I swore that if you were alive I'd find you, and that when the day of reckoning came, as it was certain to do, I'd shoot you as sure as there is a hell beneath us waiting to receive you!"

The man lay back on the ground supporting himself on his left elbow; if he was suffering pain, he showed no signs of it, but there was a look of low cunning on his face as he glanced out of the corner of his eye at Peter, which evidently showed he did not for a moment believe that Peter would put his threat into execution, and, now that the fight was over,

shoot him in cold blood.    He thought it
better, however, to ignore any reference to
Biddy, as it evidently exasperated Peter, and
so said, "And what questions would ye be
asking me, Pater?"

"What brought you here to-day?" began
Peter.

"Sure, I had orders from Dublin," was the
reply.

"What to do?" asked Peter.

"Go with the others to find the young
woman, and take her back, if possible, alive;
but if not, dead, to Limerick."

"And did you know who was with her?"

"A man disguised as a priest, and another,
a stranger, who was dressed as a car-driver."

"Did you know the name of either of these
men?"

There was, perhaps, just a shade of hesitation as Larry answered,—

"No!"

"And you could not form any guess?"

"By the Holy Mother of Jesus I swear I had
not an idea!"

"False to the very last!" Peter cried.   "You
will die with a lie on your lips.   Did you not

say as the car came along the road, ' If it's
that old blackguard Peter that's with them'?　I
could not mistake the voice; had I not been
waiting to hear it for twenty years ? "

There was something in the tone in which
these last words were uttered that caused Larry
to look up, and as he caught sight, in the
fading light, of Peter's face, he, for the first
time, began to realize the fact that his hour had
really come.　Abject coward as he was at heart,
he turned livid with fear as he watched Peter
examining the lock of his revolver.

" Ah, Pater, Pater darling," he began, re-
solved to make one more attempt to soften the
old man, "sure you remimber——"

" Hould your tongue, I tell ye," cried Peter,
interrupting him; "remimber, indeed !　Can I
ever forget my poor Biddy's face as she lay
dying in my arms—she that had been the beauty
and pride of the whole country ? and who done
it but you, schaming blackguard that you are,
with your promises to marry her, and then,
when you had had your will of her, laving her to
her fate !　Remimber, indeed!　Why wouldn't
I, only too well !　Sure, and it's that which
gives me the courage to shoot you this night

as I would a dog, for it's very like murder,
Larry, to kill a man in cold blood, and what
I'd sooner not do, if it could be anyhow
avoided."

" Listen, honey, let me say one word more!"
Larry cried, a sudden light coming into his
eyes, anxious at any cost to gain time, and
casting a despairing glance around, in hopes of
seeing some one make his appearance in that
most desolate country.

" I'd have married Biddy if I could.   Be me
sowl I would !"

"And   what   prevented   you ? "   inquired
Peter.

"Sure—sure, had I not a wife already in
Dublin ?"

" And you *dare* to tell *me* that !" exclaimed
Peter, slowly and solemnly; "you dare to
pretend that all the months you were a-
courting my poor girl, it was to ruin her
you were schaming.  Blackguard as I knew
you to be, I never could have believed this,
Larry.  However, it's glad I am you've told
me; the job's asier to do now.  Biddy," he
cried, after a moment's pause, " me darlint "—
addressing her as if the girl had been really

present—"the hour has come at last; and the villain who ruined you pays the penalty with his life. Your old father will die happy now!"

Two shots in quick succession followed, and Larry fell back—dead.

No sooner was the deed done than Peter was once more himself. Looking round, neither Cassidy nor his wife were to be seen, so Peter rightly guessed they had returned to the ruined farm. Casting his eye on the dead men, Peter now approached Conway, and in a few moments had exchanged dresses with him, thus letting it be supposed that it was the priest who had been slain. Hardly had he finished, when, hearing wheels, he observed Cassidy and his wife leading their own horse and car down the hill. Neither of them re-cognising him in the semi - darkness, they stopped the moment they perceived him, and Cassidy drew his revolver. Instantly hailing them, he assured them it was "all right," and they came on at once, laughing at their mistake. He explained to them that, in his opinion, their best chance was to get as fast as possible to the nearest station, and take the train to Dublin, that, in order to do this with any chance of success, the woman must disappear as the priest had done already.

"Choose," said Peter to Cassidy, "any of the four, and let your wife change dresses as quickly as possible.'

Meanwhile, Peter taking the mare out of the car, made her draw two of the dead men away out of sight, and then the car which Conway and his party had used, being found to be still uninjured, was once more brought into requisition, and their own mare being harnessed to it, three, to all appearance countrymen, started in it, leaving behind them, on or near the road, a nearly new car topsy-turvy, a priest, a woman, and a car-driver lying dead beside it.

Safely, without further molestation, they reached Dublin the following morning, and were duly conducted to the house in Stoney Batter by Peter, who hoped to find there either letters or telegrams from Mr. French.

# CHAPTER XIII.

## "LET HIM BEWARE."

ABOUT four o'clock on the same afternoon
on which the events recorded in the last
chapter took place, a well-appointed brougham,
drawn by a pair of horses, drew up in front
of the same house in Nassau Street to which,
as already related, the man Pat made his way
to give information of Mr. French's whereabouts. On the bell being rung and the door
opened, a gentleman, the sole occupant of the
brougham, alighted, and springing up the stairs
two steps at a time, entered unannounced into
the same library from which Pat had been dismissed on his murderous errand. The gentleman, seated still in front of his writing-table,
rose and received the new-comer with every
mark of respect and courtesy, insisting on his
taking the most comfortable arm-chair in the

room, whilst he, reseating himself at the
table, swung his chair round, so as to face
his guest.

"I called this morning between ten and
eleven," the new-comer began—"so anxious
was I to see you; but they told me you were
asleep, and I would not let them wake you."

"It was late when we arrived. We had a
terrible passage, and missed the tide, and I
found so much to do when I did get here, that
it was eight o'clock before I lay down. Still,
had I known it was your excellency——"

"And what was the result of your mission?"
asked the Prime Minister, interrupting; "it is
*that* I am so anxious to learn."

"A difficult question to answer, as I am not
by any means sure whether you will think it
satisfactory or the contrary. They agree to
come, of course, but only on their own terms,
which are very hard. Are things so very bad
that we cannot wait in hopes of getting better
conditions? They seem to know we cannot
carry on without them."

"Could hardly be worse as far as I see,"
replied the Prime Minister, with a sigh; "but
I was in hopes that the wretched state of the

country would not be known over there. This
is indeed bad news."

"Your excellency should have been aware
by this time that they possess a secret police
here, which keeps them well informed of all
that goes on. It is really a wonderful organization, which at times seems to have the
power of divulging our most secret thoughts.
Perhaps your excellency will tell me your most
pressing emergencies, and let me see if I can
in any way assist you."

"Really the prospect is so gloomy, look
which way I will, that I hardly know where
to begin. Little did I ever guess the difficulty
of governing such a country as this; and when
the G. O. M. offered us repeal, I fondly imagined our troubles were over, instead of which
they were only beginning. I sometimes think
now that he was really glad to shift the burden
on to other shoulders, and that was why he so
readily came to terms with us."

"It is useless now to cry over spilt milk.
England, having at last yielded to the universal
desire of the whole country, and allowed us to
govern ourselves, looks to us to show ourselves
worthy of the confidence she has reposed in us

—expects to see the country become daily more prosperous, law and order more respected, and the people truly happy and contented under our most enlightened Parliament."

If there was the slightest suspicion of a sneer as the last words were pronounced, it passed unnoticed as the Prime Minister replied, "How can any country prosper which not only has no money, but no credit on which to borrow any? Without this, the best Government in the world is paralysed—ceases, in fact, to be a power in the land, as, no matter what laws it may make, unless it can insure their being obeyed, it is mere waste of time to issue them. As to the people being happy and contented, they ought to be so, I am sure. They have full and complete possession of their farms, for which they have always been clamouring; they are left in perfect liberty to enjoy them ; and as to taxes, not a penny do they pay. What more can they possibly ask or hope to obtain ? "

"An *Eldorado* almost perfect, and which wants so little to make it quite so," remarked the Prime Minister's companion, who was in reality the individual so well known in Ireland as No. 1.

"And what is that?" the Prime Minister asked innocently.

"The safety for life and preservation of property. The laws are good enough, but there is no one to administer them; nor are there any means of enforcing the decrees which may be given. Is it for this the people have elected a Parliament, to whom they appeal to be wisely and properly governed—so far, alas! in vain; but the time cannot be far distant when the people in its might will surely demand from its nominees an account of their stewardship, and if they have been found wanting, there will be a terrible day of reckoning."

"If they want us to govern the country, they must give us the means to do so," said the Prime Minister, sulkily, not at all relishing either the nature of the remarks or the tone of the observations to which he had been listening.

"Unfortunately," No. 1 continued, "that is just one of the things which the people in their mighty sovereignty never have taken into account, and probably never will. Having paid you the compliment of electing you to be their representatives, they seem to consider that you

in return should show your sense of the honour
conferred by governing them according to the
most advanced Liberal opinions, as they are
pleased to term it. As to money, or means, as
you call it, if you are strong enough to enforce
payment of the taxes, with which your Parliament in its wisdom thinks proper to burden
the people, so much the better for you ; if not,
why, then, so much the better for them."

"You have not yet told me the terms on
which our friends are willing to come," said the
Prime Minister, anxious to change the subject.

"Everything is to continue, to all outward
appearance, as at present ; but, except in name,
the present Government will cease to exist."

"And how about money? will they undertake
to provide that ?" asked the Prime Minister.

"On the contrary, it is precisely to get that,
or, rather, for the purpose of repaying themselves some of their heavy advances, that they
are coming here. They propose to impose a
capitation tax."

"Impossible !" cried the Prime Minister ;
" Parliament would never vote it."

"It must be your business to introduce the
measure, gradually accustom your party to the

idea, and finally persuade them to agree to it. You understand?"

There was a short pause. The Prime Minister fidgeted on his chair; his companion watched him, but without appearing to do so.

Soon the former said, "The North will never pay it."

"Damn them! then they must be stamped out," cried No. 1, in an access of fury, such as the Prime Minister never remembered to have witnessed in his companion's usual calm demeanour; then drawing his chair closer, and laying his hand on the Prime Minister's arm, he almost hissed out, as he actually ground his teeth in his rage,—

"HE was here in Dublin, asleep in bed, dared to put himself in my power—to defy me, in fact, and escaped—slipped through my fingers in the most wonderful manner; but I will be even with him yet.  Let him beware."

"Of whom are you speaking?" inquired the Prime Minister; "not of Terence O'Grady, surely!"

"Faith and I am, the very man himself!" replied No. 1, rising from his chair, and

walking up and down the room in his excitement.

"Is it possible? but the act which passed
two days ago has not yet been put in force;
when it has, his party will be broken up, and
he must either fall into our hands or fly the
country."

No. 1 could not forbear a smile as he listened
to this remark, and then immediately rejoined,

"Did you not yourself tell me just now that,
owing to want of means, you could not enforce
your decrees?"

"But I have every hope that this case will
prove the exception. The stocks of material
are known to be so large in the possession of
the manufacturers, and which, owing to the
heavy duties now imposed, they cannot export,
and which must therefore necessarily fall into
our hands, that I believe—nay, I feel sure—we
can raise a small loan. I have therefore taken
steps to call together five hundred men of the
late coastguard, who have at once responded
to our call, and are coming in fast. There are
more than two hundred and fifty already lodged
in the Royal Barracks.

"Have you seen them yet?" asked No. 1.

"No," was the reply; "I am going to-morrow morning at ten o'clock."

"Call for me, and I will accompany you. If these men are only stanch and true to you, much may yet be done; but as to the act which you have passed, and of which every one is talking, it is *bosh*, neither more nor less; utterly useless, and a mere waste of time. With such men as you have to deal with in the North, half measures are an absurdity, and only tend to make the Government ridiculous and laughed at. Introduce, then, a short measure ordering all Orangemen to quit the country within thirty days, they and their wives and children, taking with them nothing but their clothes, and if after that time any of that damned set shall be found in Ireland, they shall be considered as outlaws, and dealt with accordingly. Get your Parliament to pass *that*, and never fear we will find means to carry it into effect."

"You are right," replied the Prime Minister; "I am quite sure you are right, but I am not omnipotent. Wait a day or two, and I will bring the matter before the council, and see what they say. I must go now"—looking at his watch; "I have just time to dine, and then be at the

House to answer questions. I expect to be nicely badgered."

"What about ?" asked No. 1.

"Oh, Mrs. Kelly, of course: her case is the Major's hobby, which he rides to death. I am sick of the very name of the woman."

"Then snuff her out, smash her up, and all her vile crew with her; make an example of her, and let it be seen that the law cannot be defied with impunity." (How truly Irish for the man who acknowledged no law but his own autocratic will, to be so indignant that another should also defy the law !)

"Easier said than done, my friend," exclaimed the Prime Minister. "Whom have I to send against her, unless some of our coast-guard just arrived ?"

"The Major is right, nevertheless," exclaimed No. 1; "and the woman must be got rid of. I must see to it myself."

They shook hands and parted for the night; but at ten the next morning the Prime Minister came, according to promise, and the pair started for the Royal Barracks.

Those who had by this time come in numbered nearly three hundred altogether, and a more likely set of men could hardly be found anywhere. They were nearly all old men-of-war's-men, who, having been drafted into the reserve, had been employed in the coastguard till the Repeal, when they were told that as smuggling was a thing unknown under an advanced Liberal Government, their services would be no longer required. As nearly all of them had been lucky enough to put by a little money, they had been able to live quietly, until now, hearing there was again a chance of employment, they had been only too glad to apply for it, and there was little doubt that in a few days the whole five hundred would make their appearance. As this was the first time that any one in authority had been to visit them, the men gathered together in a body, and requested to be allowed to have a few minutes' conversation.

"By all means," replied the Prime Minister. "What is it?"

A very fine old man, a perfect type of the man-of-war's-man stepped to the front as spokesman. Having hitched up his trousers in true orthodox fashion, he said, "We were told, your honour, that our pay would be three pounds a month and two suits of clothes. Is that correct?"

"It is," replied the Prime Minister; "that is the pay we are prepared to give."

"We suppose there is not much night-work, your honour?"

"No! Oh, no! certainly not," hazarded the Prime Minister.

"And what is the work, please your honour?"

"Well! an Act of Parliament having been passed which prohibits the exportation of all linen goods except after payment of a heavy export duty, it will be your business to watch the coast from Carlingford to Donegal, and look out that there is no infringement of the law."

"And should we discover that such work is going on, the goods are to be seized and handed over to the authorities?"

"Unquestionably! and also the men so employed, if by any means possible to catch them. Should they resist capture, you will be armed with revolvers, which you will not hesitate to use."

"And on each seizure shall we receive any bonus?"

A "no" trembled on the lips of the Prime

Minister, but before he could pronounce it, No. 1 said, "Certainly! a third of the proceeds of each seizure shall be yours."

Another of the men now said, laughing, "Some of us have been jeered at and called tax-gatherers, and we would wish for an assurance from your honour that we are not to be employed in that manner."

"Very good!" said No. 1, but the Prime Minister added: "It is impossible to bind ourselves positively as to the exact duties on which you may be employed. The work for which you are engaged I have already explained to you, but occasions may arise when it might be absolutely necessary to call in the aid of your services, and in such an emergency we should expect no grumbling, but a cheerful obedience to all orders given."

"Our wives and families are left totally unprovided for," said the first speaker; "we have also ourselves some few purchases to make. We hope your honours will give us an advance."

"How much?" inquired the Prime Minister, who seemed to think that the sooner they were away, the better.

"Two months' pay," replied the old man.

An indignant refusal on the part of the Prime Minister was forestalled by No. 1, who quickly said,—

"In other words, six pounds apiece? You shall have it."

The Prime Minister's face grew very dark as he bit his lips to prevent an angry retort, while he remarked that he could wait no longer, as he had business elsewhere.

"When are we to start, your honour?" asked the first speaker as both gentlemen were moving away.

"To-morrow night," answered No. 1; "I will let you know the hour."

No sooner were they seated in the brougham than the Prime Minister began, as he threw himself wearily back in the carriage, "I never heard anything so preposterous in my life as for men like that to be making terms with us! and you acceded to all their demands! May I ask where the two thousand pounds are to come from to pay the advance demanded?"

"I liked the appearance of the men much," No. 1 remarked quietly, "and if you want your work well done, I know how necessary it is to content those whom you employ. If it is any convenience to you, I will pay this trifle myself, and you can either give me a Government bond for the amount, or, if you prefer it, I will for the two months take the men altogether into my own employ."

"The latter arrangement would suit best," replied the Prime Minister after a few moments' consideration; "but of course on the conditions that the matter is kept strictly secret between us, that the orders issued are in the name of the Government, and that the men are to be employed only according to the promise made to them."

"To your first two conditions I agree at once; as to the third, should I attempt to employ the men in any other manner than that stipulated, they would unquestionably desert, and I should lose my money."

"And who tells you that they won't decamp now an hour after they are paid?" asked the Prime Minister. "To my mind there is nothing more probable."

No. 1 smiled, as, shaking his head, he replied, "No fear! were it necessary, I would trust those men with double or treble the amount. How could it possibly benefit them to deceive

me ? whereas it is clearly much to their interest
to serve me well and faithfully."

" I sincerely hope you are right," said the
Prime Minister, as the brougham, stopping in
Nassau Street, No. 1 alighted, and after shaking
hands with his companion, took his latch-key
from his pocket, and entered his own house.
Just inside the door he found a man waiting
for him, whom, not recognising, he asked,—

" Where do you come from ? "

" Stoney Batter—the house which——"

" Follow me," said No. 1, interrupting him.

He led the way upstairs, and having signed
to the man to precede him, followed into his
own room and closed the door; then turning to
the man, he said, " Well ! "

" I was sent to tell you that early this morning three men, to all outward appearance
countrymen, arrived, and having asked for
telegrams and letters, went to bed. They had
evidently travelled far, and were very tired.

" Is it at all suspected who they are ? "

" One is an old man named Pater, a rale
schamer; the second is a gentleman, and the
third a woman."

No. 1 gave a low whistle as he walked across

the room to where a telephone was fixed to the wall. As he unhooked the two handles, one from each side, he said to the man with him in the room, " If these three persons came early, why was I not told before ? "

" Sure, your honour was not at home," was the reply. Have I not been waiting here these three mortal hours to see your honour ? sure, you can ask the sarvint if it's not so."

" Very well," was the reply ; " you can go now, and tell him who sent you that I'll not forget him."

" Thank your honour," the man said as he backed out of the room and down the stairs, while No. 1 telephoned orders that the three persons who had that morning arrived at the old Orange Lodge in Stoney Batter were to be instantly arrested and brought to Nassau Street.

# CHAPTER XIV.

## "FLY INSTANTLY!"

WORN out and tired as John Cassidy had
been on his arrival in Dublin that morning, he had thrown himself (as had done the
others) dressed as he was, on a couch, hoping to
get some sleep. Hardly were the heads of
Mrs. Cassidy and Peter on their pillows, ere
they were off; but with Cassidy himself it was
not so. He was a man of iron constitution,
to whom fatigue was almost unknown, and
having had a few hours' sleep the night before
at the ruined farm, it seemed to him the height
of folly not to keep some sort of watch,
located as they were at the headquarters of
their enemies.

It so happened that when they arrived at
Stoney Batter, Peter had gone forward to get
admittance to the house, while Cassidy stood
for a moment in the street to pay the car
which had brought them from the station, and

also with the object of seeing whether there might be any one watching them. Observing no one, he was following Peter, when the man in charge of the house, not knowing him, laid his hand on his arm to stop him, and as he did so, Cassidy felt a cold shudder creep over him, similar to that which some people experience at the touch of a toad. Superstitious as all his countrymen are, he felt instantly an innate distrust of the man, and determined to watch him narrowly. Every sense on the *qui vive*, Cassidy lay still till daylight, when hearing, as he thought, a creak of the stairs, he crept off his couch and made his way to the door. Listening intently, he seemed to feel there was some one outside; so opening the door noiselessly, he peeped through, and could see the caretaker seated on top of the stairs with something in his hand, which he was turning over and over. Inadvertently Cassidy just touched the handle of the door, and instantly whatever the man had in his hand disappeared into his pocket. Advancing coolly, Cassidy went straight up to the man and held out his hand. He looked him full in the face, but never said a word. The caretaker hesitated ; slowly, and evidently most unwillingly, he withdrew his hand from his pocket with the letter still in it, and after looking at it again as if most loth to part with it, finally gave it to Cassidy, stating at the same time that it had just come, but that as he could not read, he did not know for whom it was intended. Cassidy did not wait to hear his explanation, but returning into the room, locked the door, and then, going over to the window, could just make out in the dim night that it was a telegram addressed to himself, the envelope of which had been already torn open.

Extracting the paper from the envelope, he unfolded it, and found only the numbers 1 6 5 4 —not a word of any sort else. Utterly at a loss to understand it, he looked to see who had sent it, when he could just decipher the letters T. O. G.

Without an instant's delay, Cassidy roused Peter, and explained to him about the telegram. With some trouble, Peter found a manuscript pamphlet, which he gave to Cassidy, who, on opening it, found it was compiled exactly like the mercantile code of signals—each number answering to a sentence on some subject or another. Turning out the number 1654, Cassidy read, "You are in the greatest danger—fly instantly!" Observing an asterisk opposite the number, he read in a foot-note, "Never to be used except in cases of the most urgent necessity, when it must always be understood that the ordinary means of locomotion are barred, and not to be attempted."

Cassidy gave vent to a low, smothered oath as he read this, and asked himself the question —what was to be done? Turning to look at his two companions, he saw that Peter was again asleep, and his wife also — the latter looking so worn and tired that he could not have the heart to wake her. Looking at his watch, and finding it was only a little after five, he decided to remain quiet till eight, as, notwithstanding the urgency of the telegram, he was convinced his wife must have rest, or she would break down altogether, and then they would be indeed in a dilemma—and so of two evils he must choose the least.

He lay down again on his couch to ponder over the situation, and while so engaged, fell asleep himself, and never woke till past nine. Instantly rousing the others, he told Peter

to get breakfast at once; and as soon as that
was finished, he called the caretaker and sent
him on an errand with a note to Merrion
Square, ordering him to be back as quickly as
possible.

Hardly had he left the house than Cassidy
told Peter the contents of the telegram, and
urged their immediate departure. To this
Peter agreed, as far as Cassidy and his wife
were concerned, and the three started on foot
to the house of a man who Peter knew was
to be thoroughly trusted, and who at once
placed his own horse and car at Cassidy's
disposal. Peter now gave him full instructions
as to his route to Drumree Station, advising
him there to take the night train (and go on
to the Cottage, as arranged with Mr. French),
and Peter also undertook to have a man at the
station to take charge of the car. Both Cassidy
and his wife were loth to part with Peter. The
man had proved himself a true friend and very
able coadjutor, and Cassidy would have been
very glad to have had his assistance for the
remainder of the journey. Peter, however,
declared he had business which detained him
in Dublin for that day, but would try and

meet them that same night at Drumree.   He
also pointed out how much better chance they
would have of escape if separate, than if they
continued together ; and as Cassidy could not
deny there was much reason in this latter
argument, they shook hands heartily and parted,
Cassidy and his wife driving off on the car,
while Peter remained in the house of his
friend.   Five minutes later the latter also left,
carrying in his hand a slip of paper on which,
at his dictation, his friend had written a few
words of which the ink was still wet.

Returning at a rapid pace to the house in
Stoney Batter, Peter mounted the stairs and
entered the room in which the three had
breakfasted.   The caretaker was still absent,
so nothing had been touched.  Peter now
proceeded to remove the cover from a packing-
case which, though empty, had been left in
one corner of the room, and this Peter proceeded to fill with books and any other heavy
articles on which he could lay his hands.   He
then replaced the cover, and fastened it with
a couple of nails.   His next job was to clear
the table, packing away plates, cups, saucers,
etc., on a tray, ready for removal downstairs

to be washed. He had hardly finished when, hearing a step on the stair, he went to the door, and found the caretaker just returned. The man smiled as he saw Peter—a sort of self-satisfied grin, as much as to say, "So there you are, all right."

"Well!" exclaimed Peter.

"I left the note, yer honour, but the master was out, and there was no answer."

"There are these cups and saucers to wash up, Mat," Peter now said; "but first help me to carry this box inside : it never ought to have been left here."

"Sure, it's empty, Mr. Pater," the man replied.

"Then carry it inside yourself," Peter exclaimed; "I've left the door open."

"Bedad and I will, your honour," and going up to the box, he attempted to lift it, but finding this to be impossible, began to slide it along the floor.

"I thought you told me it was empty," said Peter with a grin, as he watched the man's operations.

"Bedad, it's very heavy!" he cried, as straightening himself, and, taking off his hat, he began to wipe his forehead with a cotton handkerchief. He was a short, spare man, about forty years of age, and wore a long frieze coat reaching below his ankles, which greatly impeded his movements in his attempts to push the box along the floor.

"Come," said Peter, as, having taken off his coat and thrown it on to a chair, he placed himself at one end of the box; "we'll carry it together," and lifting it between them, they crossed that room and also another smaller one till they came to the foot of a short stair consisting of about six steps leading to a small storeroom on top. Turning himself round and walking backwards, Peter began the ascent, and was already up three steps, when Mat tried to ascend the first. His long coat, however, came in his way, and his two hands being both necessary to support the box, he found it simply impossible to get his foot on to the stair without at the same time treading on the coat, which, being thus held firm, quite precluded any chance of advancing his other leg.

"Come on, will ye?" cried Peter; "the box is heavy."

"Be Jasus, it's the truth you're telling this

time, Mr. Peter, and what else? Sure, it's me coat that impades me."

"Take it off then will ye, ye born omadhawn!" cried Peter as he staggered under the weight, and the box threatened to bring them both down together.

" And how would I do that at all, at all ? " asked Mat, and me hands engaged in houlding the box."

" Rest the box on your knee will ye, and be quick."

Thus apostrophized, the man had no option but to obey, and slipping first one arm then the other out of his coat, he let it, with the most evident reluctance, fall to the ground. As soon as they were up the stairs, Peter made Mat carry his end of the box first towards the far corner of the closet, and then, as it was placed on the floor, Mat was told to push it against the wall.

Apparently watching what he was doing, Peter gradually approached the stair, which he began to descend backwards till his feet became entangled in the frieze coat, when he stooped, and raising it by the skirts, shook it as if to get rid of the dust. A pistol, a tobacco pouch and pipe, also a large half-dagger, half-knife in a case fell on the floor. Another shake, and a quantity of what appeared to be letters and telegrams followed suit.

"Tear and 'ounds!" Peter heard Mat exclaim, as, observing what had happened, he made a rush towards his coat.

"Stand back," cried Peter as he took the pistol in his hand and turned to face Mat.

For one instant only Mat hesitated; then he exclaimed with a grin, "Sure, you need not be afraid of it, Mr. Pater; it's not loaded."

"In that case," Peter answered coolly, "I'll pull the trigger," and suiting the action to the word, he did so, when there was immediately a loud report.

That the pistol was pointed in the direction of Mat's head is certain, but whether Peter actually intended to shoot the man will never be known, as so intent was Mat in watching Peter, that just as the latter fired, he missed the first step of the stair, and falling head downwards on to the floor below, rolled over on to his side, and lay there motionless.

As Peter stood over him wondering whether he was really hurt or only pretending to be so, the body quivered as if a shiver had passed over it, the jaw dropped, and all was still. Kneeling down, Peter now placed his hand on the man's heart, but could feel no movement. So having collected together the letters and other articles, he unsheathed the knife—a murderous weapon nearly a foot long and as sharp as a razor—which he held poised over the man as if about to plunge it into his heart; but watching his face and perceiving that he made no sign, he forbore, and muttering, " Maybe it's better so; his neck's broke; he'll do no more harm; " then, as if soliloquizing to himself, he continued, " To think that he should turn out to be such a low, skulking traitor after all, and it's meself that recommended him to the master. Bad cess to me for that same." So saying, he pinned the piece of paper which his friend had written for him to the collar of the man's coat, and a minute after had left the house.

# CHAPTER XV.

## "WELCOME!"

HAD any stranger been shown upstairs in the house in Nassau Street on that same afternoon about three o'clock, he would have found it difficult to believe that the individual whom he saw there, more like a fiend than a human being, so beside himself was he with rage, could be truly the quiet, cool, calculating man so well known as "No. 1." He had just been informed that those who had been sent to Stoney Batter had found no one there except the caretaker lying dead on the floor of an inner room, to whose shoulder had been pinned a piece of paper, which had been brought to No. 1, who read as follows :

"A traitor his doom has met,
And with life has paid the debt,
So let 'Number One' beware,
And his soul for hell prepare."

As his passion cooled, he sat down again at the

table to consider what was to be done, muttering to himself as he did so that he'd send some
of them to hell before another twenty-four
hours were passed.    Ten minutes later the
telephone conveyed orders that twenty men
were to be sent by the five o'clock train that
afternoon to Beaupark, half a dozen of whom
were to go on to Mr. French's cottage at Slane
and burn it to the ground with every soul in
it, while the others were to watch the station
and dispose effectually of any one who might
arrive there on the way to the cottage either
during that night or the following day.

"I'll teach these fellows to give *me* advice,"
he muttered, as, descending the stairs, he hailed
a car and ordered the driver to take him to
the Royal Barracks.    "Master Terence," he
went on thinking aloud, "may defy the Government with impunity as much as he likes, but, by
God, he had better not try any of his tricks on
me, or I'll crush him as easily as I will that fly,"
and he made a well-directed blow at one of
those bravest of insects crawling over his knee;
but, somehow the fly did not quite see it, but
spreading its tiny wings before the hand could
descend, flew merrily away.    Was its escape

typical of the future?   No. 1, at any rate, did not seem to think so, to judge by the expression of his face as the car bore him on his way.

Peter in the meantime had had a busy day. He seemed literally to be ubiquitous as he made his way from house to house, never in any single instance stopping more than two or three minutes.   Informed late in the afternoon that the cottage at Slane was to be attacked that night, and also that all the stations on the line— more especially that at Beaupark—were to be watched by a set of cut-throats ordered there for that express purpose, Peter, knowing Mr. French to be far from the cottage, decided to use all his endeavours to save Cassidy and his wife from being massacred at the station, and after some consideration, devised a scheme which he hoped would be successful.

When, punctual to the minute of nine o'clock, that night the train left the Dublin terminus, Peter occupied a seat next the door of a third-class compartment, while opposite to him sat three men for whom he had taken tickets, and to whom he occasionally made a remark.

In due course the train arrived at Drumree

Station, where Cassidy and his wife, who were waiting on the platform, immediately entered a second class carriage; but as they did so, Peter's quick eye spotted two men who, having waited till Cassidy was safely in the train, and the door of the compartment closed, at the last moment swung themselves into a third-class carriage.

The train proceeded on its way, and arrived safely at Duleek, which is the station immediately preceding that at which Cassidy was to alight for the cottage. There were only two passengers waiting, and almost immediately the guard whistled and held up his hand, and the steam being turned on, the train glided out of the station. Both near and distant signals being favourable, the driver was in the act of turning on full steam, when he observed the distant signal which he was now fast approaching, suddenly change to red. Instantly shutting off the steam and whistling to the guard to put on the breaks, the speed of the train was at once checked, and in a few moments it came to a standstill. They had then about twenty yards to traverse before reaching the signal-lamp, which still showed a bright red light. As the guard descended on one side of the train, Peter,

followed by the three other men, left their
carriage on the other; both went forward, the
guard to the signalman to know what was the
matter, Peter and his companions towards the
engine.   Passing the tender, they could see that
the driver was on the other side of the engine
watching the guard, and the stoker stooping
down with his back to them opening the
furnace door.   Creeping up stealthily, they
sprang on to the engine, and while Peter with
a heavy blow from a loaded stick felled the
stoker, his companions, seizing the engine-
driver from behind, pulled him down backwards,
clapping a hand over his mouth to prevent him
calling out.   To bind first one then the other
man's hands and feet, and twist a thick woollen
comforter round their heads and over their
mouths, was the work of a moment, while the
guard, who had entered the signal-box, cried out,
" The place seems empty; there is no one here
at all;" then the next minute he continued,
" Come here, one of you—the man's in a fit."
Instead, however, of obeying, the steam was
turned on, and the train began to move ahead
—slowly for a moment, but, rapidly increasing
its speed, was gone almost before the guard

recovered from his surprise. The distance to Beaupark was very short, and at the pace at which they were going, ten minutes at most would be enough to reach it, and it was a great question whether the guard would have time to get back from the signal-box to the last station and send a telegram before the train arrived.

" There's the station," cried Peter, who had been engaged in stoking, and who at that moment cast his eye ahead. The signals were all dead against them, but there was no slackening of speed as the engine and train, bumping, jumping, and jolting, dashed into and out of the station like a flash of lightning. On, ever on, they flew; the telegraph flashed messages that the train was coming, but no one could attempt to stop it, and as to turning the points into a siding, it would be too awful even to contemplate such a catastrophe, considering the pace at which they were rushing along. They passed Drogheda at the same headlong speed, and were nearing Dundalk, when the man driving remarked in a low voice to Peter, " Water getting short."

"What's to be done ?" asked Peter.

"Stop at Dundalk," said the man; "there are the lights just showing now."

"And be clapped into a prison for a certainty," cried Peter. "No, thank you. How much longer can we hold on?"

"Fifteen minutes without much risk," was the reply.

"That means ten miles the other side of Dundalk," said Peter. "All right!"

When they were clear of the station and again in the open country, Peter, telling the driver to slacken speed for a moment, made his way along the foot-boards till he reached the carriage occupied by Cassidy and his wife. They were both fast asleep, and it was with difficulty that Peter could rouse them. He had hardly time to explain to them how they were situated when the train, which had still continued to slacken speed, in a few minutes stopped altogether. As Peter opened the door and assisted Cassidy and his wife to alight, they were joined by the engine-driver with his two companions, who whispered to Peter, "Divil a drop more water; we can't go a yard further."

Not a word more was spoken as the six

disappeared in the darkness, while heads of the passengers began to appear at the carriage windows, wondering where they were and at the cause of the delay. As under Peter's guidance the six of them left the train some distance behind them, Cassidy began to question Peter as to what had happened since the morning, but the old man would answer nothing, asserting that they had many miles to travel and no time to talk.

For three hours they walked in a N.E. direction, towards, as Cassidy supposed, the sea, without meeting a living soul; but then they soon began to overtake scattered parties, chiefly of women and children, all of whom appeared to be going in the same direction as themselves. For another three hours they continued their way, but as by this time Mrs. Cassidy showed unmistakable signs of fatigue, Peter, without much trouble, obtained for her a seat on one of the country carts, several of which they had overtaken heavily laden, all bound, apparently, in the one direction. At last Peter stopped, saying, " Listen ! " They did so, and a distant roar could be faintly distinguished. " The sea !" Peter exclaimed. " We

have not much further to go now;" but it was
more than an hour before Cassidy found himself standing on the sea-shore, holding by the
hand Mr. French, who with the other hand
was grasping that of Norah.

"Welcome! most, most welcome!" cried
Mr. French. "Matters are coming to a crisis
even quicker than I expected, and we shall
need every good man and true to hold our
own." Cassidy made no reply—he was too
much engaged in looking around and surveying
the scene. And a most extraordinary one it was;
daylight was just supplanting a pale, sickly
moon already past its last quarter, and as objects became every moment more clearly visible,
so Cassidy was enabled to see three large
steamers lying off shore, while small steam
launches were busily engaged in towing out
full barges, which, as soon as they were alongside, were not only unloaded, but as quickly
reloaded before being again sent back to the
shore, while other barges were taking off women,
children, and old men, who might be observed
on the beach huddled together like cattle waiting their turn. The quickness and precision
with which the work was being carried on,

and the order and quiet which everywhere prevailed, spoke volumes for the capabilities of the man who was the sole director of everything. At this moment a young woman approached Mr. French, and dropping a curtsey, said,—

" Plaze your honour, me heart fails me entirely, and I'm wishing to go home again."

"What's your name?" inquired Mr. French.

"Biddy O'Flaherty, your honour."

Mr. French looked her over critically from head to foot much as he would a horse he was thinking of purchasing; then he remarked, as if to himself,—

" It's good-looking and well made ye are; maybe you'd fall into good hands, and not be traited badly—at any rate, at first."

" What's that, your honour?" cried the woman, not understanding.

" I was thinking," replied Mr. French, "that when you are stripped naked, you would be showing yourself to advantage, Biddy, and some nice young man would be glad to take you home to live with him—that is, for a time, you know, Biddy."

" It's making fun of me your honour is."

" I !" exclaimed Mr. French—" never was more serious in my life."

"Was it naked your honour said ?" asked Biddy, after a pause.

" Just that, Biddy,—stripped naked."

" But what would they be doing that for ?" asked Biddy, still incredulous.

" For two reasons—first, to get your clothes for themselves ; and secondly, because they are fond of the girls, Biddy, and like to admire a well-made young woman like yourself."

"Arrah ! Mr. Terence, be asy now, can't ye ; and don't be poking your fun at me. Sure, they might be content to leave something to the imagination : it's often sweeter than the reality. And besides, looking down and getting red in the face, what would Tim say ?"

" I don't suppose the Papists would much care what he might say."

" Is it the Papists your honour said ? Sure, is it true the low blackguards are coming here ?"

" I fear they are, Biddy, and before long, too."

There was a short pause while Biddy's eyes were fixed on the ground, then, dropping a curtsey, she said, in a low voice, " Thank your honour kindly, and good-day. I think I'll be going to the boat."

" Good-day, Biddy,—a pleasant voyage to ye ! When we meet again, it will, I hope, be under pleasanter circumstances."

" You must be tired and will be glad to rest," said Mr. French, addressing Cassidy and his wife. " Come with me. It is beginning to rain, and looks like a wet day. You are safe here, and can sleep tranquilly this morning at any rate, without any uneasiness. I will order some breakfast for you at twelve, if that will suit you." At the door of a better class of fisherman's cabin Mr. French left them, and glad indeed were they both to lie down and get some peaceful and comfortable rest.

# CHAPTER XVI.

## "DON'T MIND ME!"

THE hour of twelve seemed to come only too soon, when a knock at the door aroused them, and Mr. French's voice outside informed them that breakfast was ready.

In less than five minutes they joined him in a hut close by, and were by no means sorry to sit down to a homely and most substantial meal, one of the dishes at which was a most excellent piece of pickled salmon, on helping Mrs. Cassidy to a slice of which Mr. French remarked,—

"It is bound to be good, eh, Cassidy?"

"Why?" inquired Norah, turning to her husband.

"Because he caught it," replied Mr. French.

As she looked at him with her fine eyes to see if he was in earnest, Cassidy glanced at her himself, and could not help being struck by the improvement already visible in her face. It had lost that pained look of anxiety and misery, and though she of course bore traces of fatigue, still the content and happiness of being under the care and protection of the man she had so long loved, made her appear a different being from what she had been two days before.

Before any more could be said, the tinkle of an electric bell sounded at a table behind Mr. French, who, much against his will, was obliged to leave his meal to watch the instrument.

In less than five minutes he resumed his seat, and Cassidy instantly noticed how sad was the expression of his face. Before he could, however, make any remark, Mr. French said with a sigh :—

" There is, I am sorry to say, bad news. I will read you the telegram just come," which he then did, as follows :—

" ' Mrs. Kelly attacked by coastguard-men last night, and every soul massacred.'

" Poor old woman ! " continued Mr. French, "she fought well and deserved a better fate. I warned her to come away north, but she was obstinate, and declared she could hold her own ; and we have lost a hundred men with her whom we can ill spare. It will also make the other side so cocky; it is the first real success they have gained."

"Who are the coastguard-men mentioned?" asked Cassidy.

"Have you not heard that when the bill was passed which made us all smugglers, in order to prevent exactly what you see going on outside there, the Government offered to enlist the old coastguard-men into their service, intending to send them here. They leave Dublin this afternoon, so this is our last day of smuggling."

"But what had they to do with Mrs. Kelly?" asked Cassidy.

"A question easier asked than answered," replied Mr. French; "having the men there in Dublin, sooner than let them be idle, the Government appears to have made use of them against the old woman. I suppose the Major kept worrying Ministers about her in the House, and badgered them to such an extent, they were forced to do something."

"And you say these old coastguard-men are to be here to-morrow morning," said Cassidy. "What are you going to do?"

"The special train is ordered to be ready at eight o'clock, so the men will be on their ground

before daylight.   Tell me what *you* think would
be best to be done."

"Had they not treated Mrs. Kelly so cruelly,
I might have hesitated," said Cassidy; but
now——"

A warning look from Mr. French stopped
him, and so, changing the conversation, he continued,——

"What did you mean by talking to that
young woman, Biddy O'Flaherty, this morning
about being stripped naked?"

"Simply that what the other side did before,
I firmly believe they would glory in doing
again. 'History repeats itself,' is an old and
true saying. Sooner than have our country
disgraced by the barbarity of stripping the
women naked and turning them out to be dishonoured first, and die of cold afterwards,
I am trying not to leave temptation in the way
of the league-ridden ruffians; but my hardest
task is to persuade our people that such iniquity is really possible, and that, therefore,
they must fly while there is yet time to avoid
all chance of being so treated."

"And you say they did it before?" asked
Mrs. Cassidy, now speaking for the first time.

"Do not take my word for it," replied Mr. French; "I will give you Froude's history, and, as it still rains in torrents, you shall read for yourself what he has written. Nor do I believe there has been any attempt at contradicting what he has recorded—indeed, the authorities he quotes are unimpeachable."

"I can believe anything," she sad sadly, tears being on the brink of flowing, "after what I have myself suffered, and after having also been a witness of the treatment meted out to other poor, unoffending people, who never did a ha'porth of harm to any one in their lives. Sure, the perpetrators of such atrocities must be fiends, Mr. French; they cannot be human beings."

"You are right," he replied, "and therefore the less fit to be trusted to treat poor defence-less women and children with consideration or even pity."

"Let mine be the task to persuade them to depart then," she cried enthusiastically. "When all others are so busy, I cannot be idle; and who so fit to persuade the poor heedless creatures to put themselves out of harm's way as one who has suffered herself?"

A look of approval from her husband rewarded her, while Mr. French, rising from his
chair, shook her warmly by the hand.

" I accept your offer," he said ; "to-morrow
you shall begin, and plenty of work you will
have, I can tell you. To-day you must rest,
and "—as he handed her a volume—"can read
some account of events which happened, almost
on the very ground on which we are now located, two hundred and fifty years ago. I must
be going now ;" so saying, he put on his mackintosh coat, and signing to Cassidy to do the
same, the two left the hut and walked up and
down at a short distance off, notwithstanding
the heavy rain, for upwards of an hour.
Glancing at them occasionally while perusing
her book, Mrs. Cassidy observed that Peter
had joined them, and the three were now
standing close together, Cassidy and Peter
apparently listening, while Mr. French was
explaining something to them. Soon several
cars in succession began to arrive, the new
comers all joining Mr. French outside the hut.
None stayed long : they seemed as if they
came for instructions, and, having got them,
departed. Peter then went away, and Mr.

French and Cassidy entered the hut. The former proceeded at once to open a cupboard with a key attached to his watch-chain, and taking two heavy boxes from an upper shelf, and also a coil of wire, laid them on the table, saying to Cassidy :—

" That is all you need; but remember, on no account connect the wires till the last moment. You see how it is done, and there is the button, which you must, of course, press firm when the moment comes."

Mr. French glanced at Cassidy as he finished speaking; his face was very pale, but he was examining the boxes with the greatest interest.

"I will go myself, if you like," whispered Mr. French.

Cassidy shook his head as he replied :—

" On no account ; I am quite ready."

" Take the end of the wire, and make the connection."

" This Cassidy did, and Mr. French, watching him, could observe his hand was as steady as his own.

At this moment a car drove up to the door, on which were seated Peter and another man.

Cassidy and Mr. French exchanged a glance; then the latter said, addressing Mrs. Cassidy,—

"I am forced to borrow your husband for a few hours; he is going on a most important errand, but will be back by midnight."

She rose, and going up to her husband, laid her two hands on his shoulders as, looking in his face, she asked :—

"Is there any danger, John? If so, let me share it with you."

"No, my darling," he cried, folding her in his arms and kissing her warmly; "unless it be that before my return you have eloped with— I won't say who!" he added, laughing. "The weather is so atrocious, or I would certainly take you. Good-bye! I shall be back as soon as I can."

With another kiss he left her, just as Peter, who was getting impatient, was coming to call him. The two boxes, each enveloped in a mackintosh bag, were safely deposited in the well of the car, and they started—Peter on one side, Mr. Cassidy on the other, the man driving.

They returned by the same road by which, only a few hours before, they had come on foot, but they accomplished the distance which had taken them eight hours on foot, easily now in three, and the last rays of daylight enabled them to see that they were on the side of a foaming torrent, usually a small stream, but which now, swollen by the heavy rains, came bubbling and roaring under a fine, handsome bridge, by which the trains crossed the river a short hundred yards above where they stood.

As Cassidy was still intent on surveying the ground while he had yet light, there was a distant rumble, which, as it momentarily increased, they soon perceived was caused by a train, which came puffing along the embankment, and having crossed the bridge, soon disappeared again in the direction of Belfast.

"A short hour," said Cassidy, "and very little light."

"More than enough," replied Peter, curtly. "Come along."

The two of them left the car, each carrying one of the india-rubber bags, and Peter a pickaxe also. They ascended the bank, and having reached the rails, walked along them till they came to the bridge. Letting himself down with the agility of a cat, Peter in a few minutes called to Mr. Cassidy to hand him one of the bags, and this he managed to secure under the bridge just where it left the solid embankment. They then unrolled the coils of wire and spread them down the side of, and along the bottom of, the embankment as far as they would reach. Here they placed the other box, attaching the ends of the two wires to it. As the last rays of light vanished, Peter was in the act of returning to the bridge, when a second time they heard the distant rumble of a train.

"It is the pilot engine!" exclaimed both men at once.

"Don't mind me," cried Peter; "it is impossible I can have time to return here. I'll take care of myself, never fear."

Before Cassidy could reply, he had disappeared into the intense darkness, and Cassidy remained alone, while the rain pattering around him, the roar of the river in front, the rumble of the engine, now close by, above, seemed for a moment to bewilder him. He crouched down instinctively as it went by; he did it without knowing why, as an instant's consideration would have told him it was impossible in so dark a night for any one to see him.

Glancing upwards, he saw the engine's bright lamp lighting up the drops of rain as they fell. A moment more it was past, and the dull red light behind alone remained visible, as the monster, surging ahead, crossed the bridge and sped on its way.

The patter of the rain-drops, the roar of the river, were soon again the only sounds audible to Cassidy, who, as he still crouched at the base of the embankment, wondered where was Peter. Had he already been able to make the connections? and if so, where had he gone to secure his own safety? It was a terrible moment, but his only anxiety was for his companion Peter; if for an instant he gave a thought to any one else, he said to himself, " The poor old woman was alive this time last night. Why could they not let her alone ? "

His quick ear caught only too soon the distant rumble of the train which was now coming, and though nothing could shake his determination, he involuntarily shuddered. As the train came nearer, a sound different from any which he had heard before became audible. He listened intently, wondering what it could be. Nearer and nearer it came, and then he could distinguish loud and continuous shouting. He started! Was it possible they could have discovered anything, and were calling to the engine-driver to stop. He could not forbear a smile at the absurdity of the idea as he immediately after became aware it was only a carouse; the men had been drinking, and were now singing at the very top of their voices, each carriage trying to drown the others. They were exactly above him now, and as he gave one glance only up at them, he observed that the engine-driver was standing facing the train, singing with the others; then Cassidy, stooping, placed his finger on the button, and waited yet a moment more. In the intense darkness he could only guess the position of the bridge; so as soon as the engine was past him, he pressed the button and held it hard down. So great was the hubbub, he heard nothing, but fancied he felt the earth quiver rather more than before. " Oh, Peter, Peter! where are you ? " he cried, as with straining eyes he looked again up at the train. The seconds could probably be counted on the fingers of one hand ere the engine reached the bridge; but to Cassidy it seemed as many minutes. In an agony of sus pense he watched. " Had their plot failed ?" he said to himself; but no! even before he could ask himself the question, the huge monster seemed to stop as if arrested in mid-air; then he could see the blaze of light which it emitted begin to sink down, down, down, lower, lower, lower.

With eyes starting from their sockets, Cassidy remained spellbound as lighted carriage after carriage arrived at the one fell spot with its jovial, singing crew, and toppling over, followed the engine into the yawning abyss below. As the first disappeared, so did the last : not one escaped. The whole train, which only one moment before was speeding on its way full of over three hundred living souls, to all appearance happy and in full enjoyment of health, now lay heaped together a shapeless mass in that foaming torrent beneath.

" Poor wretches !" he exclaimed aloud. " I believe they were all drunk, and have met their doom with shouts of revelry on their lips, for that one of them will ever see to-morrow's sun rise, I cannot credit."

All had been so sudden, so quick, the manner in which the train had literally vanished so

terrible, that Cassidy sank down on the wet
ground, and as he covered his face with his
hands, groaned aloud, horrified to think that he
alone had a moment before been the means of
sending over three hundred souls to eternity.

He was roused by a voice coming out of the
intense darkness before he could see any one.
It was Peter, who was coiling up the wires
while following them as a guide to find
Cassidy.

"Sure it's time we were out of this, your
honour, as soon as we can reach the car. It
was a grand night for the work, and it was
foine to see them go over, the skulking blackguards! Sure, and it's scarcely more than
twelve hours since they traited the poor harmless old woman in the same way. Bad cess to
them for that same! they have only got what
they desarved!"

Cassidy made no reply : his heart was too
full. It might be true enough what Peter
had just remarked, that they deserved it,
but was it not rather those who had planned
the old woman's destruction, and despatched
these poor wretches as their tools to carry
out the cruel deed, who ought to be lying

there in that foaming torrent. Those that ordered Mrs. Kelly's murder, as well as that of her crew, were clearly more guilty than those who only carried out their instructions. But did not this same reasoning also apply to himself? had he not been sent to do this deed, and did not the responsibility of it lie on other shoulders than his own? Unquestionably it did; and the thought of this fact gave him immense relief, even though he still saw vividly before him the brightly-lighted train, the crowded carriages, out of the windows of which heads were protruded, and in many instances arms waving hats, while the noise of the singing and shouting still rang in his ears. What a sight it was! Suddenly in the dark wet night it burst into view; as suddenly it vanished, not to pass on to its destination, but to be swallowed up in that foaming river—to be hushed for ever in the stillness of death. Slipping on the wet, greasy soil, stumbling in the darkness over stones and sticks, Cassidy and Peter at last reached the high road, and in due time, having found the car, started back by the same road by which less than an hour before they had come.

# CHAPTER XVII.

## "IS IT ME NAME?"

WHAT a different scene was being enacted in Dublin at the same moment as Cassidy and Peter started on their homeward journey! In the brilliantly-lighted hall in which the Irish Parliament held its sittings, the whole two hundred members were assembled, and while waiting the advent of the Prime Minister, were all talking and laughing together, evidently in the very highest spirits. Suddenly the door behind the Speaker's chair opened, and instantly every voice was hushed; then as the great man appeared and advanced to his place, ringing cheers broke forth from every part of the House, which were renewed again and again. He stood with a pleased, proud smile on his face, looking round, until when at last from sheer exhaustion silence was restored, he said :—

" Twenty-four hours ago, in answer to a question from the gallant Major, I stated to the House that means were being taken for the vindication of the law, and that the monstrous anomaly of an old woman with a few of her dependants daring to defy the Government of the country, must be at once and for ever put a stop to.    I have much pleasure now in being able to inform you that our efforts have been crowned with complete success.    Lulled into security by the immunity she has so long en-joyed, and without the slightest suspicion of an attack, Mrs. Kelly and her gang seem to have kept no sort of watch, and consequently we were enabled to place boxes of dynamite against the gate without any one inside being a bit the wiser.    These being simultaneously fired by means of a battery the large doors and part of the wall were blown down, and before those inside had recovered from their surprise at the shock, our people were upon them ; and as it was considered necessary to make an example, orders had been issued that no quarter was to be given, so every man was killed on the spot.    Nothing could have been better than the way the whole affair was managed, more especially taking into consideration the fact that the casualties on our side were almost nil, one man only having received a slight wound in the shoulder from a shot fired by the old woman herself. I had given orders that, if possible, Mrs. Kelly was to be spared and brought alive to Dublin to be publicly tried ; but the man whom she had shot, irritated at being wounded, instantly stabbed her to the heart."

As the Prime Minister finished speaking, the members, led by the Major, testified their approval of what had been done by loud and prolonged cheering. As this died away, and the officials, who, with a few others, had crowded in to hear the statement, anxious to learn the exact truth, now returned to their several posts, a spare, rather tall, elderly woman was left standing on the floor of the House a short distance from the entrance. For a few moments no one noticed her ; but perceiving that she showed no signs of retiring with the rest, the official at the door, advancing to her side, motioned her to be off. She paid no heed, however, but looked round the House with the greatest *sang-froid*. Several members having observed her, the inquiry began to circulate as to who she was, and the official was told to inquire her name.

"Is it me name?" she replied. "Faith, I am wondering meself what it can be, as I have heard Mrs. Kelly was kilt entirely last night. But maybe the Major can tell ye who I am."

There was something in the sound of the voice which made the Major start and look up; then, leaving his seat, he made his way to the door, but instead of going out, advanced up the floor of the House. He was painfully short-sighted, so was forced to come close to the woman and peer into her very face before he could make out who she was. Having satisfied himself on this point, he turned towards the Speaker, saying,—

"I am damned if it is not that old she-devil Mrs. Kelly herself!"

A loud murmur ran through the whole House as all pressed forward to have a good look at the woman who had gained so much notoriety, and who, they had just been informed, had been stabbed to the heart; whereas there she was standing before them in perfect health. She smiled slightly as she heard the Major's remark. Then, as he again turned his head as if to have a second look at her, she lifted her arm and gave him a slap with the open palm of her hand in the face, as she exclaimed,—

" I'll tache ye to call me names, Major, me darlint ! "

There was a roar of laughter from one end of the House to the other, while the Major, stepping back to avoid a repetition of the blow, shook his fist at her, as he stammered out,—

" You infernal old hag! you dare to raise your hand to me, a Mimber of Parliament, in the House itself! Here, doorkeeper, turn her out! Do you hear what I say? Turn her out at once ! "

The man advanced, but without taking any further action in the matter, awaited his orders from the Speaker. The Prime Minister, as soon as he could speak for laughing, now intervened, and turning to the woman, said,—

" You tell us your name is Mrs. Kelly ? "

" It was the Major said so, not I."

" How comes it," he went on, biting his lips not to laugh, " that you are here alive and well, when we heard that you and all your servants had been attacked and killed last night ? "

" I left home two days ago, and have been

in Dublin ever since, or it is a different tale ye'd have to tell of last night's work."

"What do you mean?" inquired the Prime Minister.

"Is it what I mane? Sure, it is simple enough. Had I been at home, your attack on us would have failed; but there, they let themselves be surprised, and so you were able to work your wicked will on them."

"How came you here?" asked some one in a loud voice.

"Is it how I came here? I just walked,— how else? I was lodging close by, and seeing the doors open and no one to hinder me, I came in, and was in time to hear how the 'monstrous anomaly of an old woman daring to defy the Government of the country must be at once and for ever put a stop to,' how 'lulled into security by the immunity she has so long enjoyed, and without the slightest suspicion of an attack, Mrs. Kelly and her gang seem to have kept no sort of watch.'"

She went on quoting the very words of the Prime Minister's speech, and admirably mimicking his tone of voice and his jaunty, *nonchalant* manner, till every soul in the House literally roared with laughter. When she came to where the man "received a slight wound in the shoulder from a shot fired by the old woman herself," she remarked, by way of parenthesis, " Bedad ! it was a long one," alluding, of course, to the fact of her having been in Dublin at the time. Then, as she concluded by relating how the wounded man had "stabbed her to the heart," she put on such a comical look that again there was a general laugh. She was clever enough to know that to get a hearing among such an audience as she was addressing, her only chance was to try and amuse them, and she had come there to tell them a few home-truths before she was tried and hung, as she knew only too well would be her fate.

"You may laugh," she exclaimed as soon as silence was restored, "and it's mighty proud ye are, one and all of ye, to have murdered in cold blood a hundred quiet, inoffensive men as never did any harm to one of ye, nor, for the matter of that, to any one else either. And what were they murdered for? I ask ye, is there one of ye can answer me that question? What were they murdered for ? "

She waited a moment for a reply, and some

one said something about having broken the law.

"The law!" she retorted scornfully; "is it the law ye said? Faith! that is dead and buried long ago. Didn't I obey the law, and pay my taxes long after my neighbours? and was I a bit better off, or as well off, as they were? Sure, was I not bred and born in the house ye have just destroyed? Didn't I spend my whole life and all my money in helping the boys and girls on me estate? Was one of them sick—was not I there to nurse them? was one of them in trouble—who was there to help him but meself and his Rivirence? Ah, me! it was a sad day for us all when he was took from us. May God have mercy on his soul! for a better man never was born; and had he lived, none of this trouble would have come upon us. They sent another priest to take his place, and from that moment there was no peace. It was jealous of me he was,—jealous because the poor people liked me. Sure, had I not been a mother, ay, and father too, to them all? And though I was warned that he'd be too clever for me, sure, I did not believe it. It was true though, as I discovered when it was too late.

One after another he won the people over, till there were only three or four families would spake to me. Then they boycotted me, and, as they thought, left me to starve. But I was not to be bate as easily as they supposed. I offered them money for the food I wanted, but they refused it; they could do without it, I suppose. But, faith, I could not do without the food, and so I took it, telling them that they could have the money if they sent the bill. Even then I believe all might have come right. His Rivirence was going to be moved to Limerick—at least, so we heard; and the people, who in their hearts loved me still, would have been only too glad to make friends, when the Major brought the whole business up in Parliament, and night after night I was told he rose in his place 'to bring,' as he said, 'the case of that accursed she-devil, Mrs. Kelly, to the notice of this House. This damned old woman, having been boycotted as she richly deserved, set to work to fortify her house.'"

The swagger, the bullying manner, the loud, coarse voice of the Major were so admirably mimicked that again the whole House roared with laughter, except the Major himself, who, instead of returning to his place, had taken a vacant seat just in front of Mrs. Kelly, and who, evidently not seeing the joke, sat with his arms folded, his legs stretched out, looking straight at her.

"Arrah, Major! It was not this way ye'd be going on," Mrs. Kelly continued, taking him off with his folded arms and stern, defiant look, "when ye used to be coming courting Barbara Maguire thirty years ago now, Major, and more. Sure, there was nothing good enough for me then, and it was kissing me you'd be one moment, and your arm round my neck the next;" and as she spoke, her whole manner changed to one of softness, and she mimicked the kissing and love-making admirably. "And do you mind, Major, the evening I was sitting on your knee, and you asked me to be your wife, and go off with you to Dublin and be married there; and when I would not consent, and you asked me why, I just told you the plain truth, because you had a wife already; and though I thanked you kindly, I was not ambitious to be your mistress. And oh! but you were angry, and swore it was a lie——"

"Peace, vile woman!"—the Major now roared

in a voice of thunder, as, rising from his seat, his fists clenched, and his whole body contorted with passion, he approached her—"or, by the blessed Virgin, I will break every bone in your cursed body."

The most intense silence reigned through the whole House as all watched to see what would happen. Mrs. Kelly, however, instead of retreating, advanced a couple of steps towards him, and then, crossing her two hands on her breast, she dropped a low curtsy as she said,—

"It is the kindest act you could do me now, Major. I'd sooner be kilt here this moment by you than go through the farce of a trial and be hung, as I know I shall be. But mind what I say, Major, and not only you, but every one of ye who are listening to me this night, and it is the very last word I'll say to you: the curse of a dying woman rest on ye one and all, forasmuch as ye have been instrumental in shedding innocent blood. Not for one instant while I live will I cease to pray that God will have vengeance on ye for what ye have done; and, further, that He will also spare me to see it, for that a day of bitter reckoning will come, and soon too, is as sure as that I stand here."

Several times during her long harangue had the officials of the House approached with the object of removing her; but the wish of members seemed to be to let her have her say. Now, however, that she had anathematized them all in so impudent a manner, the quicker she was taken away, the better. As three of the police now laid hands on her, and she, nothing loth, turned to follow them, she called out,—

" ' Vengeance is Mine, and I will repay, saith the——' " The last word was lost by the closing of the door of the House.

END OF VOL. I.

Butler & Tanner, The Selwood Printing Works, Frome, and London.

# CONTENTS.

———•———

# IRELAND'S DREAM.

## CHAPTER XVIII.

### "NO! IT SHALL NOT BE."

EARLY next morning rumours began to circulate in Dublin of some calamity having happened: no one as yet knew exactly what, but people went about as if conscious of some terrible catastrophe. Every one inquired, "What is it?" but as yet people only shook their heads and looked wise, but said nothing.

Soon after eleven o'clock a brougham drew up at the door of the house in Nassau Street, and the Prime Minister, alighting as soon as the door was opened, mounted the stairs and entered the same room as before. Its occupant, the individual who was known as No. 1, was seated at the table with his head resting on his two hands. He looked up when the door opened, and seeing who it was, extended one hand, but without rising.

"Well!" said the Prime Minister, as he took a chair. "It is true, I suppose?"

"True! there can be no question about that. I only wish there was."

"But how did it happen? have you any idea? Was it an accident, or was it brought about on purpose?"

"Who knows? The only three survivors have just left me, but they could tell me nothing except that in a moment the engine left the rails, and fell headlong into the river, dragging all the carriages after it. How even these three were saved is little short of a miracle."

"How very terrible!" exclaimed the Prime Minister, and for several minutes both men were silent; then No. 1, looking up at his companion, said,—

"It is seldom an accident of this kind cannot be turned to account, and in this instance it comes most opportunely."

"I confess I do not understand you," replied the Prime Minister.

With a smile of pity for his companion's dulness of comprehension, No. 1 went on:

"Do you not remember my telling you how necessary it was for the sake of peace and quietness to drive the whole set of those damned Orangemen out of the country, and that this could only be done by passing a bill, allowing them so many days' grace to decamp, after which time they would all be declared outlaws, and treated like mad dogs. I have already paved the way by telling those three poor devils who were saved, that there could not be a shadow of doubt that the whole thing was planned and carried out by the Orangemen. This story, promulgated by them, will, of course, soon get wind and be universally believed. It must be corroborated by you to-night in the House, and then will be your opportunity to introduce your bill; and unless I am much mistaken, there will be no difficulty in reading it a first and even perhaps a second time before you separate. At any rate, you can but try. Have you a bill drafted?"

"No!" replied the Prime Minister—"not altogether; but it will not take long—it is a simple matter."

"Let me help you," said No. 1, and in little

over an hour the bill was drawn up, and by the Prime Minister himself at once placed in the hands of the Government printers.

It was a very different aspect the House presented that night when it assembled, and, as usual, awaited the arrival of the Prime Minister. There was no joking nor laughing in loud voices among the members as on the previous evening, but what little was said was in whispers, nor did scarcely a single member enter who did not look crestfallen and unhappy, the fact being that they could not forget Mrs. Kelly and the curse she foretold would overtake them, and it really looked as if her prophecy had only too soon come true.

When the Prime Minister entered, as usual, behind the Speaker's chair, there was some faint applause; but as he took his seat, there was a dead silence. The few questions on the paper were put and answered; then, with a grave face, but firm, determined air, the Prime Minister, without waiting to be questioned, rose and said,—

" Seldom, if ever, has it been the misfortune of a Minister to have to relate to any House the circumstances of so cruel, devilish, and iniquitous a plot as the one which occurred last night, and which must for ever be remembered as a disgrace to our whole nation.

"It will doubtless be present to the memory of all here that a bill was lately introduced into and passed by this House, imposing certain duties on the exportation of linen goods. In order to be sure that the provisions of this bill should be duly enforced, and to prevent any chance of smuggling, between three and four hundred of the men formerly employed in the coastguard were enlisted in the Government service, and all matters as to their pay, etc., etc., having been satisfactorily arranged, a special train, preceded by a pilot engine, was engaged yesterday afternoon, and timed to leave Dublin at eight o'clock to convey these men to their destination.

"All went well till they passed Dundalk, where there is a bridge over the river Kilcurry. Here—it being by this time a wet night and very dark—the Orangemen had been able to place a quantity of dynamite, and having watched the pilot engine safely over the bridge, they then blew it up, and a large crowd which had assembled at the spot actually cheered lustily as the train containing these old public servants was precipitated into the river below. A more monstrous piece of iniquity never was perpetrated, and I give any one leave to search history through, and defy them to produce a deed to be at all compared to it in infamy and bloodguiltiness. Here were these poor but most honest and most deserving men, who had spent their lives in the public service, and only retired a short time ago on their pensions, but who, without a moment's hesitation, at the call of their country were willing to again come forward and offer their services. These having been accepted, they were on their way to the several stations to which they had been appointed, when, with an ingenuity which can only be styled devilish, a trap was laid for the poor innocent men by a set of fiends—for I can call them by no other name—and as the train in which they were boxed up was precipitated into the torrent below, and nearly four hundred souls hurried without one moment's warning into eternity, the last sounds ringing in the ears of the poor dying men were the loud, exulting cheers of the inhuman wretches who had murdered them.

"Words altogether fail me to describe my sensations when this horrid story was, on incontrovertible evidence, related to me this morning; and then, when I remembered that the fiends who could act in such a manner were, like ourselves, Irishmen, or rather called themselves so, I said to myself, '*No, it shall not be; we will not own such inhuman monsters as fellow-countrymen. We will drive them forth, and purge the soil of our dear country from contact with such iniquity.*' And I then and there sat down and drafted a bill which is now in the hands of the printers, and which I hope and trust will be in the possession of all of you to-morrow morning.

"This bill, as you will see, provides that, taking into consideration that there is no chance of peace or quietness here as long as the people are broken up and divided into two sects, so diametrically opposed in every way to each other, and, further, that as the vast majority of the Irish nation are of the Roman Catholic religion, so it is enacted that thirty days be granted to all persons professing any other faith, either to join the true Church or leave the country; and if at the expiration of the said period of thirty days such persons shall still be found located in this country, without having become members of our faith, then that they shall be considered outlaws, and it shall be permissible for any one to seize any property, goods, or chattels of which they may be possessed, turning them out as vagabonds on the face of the earth; and should they under any circumstances, either singly or banded together, attempt to oppose such seizure by force, then it shall be lawful to shoot them down as you would a dog, either by night or by day. Such is the purport of the bill which I propose to the House to now read a first time, and for which I ask to be granted urgency in all its future stages." There was loud and continued cheering as the Prime Minister resumed his seat, the feeling of the large majority of members evidently being that some such bill had become a necessity, and the sooner it became law, the better.

One of the members for Belfast, however, having caught the Speaker's eye, rose and said,—

" Mr. Speaker,—Sir, may I claim the indulgence of the House while I occupy its time and crave its attention for a few moments only. No one, no matter to what religion he may belong, could have listened to the detail of facts as related by the Prime Minister, without a feeling of horror and disgust that in a so-called civilized country such atrocities could be perpetrated ; but may I be allowed to call the attention of members to the fact that no proof whatever has been given us that the Prime Minister may not have been misinformed, and that the fall of the bridge may have been nothing more than a pure accident. Under these circumstances, before you proceed to pass a law expatriating some millions of your fellow-subjects, I move as an amendment that a commission be appointed to inquire upon oath into the circumstances of this most sad affair, as I cannot help feeling certain that not one particle of evidence will be forthcoming to connect the Orangemen, either directly or indirectly, with this most terrible catastrophe."

The amendment was seconded by the member for Londonderry, who, in a short but very forcible speech, warned the House to be careful how they proceeded to pass a bill which would probably sound the tocsin of civil war. It was not to be expected that the Orangemen would tamely submit to be driven forth from their homes and their country without a struggle; and did such a strife once begin, who could possibly say where it would end ? Several other members having spoken both for and against the amendment, the House divided, when the numbers were—against the amendment, 180, while to vote in favour of it there were only 12, which latter members, on the announcement of the numbers, immediately left the House. The bill was accordingly read a first time without a division; and urgency being agreed to, it was on the following night read a second time, passed through committee, reported, and read a third time in the short space of one hour and a half.

# CHAPTER XIX.

## THE TRIAL.

ON the day following the events related in the last chapter, Mr. French—or as he was more generally called among his own people, Terence O'Grady—was standing on the banks of Carlingford Lough about two o'clock in the afternoon, watching the embarking of bales of goods and large numbers of women and children, and also the disembarkation of heavy cases as already described, which now went on without intermission day and night. One by one, cars with hot and tired horses drove up, and their occupants alighting, joined Terence, who welcomed them with a hearty hand-shake and a pleasant smile. Waiting till about a dozen had assembled, Terence, addressing them, said,—

"Great and stirring events, as you all doubtless know, have taken place since last we met, of which the most momentous to us was the bill passed last night by our Parliament, per-

emptorily ordering us to abjure our faith or be
turned out of our houses, homes, and country;
in one word, in thirty days we shall be outcasts
on the face of the globe.    It is not difficult to
guess whom we have to thank for this sweeping
measure, nor who, himself unseen, is pulling
the wires and wheedling Parliament into passing
whatever bills he may think necessary for his
own purpose.    Were there any means of ascer-
taining the truth, I would wager a good round
sum that this very bill was drafted by himself in
revenge for the giving way of that bridge over
the river Kilcurry, and the hurling to destruction of the coastguardmen whom, elated and
red-handed from the murder of Mrs. Kelly's
unhappy crew, he was sending down here to
prevent not only our smuggling out of the
country our own property, but also the exportation of the poor women and children; on
whom, as on previous occasions, he and his
villains were doubtless looking forward to
working their abominable cruelties, revelling in
anticipation in the chance of dishonouring our
women and murdering our children, large
numbers of both of whom, I am thankful to
say, are already out of harm's way.

"Gentlemen, by what means the Government intend to put in force this most cruel law, I know not; but it behoves us to take immediate steps to resist to the uttermost the treatment to which they are about to subject us. This can only be done by combination; should we not work together, we are hopelessly, irretrievably lost. As I have already told you on more than one occasion, we must be prepared to rise *en masse;* and in order to put it out of the power of the Government to interfere with us, we must establish ourselves in a part of the country which we can, if necessary, hold by force, and allow no one but those whom we choose to come among us.

"That I can depend on the Orange Lodges, I know well; for have I not again and again received assurances of support from one and all of you? Gentlemen, the time has now come to put your professions to the test: you must be prepared to rise at a moment's notice, and march to any spot to which I may direct you. Half an hour after you receive my order, you must be under arms ready to start. I trust to you to see to this."

"We will, we will! never fear! We are quite

ready—this moment if you like," were the
remarks of those to whom Terence had been
speaking. Then in a lower voice, and glancing
round to see that no one could possibly overhear him, he continued,—

"In a few days we fall back from here, and
establish our headquarters at Belfast, which
city I propose to seize by a *coup de main.* In
these instructions," Terence continued, taking
several official-looking documents from his
pocket, and handing one to each of those
present, "which are so clearly and simply
worded that I do not see any possibility of a
mistake, you will find full directions as to what
it will be the duty of each lodge to do, how
secretly to make preparations for the decisive
moment, and, when the signal is given, how to
act. By these means, twenty-five thousand
men will at the same moment take possession
of every point of vantage in the city.

"Should the Catholics attempt any opposition,
which is hardly likely in the presence of such a
force, they must be instantly shot down. Once
the city is ours, ten thousand men must be left
to garrison it; and fifteen thousand, who will
be increased by contingents constantly arriving

to twenty thousand or more, will march south to Lisburn, Moira, and Lurgan, striking the river Bann to the west of the last-named city. This will be the extreme right of our lines, which will stretch from thence to Comber, at the head of Strangford Lough. The whole of this country once in our possession, not a moment must be lost in digging trenches and throwing up earth-works, the Catholics of Belfast and all the other towns being made to take their share of the labour, the option being of course given to them of going South with their wives and children should they prefer it. Thus, in case of any contretemps, we shall always feel we have a fortified camp with the town and harbour of Belfast to fall back on, and no matter what measures we may ultimately undertake, shall sleep comfortably, knowing that in case of dire necessity we shall have a haven of refuge."

A desultory conversation, lasting over an hour, followed, during which many questions were asked and answered by Terence, and then the meeting terminated, each man, as he returned home on his car, congratulating himself that they had so first-rate a leader, and firmly believing that, under his able management, ultimate success was not only probable, but certain.

Meanwhile, in Dublin, the trial of Mrs. Kelly was pushed on with the utmost haste. It was on a Wednesday that she suddenly made her appearance in the House, and the following Monday was to be her trial day, two or at most three days after which she was to be hung. Such were the instructions given by No. 1 to the Prime Minister, which must necessarily be acted on to the letter, the fact being that No. 1, who had of course organized and carried out the attack on the old woman's farm, was, beyond measure, annoyed to think that Mrs. Kelly should have herself escaped, and be actually living in Dublin without *his* being the least aware of the fact.

He wished, therefore, for once and for ever, to get the poor old woman out of the way, in order to be able to concentrate all his energies on getting together a large body of men to despatch to the North. He had no ridiculous scruples as to waiting thirty days for the Orangemen to decide whether they would change their religion or leave the country. He knew too well that there would be as much chance of either event happening, as of the sun ceasing to shine. He also gauged at their full worth the capabilities of the Orange leader, Terence O'Grady, and was not slow to realize the fact that, search the world through, a better man for the post could hardly be found. But while truly recognising this, and also that, if Terence only had time, he would make the Orange position so strong as to be unassailable, No. 1 believed that, on a sudden emergency, Terence would not be found equal to the occasion. His idea therefore was to endeavour, by promptitude and decision, so to force his adversary's hand as to upset all his calculations, hoping that he might be able to shake the confidences of the Orangemen in their leader; and in the hesitation which must then ensue, that he, aided by the rising of his own people in all the towns, would be able to seize them one after another, and by thus paralyzing all efforts on the part of the Orangemen to concentrate and act together, it ought not to be difficult to destroy them utterly. It was a bold scheme; whether it would be successful, time alone could tell; but he had, in the sacking of Belfast and other nearly as rich cities, and in the rape of the women, a rare bait to hold out to his own people, which he rightly guessed would draw thousands to follow him.

Such was the state of affairs on Sunday night, the next day, Monday, being that appointed for the trial of Mrs. Kelly; and accordingly on that morning the miserable farce was enacted, and the old woman, on being brought into court and asked in due form whether she was guilty or not guilty, replied that it was impossible she could answer the question until she knew of what she was accused.

This being interpreted to mean not guilty, a single witness was called, who related how she had proceeded with a party to the house of a farmer, and interfered in a most unwarrantable manner in a matter that in no way concerned her; and finally, when remonstrated with, had herself struck the man with her whip, and then ordered one of her own people to stab him to death before her face.

" How many men did I strike on that occasion ? " inquired Mrs. Kelly of the witness.

" Only one that I saw," was the reply.

" Which one was yourself," said Mrs. Kelly.

"There is the mark plainly visible on your cheek now; and if you were stabbed to death, how comes it that you are here alive and well?"

"Sure, it was not me at all," said the witness, "but me twin brother. Did not his Rivirence bury him the next day? And he'll tell you it is the truth I'm spaking."

"It was he, then, that I struck," said Mrs. Kelly, "and the mark is on your cheek! Did you feel the pain of the blow also?"

"Bedad and I did, and do now. Faith, if it is touched, and if I turn my head in my sleep, I wake directly. Och! it was a cruel blow!"

"It must have been," remarked Mrs. Kelly, as if to herself; "but it is curious how a blow given with a whip to one twin should cause so much pain and suffering to the other brother, whereas the stab of a knife which killed one had no sort of an effect on the other at all, at all."

There was a slight laugh at this remark, but it was instantly suppressed.

In less than two hours the farce was played out, and the judge, having put on the black cap, informed Mrs. Kelly that, after a fair and impartial trial, she, having been found guilty by a jury of her fellow-countrymen, the sentence of the court was that, on the Thursday following, at eight in the morning, she should be hung by the neck until she was dead, and concluded with the usual formula, " May God have mercy on your soul ! "

" I thank your lordship kindly," Mrs. Kelly said. " I have no wish to live. My home destroyed, my people all foully murdered, the old woman would be an outcast and a wanderer on the face of the globe. She is much better out of the way and under the sod."

She said no more, and was taken back to prison. The trial was over, and though it may undoubtedly have been considered a foregone conclusion, still, when Terence O'Grady heard of it that night, he was strangely affected, and swore he would leave no stone unturned to effect her escape.

Long and anxiously did he ponder on the means to be adopted, and though in all the hurry of departure—for the last steamer had just finished loading, and within an hour he was to leave Carlingford Lough— still, during that whole night, Mrs. Kelly was hardly ever absent from his thoughts.

Late in the evening Terence proceeded to Lisburn, and immediately after his departure the banks of the lough and the country in the immediate vicinity resumed ,the quietude and repose to which, for the past two weeks, they had been strangers.

At Lisburn, Terence found Cassidy awaiting him, and for an hour the two were engaged in close conversation, when they were joined by Peter, and for another half-hour the conference continued, at the expiration of which time Peter and Cassidy left, each going in a different direction, while Terence, tired and worn out, went to bed, and slept soundly for the remainder of the night.

It was past ten next morning before he awoke. He had intended going on to Belfast after breakfast, as he wished by another personal inspection to make sure that, in the directions which he had given for the seizure of the city, no single point of vantage had been overlooked ; but while in the act of drinking his first cup of tea, news was brought to him which at first he positively refused to believe, but when a second message, and again a third, arrived to confirm it, he could no longer doubt that the whole country round Newry, which he had himself left only the night before, was "up," that some person high in authority was on the spot superintending and encouraging the movement, and that train after train was arriving there packed with men from Dublin and the South.

For five whole minutes Terence sat silent, apparently dazed at what he had heard, his breakfast lying untasted on the table before him. During that time, he not only realized the mistake he had made in not utterly destroying the railway, but also grasped the whole situation, and at once decided on his own line of action.

Never, perhaps, had No. 1 made a greater mistake than in imagining his adversary Terence not equal to an emergency, " as he will find to his bitter cost," Terence remarked to himself, with a smile, as he finished his breakfast.

# CHAPTER XX

## "ALL'S WELL THAT ENDS WELL."

MESSAGES were now instantly despatched to the different lodges, cancelling all instructions previously given, and issuing fresh orders that men were to be at once called together, and advance without one moment's delay to Portadown, there to await further instructions. The utmost secrecy was to be observed, even the men themselves not being informed of their destination.

At eleven o'clock Terence himself started for Belfast. Before twelve he had chartered ten steamers for twenty-four hours, each capable of carrying five hundred men. Before three the Orangemen from the nearest lodges were on board, and the vessels under way steaming out of the lough. By four, Terence was back again at Lisburn, where he remained one hour for dinner, and then himself started for Portadown, which he reached on an engine at six.   He found about three thousand men already assembled, and trains kept arriving, bringing in more, but it was a small force with which to attack twenty thousand, the number at which the latest accounts computed the enemy.   Terence, however, was not a man to hesitate.   He addressed a few stirring words to his men, reminded them of the past, and the glorious deeds of their ancestors, of which he knew they would one and all show themselves worthy.   He then went on to speak of the situation in which they found themselves placed —how the quarrel was not of their seeking, but forced on them by the other side, who were endeavouring to rob them of all they possessed, and who would, were they the conquerors, after ravishing their wives and daughters, turn them out naked to die in the cold and wet.

" Will you permit this ? " he went on.   " No ! I know you won't !   There is not a man who listens to me who will not fight to the last to prevent it ; and let the thought of what is in store for your dearly loved, helpless ones be ever present to your minds.   Let it nerve your arms to strike a blow this night that shall be the talk of all Europe, and that will go far to settle this unhappy quarrel, and decide the future destiny of our ill-fated country!"

A murmur of applause ran through those there assembled as Terence finished speaking; but they were not men of words, but of deeds, and there was a something in the firm, determined way in which, catching up their arms, they prepared to follow, that told him there was not one among those present who would not fight to the death.

Leaving orders that all trains which arrived with more men at Portadown were to be sent on to overtake him, Terence about seven o'clock started on his march of fifteen miles. He was in no hurry, but halted nearly every hour to rest his men and allow more to come up. He was much disappointed at the smallness of his force, and expected to have found at least double the number awaiting him at Portadown. He guessed, however, that the fault lay rather with the railway than with the lodges, and in this he was correct, every station being besieged by men anxious to get to the front. At midnight he was within five miles of the enemy, and calculated that his force numbered about six thousand men. The night was still,

but very dark : there was no moon.  The
Catholics in the meantime had not been idle.
Their leader had posted his men well, massing
them together much in the Russian mode of
fighting, which he believed to be the sole
method by which raw and undisciplined levies
can be pitted against drilled and disciplined
men.  He had good information as to Terence's
leaving Portadown, but his spy underrated the
number of the Orangemen, declaring them not
to exceed two thousand.   Under these circumstances, the Catholic leader did not believe
Terence would be so mad as to attack him ; but
if he was foolish enough to do so, the result
could not be doubtful, and no one knew better
than No. 1 the immense advantage of the first
success in a struggle of this sort.  Again and
again during that long night, how he wished he
had his trusty coastguard, just a few hundred old
disciplined men, on whom he could thoroughly
depend, either to bear the first brunt of the
assault, should it really come, or, if not, to lead
in any offensive operations which next day he
might attempt.

Half an hour before the first glimmer of
dawn lighted up the eastern horizon, the din

and noise, the talking, singing, shouting, which had been going on all night among the Catholics, suddenly ceased, and a rumour flew from mouth to mouth, "They are coming! they are coming!"

The parties which had been out on patrol came hurrying in, and though still invisible, there was no longer any doubt a body of Orangemen were advancing to the attack. The place where the Catholics were encamped was close to the railway station of Goragh, where the branch to Newry, Rosstrevor, etc., leaves the main line. Here, just over the crest of a low hill, they were massed together, their leader intending, as soon as ever time allowed, to throw up earthworks round the summit of the hill, and thus form a fortified camp. Terence had halted for the last time just over the crest on the other side, and here he formed his small force into three divisions, each with its own commander. He then again addressed them as follows :—

"My men," he said, "you will advance steadily till within twenty yards of the enemy; then, on receiving the word from its separate commander, each party will deliver its fire, and without waiting to reload, charge with the bayonet. Should you be obliged to fall back, the rallying point will be the commanders, who will remain on horseback on the crest of the hill. The result is in the hands of the Almighty, to Whose care and protection we commend ourselves, Whom we call to witness as to the justness of our cause, and that for the blood which may be shed this day we are in no wise responsible. He knows the quarrel has been forced on us, and to His safe keeping we commend our souls and bodies, ready, as every true Christian should be, to say, no matter what may be the result, ' Thy will be done.'"

As steadily and as coolly as if on the line of march, each division passed over the crest of the hill and advanced to the attack. Though exposed to a galling fire from the moment they became indistinctly visible, Terence's orders were carried out to the letter; but, contrary to their expectation, they found the enemy had commenced to throw up earthworks, and were altogether much more strongly posted than they expected. Three times they charged, but each time were driven back; and though they fought like demons, and the slaughter was fearful, they seemed to make no impression on the masses of their enemies. It was by this time

past five, and daylight was fast coming. As
the men went steadily, and with a determined,
dogged obstinacy forward the fourth time to
attack, the smallness of their numbers, compared
with the other side, was painfully apparent, and
Terence noted that the Catholics were moving
forward their two flanks, so as to form themselves into more or less of a semicircle, and he
knew that under such circumstances to attempt
an attack on the centre with so small a force
would be suicidal. When his men, therefore, a
fourth time repulsed, retired to their rallying
point, they found the three commanders themselves in full retreat over the hill.

The Catholic leader had determined, and
had again and again impressed on those under
him, that with a raw and undisciplined mob
such as he commanded, they must be content
to act purely on the defensive. It would be quite
sufficient to hurl back the attacks of the enemy ;
and if successful in doing this, they might safely
claim the victory. Thus it was the men were
kept back, and the Orangemen were allowed to
re-form and renew their attacks so often without
molestation ; but now, when these latter disappeared altogether out of sight over the hill,

the Catholics, believing the enemy discomfited and in full retreat, broke through all restraint, and, with ringing cheers, rushed off in wild pursuit.    Helter-skelter on they came till they arrived on the crest of the hill, where they were received with a volley, and then a charge from the Orangemen, whom Terence had re-formed just out of sight on the other side, and now led in person against their assailants.    The Catholics, surprised by the sudden onslaught, gave way at first, but it was only for a moment. Their leader, guessing what would happen, pushed on strong reinforcements to their support, and again the Catholics had decidedly the best of the fight.    It was now seven o'clock and broad daylight, and the Orangemen, though fighting with a desperation and valour beyond all praise, were already nearly decimated, and could not much longer continue the unequal contest.

It was now that Terence O'Grady, whose eyes had been again and again directed down the valley towards Carlingford, fancied he could descry in the distance a large body or mass moving in his direction.    Ten minutes later there could be no longer any doubt on the matter ; but they were still a great way off, and it was questionable whether his own men could hold out so long. He feared not, and so did some of the heads of the lodges whom he consulted. What was to be done? There was nothing for it but to retire out of range, and make his men lie down. This course was adopted, and the Catholic leader, who was momentarily expecting more ammunition, of which he was getting very short, was this time able to restrain his men, and at once ordered them to cease firing. It was a fatal mistake; for had he now rushed on, victory would almost certainly have been his. Hardly had the truce begun when Terence despatched a messenger to the advancing force, which was no other than the five thousand men who had embarked at Belfast on the previous day, and who having come round by sea, had landed at Carlingford Lough to attack the Catholics in their rear. He sent orders that the men were to take their time, and on no account to be hurried.

Meanwhile, reinforcements on both sides were fast arriving by train; and though the Catholics benefited most in numbers, receiving nearly three to one more than the Orangemen, there was some compensation in the fact that the latter had any amount of ammunition, of which the former were very short. The Orangemen also were far better armed, many of them having breechloaders of the very newest and best type, and of this Terence, at the end of half an hour, determined to take advantage. He ordered two hundred picked shots to creep forward until within range, and then to open fire while still themselves out of reach of the more obsolete weapons of the enemy. The Catholic leader, knowing how impatient his men would get if shot down and not able to return the fire, ordered several parties to push forward within range, but before they could do so, the Orangemen had retired, firing—Terence's object being only to keep the attention of the enemy fixed on himself, and so gain time. This he had now accomplished, and accordingly once more formed his men as before and advanced to the attack. With as much coolness and determination as on the first occasion, the assault was renewed; but the Catholics having by this time become accustomed to this mode of warfare, and believing themselves already certain of success, now received the Orangemen with loud shouts of derision and contempt.

They consequently failed to hear the ringing
cheers and a volley of shots immediately in
their rear, as, carrying all before them, a body
of fresh Orangemen having attacked and carried the position which the Catholics had occupied the night before, drove out those still
remaining there, who, surprised and utterly demoralized by the suddenness of the onslaught,
took to their heels in all directions.

It is a positive fact, deny it who can, that,
even among regular troops, running away is
infectious ; the very sight of a body of their
comrades flying for their lives, without being
able even to guess the why or the wherefore,
makes men suspicious and frightened at they
know not what.   How much more would an
undisciplined mob experience the same sensations ; and so now, when some of the fugitives
running up the incline precipitated themselves
for shelter into the midst of the mass on the
crest of the hill, the whole body were within
an ace of taking to their heels.   This was the
moment for which Terence had been waiting
all the morning.   Calling on his men for one
last effort, he led them himself to the attack.
They had hitherto fought in dumb silence, but

now, as they came on, they pealed forth cheer after cheer, which, taken up and repeated by their comrades coming up the hill, seemed altogether to paralyze the Catholics. As if at a given signal, both parties of Orangemen opened fire at the same moment, and then, rushing forward, threw themselves on the mass of Catholics with a force that nothing could withstand. They had hitherto used the bayonet only, but many of them now, discarding that weapon, clubbed their rifles, and swinging them round their heads, dealt fearful destruction on those to whom they were opposed. As so often happens with a mob, for some reason unknown even to themselves, they suddenly seemed to lose heart. Those in front, as soon as they were aware that an attack was being made on their rear, at once concluded that all was lost, and were prepared to sue for mercy.

Huddled together as they had been, flight was for a time impossible. Until those on the flanks moved off, none of the others need attempt to fly; but the fight was over, the victory was won, the carnage had begun. Irritated at the stubborn resistance which their adversaries had made, smarting under a feeling of unjust treatment, to which, whether rightly or wrongly, they considered they had been subjected for years in favour of the Catholics, the Orangemen would give no quarter; their hour of retaliation had come at last, and they would not be baulked of it. Nor was any attempt made to stay their hands, for Terence, a most ardent admirer of Oliver Cromwell, and remembering how that great leader had acted at the taking of Drogheda, implicitly believed that "the wisdom of making a severe example would be justified in its consequences," and that now was the time to teach the Catholics a lesson which they would not in a hurry forget. Besides, who had been the originators of the quarrel? The Orangemen had been quite willing to live on terms of mutual forbearance with their Catholic neighbours, but it was the latter who had said "No," peremptorily ordering all Protestants to change their religion or quit their country; and so, for whatever chastisement they might receive, they had only themselves to thank.

"Charley," said Terence, as he met one of the leaders of the party who had been sent to Carlingford by sea, "it was a near shave: too

much so a great deal to be pleasant. What
made you so late?"

"The pilot of the first steamer, on entering
the lough, ran her aground, and it delayed us
nearly three hours to get her off. Believing
the man to have done it on purpose, I gave
orders to run him up to the yard-arm, and
warned the others we would serve them the
same if a single steamer touched the ground.
They took the hint, and brought us up first-
rate."

"You did well," said Terence; "it is the
only way to serve these fellows. Punishment
must be summary and instantaneous to have
any effect on them. If you had not come, God
alone knows what would have become of us,
or of our country either. The very thought
makes me shudder."

"All's well that ends well," replied Charley.

# CHAPTER XXI.

## "LUCY, I PROMISE."

IN a small but beautifully situated house at Blackrock, just outside Dublin, on the evening before the fight near Newry, about the same time that Terence O'Grady started with his men from Portadown, a young and very lovely girl (for she looked little more), having finished her dinner, rose, and leaving the dining-room, passed into the adjoining boudoir. A prettier little room than the one she now entered it would be impossible to conceive. Both the decorations of the walls as well as the furniture, were simply perfect. Everything seemed as if made to suit the room, nor would it be possible anywhere to imagine more luxurious armchairs, divans, and sofas, than were here to be found. Lucy O'Connor, as the young lady was called, was very proud of her room. She had furnished it entirely herself, and there was no surer way to her good graces than to praise the taste with which everything had been chosen. Nor was there anything of which she was more fond than to stand at the door, and, looking round the room, try if by re-arranging either the furniture or the many objects of art scattered about, she could by any means improve what was as near perfection as possible.

On the present occasion, however, she seemed very weary and apathetic; for, without even once glancing round the pretty boudoir, she pushed a crimson velvet couch close to a small table on which a very handsome lamp was burning, and, taking up one of Zola's novels, threw herself at full length on the comfortable sofa.

As she remained for some minutes absorbed in her book, it will be a good opportunity to describe her.

Though apparently still a girl, she was in reality three-and-twenty, decidedly small, under medium height, rather slight, but still a delicious figure; her every movement was graceful; while, as to her face, it was one which, when seen once, would never be forgotten. Her features were all small except her glorious eyes, which were of that wonderful Irish chameleon colour so impossible to describe ; her nose was the least little bit in the world *retroussé*, just enough to give piquancy to her face; while, as to her mouth, with its too lovely red lips, not too full, but sufficiently to make a kiss so truly delicious as to stir the blood in the veins of an anchorite.

As, weary of reading, she put up one arm round her exquisitely shaped little head, the wide sleeve fell back and exposed to view an arm which must be imagined rather than described; while from under her soft foulard silk dress peeped forth a foot and ankle such as any sculptor would be proud to model. She was deliciously comfortable, and as gradually her eyes closed, she would in another moment have been fast asleep had she not been startled from her recumbent position by a ring at the front-door bell.

She was on her feet in a moment, as she muttered the French word *déjà;* and then, having smoothed her hair and shaken out her dress, she opened the door of her boudoir, and with a bright light of pleasure and expectancy in her eyes, went herself, and having unlocked the hall door, waited, evidently believing the new-comer would enter. Finding he did not do so, she turned the handle, and standing behind the door herself, held it, with her right hand, sufficiently open for any one to pass through.

"Come in, come in!" she cried, in her sweet, merry voice; and then, as she felt some one coming through the aperture, she watched till the brim of his hat appeared, which she instantly tilted up, and waited till she heard the hat itself drop on the stone outside and roll down step by step to the ground below. With a ringing laugh, she flew across the hall to the boudoir, which she entered, and stood with the door about an inch open, looking out. Her astonishment, not to say horror, can be easier imagined than described, when she observed that the gentleman who, after having picked up his hat, now came into the hall, was by no means the person she expected, but a perfect stranger to her. Instead, however, of looking annoyed at the trick which had been played on him, he was laughing, as he said interrogatively,—

"Miss O'Connor?"

"I am Miss O'Connor," the girl said, as she threw open the door of the boudoir, looking very confused and sheepish. "What do you want with me?"

He closed the front door, and crossing the hall, handed Miss O'Connor a card, on which was his own name, and a note addressed to herself, which she evidently at once recognised, as she started the moment it caught her eye.

"Pardon my calling at so late an hour," the visitor began; "but Mr.——"

Before he could pronounce the name, Lucy had placed her hand over his mouth, while, like a frightened gazelle, she glanced timidly round in all directions, and her visitor instantly observed that her pretty face had turned so deadly pale, she seemed about to faint.

"Hush! hush!" she cried; "for God's sake be careful what you say." Then, as he followed her into the boudoir, and the door was closed, she continued :—

"Pardon my want of ceremony, Mr. Cassidy," glancing at the card; "but," in a whisper, "had any one seen you give me this note and heard you mention that name, the result to me it would be impossible to foretell; it *might* have been——" and she made a gesture significative of being hung up by the neck. She opened the note and rapidly scanned its contents, while Cassidy, having glanced round the room, stood watching her.

"Come and sit down here beside me," Lucy said, placing herself on the sofa. "All *his* friends are my friends; and now tell me first how he is and what doing."

"As well as a man who is worked to death can be," replied Cassidy. "It is simply marvellous what he gets through in the twenty-four hours, and what they would do without him no one can even guess."

"But what work is it which he has to do, and which keeps him away so long from Dublin?" asked Lucy.

"He is busy now sending as many of the poor women and children out of Ireland as he possibly can. Once the fighting begins, the Protestant women would be at the mercy of the Catholics, who will probably treat them again pretty much as they did before."

"And are they really going to fight?" inquired Lucy.

"Indeed, and they are, and before long too.

The Orangemen are not going to allow themselves to be turned out of their country, where
they were bred and born, without a struggle, I
can tell you."

There was a pause while Lucy seemed considering; then, looking her visitor full in the
face, she asked, naïvely,—

"And is it to ask me to try and stop the
fighting he has sent you here?"

Cassidy smiled as he replied,—

"Oh, no! It was to try and save the life of
that poor unfortunate old woman, Mrs. Kelly;
for, after all, what has she done? She was
boycotted, and when she found it was impossible to buy food, she went with her own servants and took it; and because she did this,
she is sentenced to be hung."

"I know, I know," said Lucy. "I read her
trial, and felt much for the poor old body, and
will certainly try if anything can be done to
save her. You may rest assured that no effort
shall be wanting on my part, though I tell you
plainly beforehand that I do not think there is
much chance of my succeeding."

"How shall I ascertain whether you do o
not?" asked Cassidy, as he rose from the sofa.

"You do not know *his* house close by?" asked Lucy.

"I have a man outside who does, of course," replied Cassidy. "But is the telephone working?"

"We will soon make it do so," said Lucy, springing up and leaving the room, followed by Cassidy, who, however, remained in the hall while she passed through an inner door. In less than a minute she rejoined him, and holding out her hand, said prettily,—

"*So* glad to have seen you. Come and pay me another visit if you can manage it before you leave."

"Any message?" asked Cassidy.

Lucy paused before replying. Then, as a pretty blush covered her face, she said,—

"Tell him to take care of himself, and to remember that if anything happened to him, Lucy would *never, never* get over it."

As the door closed, Lucy went back to her boudoir; but all the life and spirit seemed to have gone out of her. Whether it was the remembrance of the poor old woman in prison so near her end, with whom she had once as a child been slightly acquainted, and of whose good deeds and kindness to the poor she had often heard, or owing to some other cause, certain it is she felt low and hipped, and as if there was nothing she would like better than a good cry. Nor had she by any means recovered herself, when, two hours later, the grating of wheels on the gravel outside and a ring at the bell told her another visitor had arrived. She admitted him herself, when, putting his arm round her neck and kissing her, he said,—

" How now, little woman ! what's the matter ? You do not seem in spirits to-night."

" No," she replied ; " a fit of the blues which I cannot shake off ; " and then, as he followed her into the boudoir, she turned towards him, and laying her pretty head on his shoulder, said : " Oh, George, George ! I have been thinking all day of that poor old woman, Mrs. Kelly. I knew her so well when I was a child, and she was always kind to me, as, indeed, she was to every one ; and now she is in prison, and in thirty-six hours is to be hung —*murdered*, I call it, for what has she done to deserve death ? Nothing, absolutely nothing ! " and Lucy's eyes filled with tears.

"You are hipped, darling," George said, looking down at her pretty face, and kissing away her tears. "Forget all about the old hag, and let us enjoy ourselves. I come here for peace and quietness, and God knows it is the only place where I have a chance to get it; so don't *you* worry me, please, darling."

He threw himself wearily into an armchair as he spoke, while she stood beside him, tears still stealing down her cheeks.

Seeing her look so miserable, he took her hand and drew her down beside him.

"Come, Lucy, come," he went on, "dry those pretty eyes, and give me a kiss with those sweet lips. The only few hours of real pleasure I have in the whole twenty-four are those I spend with my darling, and I can't afford to have them spoilt by any old woman that ever lived; and what is more, I *won't!*" and slipping his right arm round her, he pulled her to him, and as she lay passive in his embrace, he pressed his lips again and again on hers.

"How cold you are to-night, Lucy!" he said a moment after, finding she did not respond as usual to his ardent kisses; "what's the matter with you? You are not yourself at all."

"I know it," she replied; "but I cannot help it. It seems almost like sacrilege to *enjoy* anything, even you, you dear old darling," accompanying the words with a look that spoke volumes, "when that old woman——"

"Oh, damn the old woman! Let her go to hell, and the whole world follow her! What do I care, so long as I have *you*, my sweetest?" and again he caught her in his arms and covered her with kisses. Again she lay passive in his embrace. There was no response to his ardour. Had she been a statue, she could not have been colder. He felt it, and it vexed him to find that the few happy moments he had been looking forward to during his long and toilsome day were to be spoilt by an old woman. So letting Lucy go, he gave a long, deep sigh as he said,—

"Poor me! I am indeed down on my luck, when even you give me the cold shoulder."

Lucy had got up from the chair and seated herself on the sofa, and with her face buried in her hands, she replied,—

"It is the fact that she does not deserve it, George, which has such an effect on me—a useless sacrifice of a life for nothing at all.

You ought all to be ashamed of yourselves to allow any one to be murdered in cold blood in such a cruel manner. A man would be bad enough, but a woman! Oh, George!"

"I, Lucy! What have I got to do with it? It was not I who condemned her to death, and it most certainly will not be I who will hang her!"

"Perhaps not," replied Lucy; "but, nevertheless, it is you who are responsible for it. One word from you, and she would be allowed to go free directly. And oh, George!" she went on, the tears streaming down her cheeks, "if you really love me, as you so often say you do, listen to me, and let me plead for the poor old creature. Don't! *please, please* don't let her be killed. Punish her in some other way, but spare her life for my sake, George—for the sake of"—sob—"your"—sob—"own loving"—sob—"little Lucy, don't—murder—a—harmless —old—woman;" and Lucy threw herself on her knees beside him, and tried to take possession of one of his hands. But George was getting angry now; no one hated to be worried more than he did, and having had enough of it in the day-time, he thought that surely at night he might enjoy himself; so, pushing back his chair, he said curtly,—

"Good God! Lucy! how can you be so foolish? Get up, child, get up! Why, if the old hag was your own mother, you could not make more fuss about her!"

"Perhaps—she—is," Lucy replied, in a very low voice, as, instead of rising, she sank into a sitting posture on the floor.

Had a bomb exploded at his feet, George could not have been more astonished.

"What did you say?" he cried, as, springing out of the chair, he went up to her and raised her from the floor; "but it's joking you are," as an idea seemed to strike him, "for if this woman was your mother, your name would be Kelly, the same as hers is."

Lucy shook her head as she answered almost in a whisper,—

"*She* was my mother, but my father, I have always understood, was a gentleman."

"Good God! Is it possible?" George cried, as he began to take one or two short turns up and down the room, when, as he came close to the sofa on which she was now again seated, he bent over her and said,—

"Why did you never so much as give me a hint of this before, Lucy?"

She covered her face with her hands, but he could see that the roots of her hair and even her neck became crimson as she replied,—

"Can you not understand that even to you it must be pain to me to publish my mother's— mother's shame?"

"My poor child!" said George, as he stroked her soft hair.

"Oh, George, George!" she cried, springing up and throwing her arms round his neck, " now you know all, you will not, you cannot, you dare not refuse to spare a mother's life at the prayer of her daughter, more especially when you remember that that daughter has sacrificed for you all—everything that a woman holds most dear. Not that I regret it; oh, no, George, far from it, for you have made me *very, very* happy! But just think for one moment how we are now placed, and tell me yourself if I can ever enjoy those same delicious hours with you when the memory must always be present with me that my poor innocent mother was unjustly condemned to die a felon's death, and that when, on my knees, I implored you to save her life, you not only refused to do so, but cursed her, and said she might go to hell for all you cared. No, George, no! It is impossible the old relations should ever again exist between us, so it is better we should part at once, for I should get to *hate* you soon. You know they say, 'love and hate are very closely allied together.'"

"Hush, hush! Lucy, darling," George cried; "you are talking nonsense,—allowing yourself to be carried away by morbid sentimentality. You forget that I have never said I would not do my best to save Mrs. Kelly's life. On the contrary, I *will* do so. Nor is it fair to accuse me of consigning her to a certain place which shall be unmentionable; for at the time I did so, I had not the faintest idea who she really was, or I should most certainly not have been so cruel."

Lucy had, while he had been speaking, seated herself at her writing table, and having scribbled a few lines, called him over to her side.

"You will sign that," she said, rising, and handing George the pen.

Glancing at the paper, he read, "Admit Miss

Lucy O'Connor to see Mrs. Kelly," and seating himself instantly signed it.

"It ought to have the office seal," he said. "Try if they will admit you; but if not, come or send the order to the office, and I will see it is duly stamped."

She put her arm round his neck, and lowering her head, kissed him with her rosy lips, as she whispered,—

"You will forgive your poor Lucy?"

"You darling!" he answered, as he caught her in his arms.

"And you promise to do your very, very best to save my mother's life?"

Was there, or was there not, a second's hesitation as she pronounced the word "mother"? George was not sure; he replied, however,—

"Of course I will; but I am not omnipotent, Lucy."

"No, no!" she said; "but you must say 'Lucy, I promise,' and then——" She finished the sentence with her eyes, which spoke her meaning far more eloquently than any words.

"'Lucy, I promise,'" repeated George. "Are you satisfied now?"

The reconciliation was complete; there was

no need of any further words, and assuredly, as George soon found, he would have no reason to complain of any coldness on the part of his inamorata now. But they were not fated to remain long undisturbed, for ten minutes had scarcely elapsed before wheels were again heard crunching the gravel outside, and a moment after there was a ring at the front door.

# CHAPTER XXII.

### " WELL MET !"

WHEN Cassidy left Miss O'Connor, as already described, he found Peter waiting, who at once conducted him to the house where, by means of the telephone, Terence had before been able to pry into the secrets of the Prime Minister, and where Cassidy now hoped to hear whether there was any chance of saving the life of Mrs. Kelly.

Ten, eleven, and even midnight sounded, but not one word had Cassidy heard, and he was just coming to the conclusion that the telephone could not be working, when Peter (who, after taking Cassidy to the house, had left him there) entered.

" Well ? " he at once asked in a low voice.

" I can hear nothing whatever," replied Cassidy. " Has he ever come, do you think ? "

" Of course he has, more than an hour ago."

"Damn the infernal thing!" exclaimed Cassidy; "it must be out of order, then. What's to be done?"

"Safer to act as if she had failed," said Peter; "which you know I always thought would be the case. Everything is quite ready, and the sooner he is away, the better."

"Why, what have you done since?" asked Cassidy.

"As soon as the Minister's carriage had left him at her door, the coachman started off for town; but about a mile off there is a whisky shop, where the man often stops for a drop; and as there was singing and other signs of conviviality," explained Peter, "going on there to-night, the carriage was pulled up, and the horses being left in charge of a gossoon, or small boy, the coachman comes in. Well, he stayed nearly an hour, and we took care to give him plenty of drink. When he went out, he had to take my arm for support. We helped him up into the box, and I took my place beside him. Before we had gone half a mile, he was fast asleep; so I stopped, and as the two others who were inside gave me a hand, we lifted him down, laid him beside the road, and having poured a lot more whisky down his throat, left him there and came back at once."

"And the carriage?" asked Cassidy.

"Is outside," was the reply, "and I brought the man's great-coat and hat; it will be better to put them on, I think."

"All right," said Cassidy; "you have the letter?"

"I have, in me pocket."

"Come then," said Cassidy; "let us set to work at once."

The two quitted the house, which they locked up. In the road they found the carriage, on to the box of which Peter, having donned the coachman's great-coat and hat, mounted, and having taken the reins, drove up to the door and rang the bell of Miss Lucy O'Connor's house.

There was a short delay before any one answered; then a man's voice called out,—

"Who's there?"

"Sure, it's a letter for your Excellency," was the reply.

"Who from?"

"Sorra a one of me knows, your Excellency."

" It's my carriage and horses you have there ? "

" It is, your Excellency.   What else ? "

" And where's the coachman ? "

" Sure, he could not come, your Excellency;
he's got the headache."

" Why don't you tell the truth, and say he's
drunk ?   It's to-morrow morning he'll have the
headache."

" Your Excellency knows best, in course,"
the driver replied.

Opening the hall door, the Prime Minister
called out,—

" Here, give me the letter," which, as soon
as he had taken it from the coachman's hand,
he entered the house to read.   The light in the
hall was so bad, he went on into the boudoir,
and Lucy stood by, watching him as he tore
open the envelope, and having extracted a sheet
of note-paper, unfolded it, and glanced at its
contents.   There was only one line written in
cypher, quite unintelligible to Lucy, but its
meaning was clear enough to the Prime Minister, who, as he crumpled the paper in his
hand, and tossed it into the grate, exclaimed,—

"Damnation !   I declare it's too bad not to
be left in peace for even an hour in the middle

of the night. If it was from any one else, I
would not go a yard; but from *him*, I suppose I must. There is no help for it."

The last sentence was spoken in a low voice,
as if half in soliloquy; but Lucy heard it, and
crossing the room, prompted by a woman's
curiosity, took the paper from the grate, and
smoothing it out again, tried to master its
contents.

"Who is it from, George?" she asked, as
she again came to his side, and put her arm
round his neck. "Do tell me."

"The real master of this country," he
answered bitterly; "the man who pulls the
wires, while we, the puppets, are made to do
his bidding, and take all the responsibility if
anything goes wrong."

"And is he really there in his own carriage
waiting for you?" Lucy asked, glancing ner-
vously at the door.

"No! Oh, no!" the Prime Minister replied,
with a smile. "It is my carriage, which he has
sent back to bring me that note, which means
that something of great importance is either
occurring or near at hand, and my presence is
urgently required. I fear I must go, as such a

note as this would only have been sent in the case of the last necessity."

"Go!" cried Lucy, "indeed you shall not— that is, not at present. Tell the man to wait, and then for one short hour—only one out of the whole twenty-four—let us——" She whispered the remainder of the sentence in his ear.

Who could resist her? Certainly not George, who, seizing her in his arms, and mentally consigning the letter, its writer, horses, carriage, and all else besides, to the lowest depths of the infernal regions, determined that if it was the last hour he had to live, he would spend it *with her*.

How bitterly Cassidy, Peter, and those waiting outside cursed and swore at what appeared to them as this most unnecessary delay, can be easily imagined. Every minute seemed to them as if multiplied by fifty; and so fearful was Cassidy of a trap, that he was several times on the point of jumping into the carriage, and telling Peter to drive off.

At last, however, their patience was rewarded : the hall door was thrown open, a gentleman came hurriedly out, and entering the carriage, cried,—

" Home ! and drive as if for your life ! "

Peter grinned as the door of the carriage slammed and the horses started, but between the drive up to the house and the high-road there was a gate, which was now shut, and which caused Peter to pull up his horses.

Fretted and cold at the long delay, the animals were most impatient to be off, and Peter did not dare get down to open the gate, as, had he done so, the animals would most certainly have been off before he would be able to regain his seat, and yet, in order to get to Dublin, the gate *must* be opened. Chafing at the delay, the Prime Minister now put his head out of the window, and called out to the driver,—

"What the devil are you stopping here for, you idiot ? "

" Sure, the gate's shut, your Excellency, and the bastesses is that impatient I daren't get down, or maybe they would be off, laving me behind."

"Wait a moment, I'll do it," was the reply, as, opening the carriage door, the Prime Minister himself jumped out, and going to the gate, pulled it open, and held it there for the carriage to pass through. Immediately behind him were some high, thick laurels, with his back to which the Prime Minister stood as, stooping down, he tried to find the hook which usually kept the gate open. He was in the act of placing it over the lower bar, when two men who had been waiting concealed in the laurels seized him, and before he could offer the slightest resistance, one slipped a cord round him and pinioned his arms to his side, while the other twisted a woollen comforter tight round his head, completely covering his mouth. Lifting him as they would a child, they carried him to the carriage, inside which they placed him, Cassidy and one of the men entering with him, while the other mounted beside Peter. Instantly the horses started at a rapid pace in the direction of Kingstown.

It did not take long to travel the short distance, and at the same headlong speed they passed in front of the railway station, descended the hill, and keeping to the left, drew up close to the harbour at the water's edge, where a small steamer lay smoking from both funnels. There was not a living soul to be seen, as Peter and his companion opened the carriage door, and the three together carried their prisoner on board, Cassidy alone remaining with the carriage.

"To sea!" he cried, as soon as the others set foot on deck; and a man on the bridge of the steamer, lifting his cap, spoke through a tube to the engine-room below. Instantly the steam was turned on to a winch, round which was a wire hawser fast to a buoy in the centre of the small harbour, and the vessel's head, being thus hauled seawards, "Turn ahead" was signalled, and then, a minute after, "Full speed," and as Cassidy watched her pass out to sea, and begin to tumble about as she felt the motion, he smiled as he said to himself,—

"Prime Minister though he be, he won't be long in that cockle-shell before he'll feed the fish;" and then, as the vessel disappeared in the darkness, he mounted the box, and turning his horses' heads, drove slowly back to Dublin, where, having left the carriage at the first livery stable which he saw, he went on foot to his old quarters at the Imperial Hotel, at which, after having, with some difficulty, gained admittance, he was shown upstairs to a bedroom.

It was by this time so near daylight, that

it was not worth while to undress, so throwing
himself on the bed, he hoped to get three or
four hours' sleep, but in vain. The excitement
of the work in which he had been that night
engaged had not yet subsided; added to which
his thoughts reverted to his wife and Terence
O'Grady far away in the North, and he began to wonder what was taking place, and to
long to be with them to share in the fight,
which, though he felt sure it could not be far
off, he but little guessed was just then beginning. As he lay there restless, the events of
the past fifteen years all came back to his
memory, and he remembered how he had again
and again pictured to himself his return to his
native land, his arrival in Dublin, whence he
would send a message to Norah, as to the train
by which he should leave ; how she would
meet him at the station in Limerick ; her
delight at seeing him return ; their marriage and
departure for the home he had prepared for
her far away. It had all been mapped out
and settled so often, and had thus become so
engraven on his mind, that it almost seemed to
him as if the events which had really occurred
(so different from what he had imagined !)

must be a dream—a wild chimera of his brain,—
and that the reality had yet to come.  He dozed
off at last, but it was a troubled and broken sleep
which did not last long, and at ten o'clock he
went down to the coffee-room to get some
breakfast.  Hardly had he entered the room
when, from the excitement visible on the faces
of all present, he felt sure that something of
importance had occurred.  His thoughts instantly reverted to the abduction in which he
had been himself engaged the night before; but
a moment's consideration convinced him that
as yet nothing could possibly be known in that
quarter.

As a waiter came to take his orders, the
man's face was so beaming with delight that
Cassidy could not refrain from asking what
was the news.

" Sure, it is great news entirely, your honour.
There's been a battle near Newry, and the
Orangemen were defeated — some say, destroyed entirely; anyway, the whole country's
' up,' and they are determined now to drive the
Orangemen into the sae, and so have done
with them altogether."

Cassidy had sufficient command over his

countenance not to show his real feelings at the receipt of this intelligence; but it was with a sorry heart he ate his breakfast, and then leaving the hotel took his way along the quay towards the Law Courts, where he hoped to find his friend O'Shaughnessy.

Never in his life did he remember to have felt so low-spirited as at that moment, and often in after years did he look back at that walk as the most miserable one he ever took—partly, no doubt, owing to his having had no sleep on the previous night, partly to the news he had just heard, and his uncertainty as to the fate of his wife and friend, and also owing not a little to the sight of the city which he had once known so different, but which now was so forlorn and wretched, three-fourths of the houses with their shutters up, more than half the shops closed, while those that were open were empty both of customers and merchandise. The very streets even looked deserted, and, except here and there a woman or a child, not a soul was to be seen the whole length of the quay.

As Cassidy reached the Law Courts, he met O'Shaughnessy, in wig and gown, coming out, who, as he shook hands with his friend, re-marked,—

"Well met! but where on earth did you spring from? Heard the news? I suppose not, or you would hardly look so awfully down in the mouth."

"If you mean about the defeat of the Orangemen, yes," replied Cassidy.

"Who told you that?" asked Mr. O'Shaugh-nessy.

"It was the talk of every one in the hotel; so of course I heard it. You can imagine how anxious I am about Norah, and—and ——" He hesitated, and finally stopped.

"You are married then, after all?" said Mr. O'Shaughnessy. "Allow me to congratulate you; but Mrs. Cassidy—Norah as you call her —what on earth has she got to do with the Orangemen? She is surely not up in the North."

"Indeed, she is," replied Cassidy. "We had to go straight there from Limerick; it was the only chance we had for our lives."

"But you! what brings you then to Dublin? Surely, so lately married, your proper place is with your wife."

Before Cassidy could reply, a young barrister passing called out to O'Shaughnessy,—

"Another telegram just come, Shaugh, which says that French, with ten thousand men, is in full march on Dublin."

Mr. O'Shaughnessy laughed as he replied,—

"Tell that to the Horse Marines, dear boy; though I almost doubt if even they would believe it."

"Then the Orangemen have not been defeated?" cried Cassidy, staring in amazement at his friend.

"Defeated! not a bit of it," was the reply; "they have carried everything before them, but I fear they have been so elated at their victory that they have shown no quarter. They say the carnage has been something awful." If Cassidy had found it difficult to control his face at the hotel, it was ten times more so now. He felt inclined to throw up his hat and shout for joy; but to act thus in such a place would have been simple madness. "Oh, yes," O'Shaughnessy went on, "French has shown himself a general fit to command an army in the field, and no mistake about it; but for that very reason I feel sure he will be content for the present with what he has already done. There would be nothing to be gained by hurrying on here, and he has plenty to occupy him in the North;—that turbulent city of Belfast to take possession of and hold, also Lisburn and Lurgan, to say nothing of the wounded to be cared for. But what brings *you* here? no law business, eh? Anything I can do for you?"

"It was in hopes of finding you that I came to the Courts," replied Cassidy; "but, thank God, I have nothing to say to law. Are you going home?"

"Yes!" said O'Shaughnessy, taking Cassidy by the arm; "there is nothing to be done here. If the truth were told, it is a mere farce opening the Courts at all. A plaintiff or defendant is fast becoming the *rara avis*. There is no money in the country to go to law, nor for anything else, for the matter of that."

As they strolled on, Cassidy told Mr. O'Shaughnessy that what had brought him to Dublin was the fate of the poor old woman Mrs. Kelly, of whom he hoped to be able to "But yde; and though Mr. O'Shaughnessy Surely, so lattotion of such a thing being pos- with your wife." ng pressed hard by Cassidy,

he at last consented to bring the case before
the House that night, and Cassidy would, if he
came there, at once see how strong the feeling
was that she must die to vindicate the law.

"Which does not exist except in name," said
Cassidy, *sotto voce.*

"The more reason a victim should suffer to
prove you are wrong," replied Mr. O'Shaughnessy.

No more was said. Cassidy spent the remainder of the day and dined with his friend,
and, as before, in the evening they both walked
to the House, when Cassidy was lucky enough
to obtain the same seat as on the last occasion.
But how different was the aspect of the House
now from what it had been then! There was
no laughing, talking, joking. Members entered
the House silently, and if they spoke at all,
it was in whispers. An unmistakable gloom
pervaded everything and everybody. Time
passed ; half an hour's grace had already been
granted to the Prime Minister, and as it was
known no one had seen him all day, a rumour
began to circulate that he had himself gone to
the North to see what could be done, and to
ascertain how far the tidings which had been

received were correct. It was curious, of course, he should not have sent a line to the Speaker, or to one of the other ministers, stating his intention; but he might have gone off in a great hurry, intending to be back before the House met, and then been unavoidably detained. It amused Cassidy much as he listened to these rumours, and he smiled as he thought how near the truth they were as to the journey to the North, but how far from it in all other respects.

There was also another man standing near Cassidy, who had entered the House after him, and who, though evidently wishing to avoid observation as much as possible, listened with an amused smile to what was being said. Several times Cassidy had tried, in the dim light pervading that part of the House, to catch a glimpse of that face, but had not been able to do so. How much more strenuous would have been his efforts had he only known that the individual so close to him was the redoubtable No. 1, the only man who had any semblance of authority in the whole country, and who, when his orders were not instantly obeyed, punished disobedience with death.

Immediately after his crushing defeat that morning he had started for Dublin, leaving his unhappy followers to their fate. He arrived about four, and had sent at once for the Prime Minister, but was told no one had seen him since the previous night, nor had any one an idea where he was.

Guessing that the proper place to inquire was at Blackrock, he despatched several clever detectives to make a few inquiries, who, having very quickly got a clue, soon learnt how a carriage had been observed to drive rapidly towards Kingstown—how it had passed the railway station and stopped close to a small steamer lying beside the quay, and how the vessel immediately after had put to sea.

" Was anything known as to what steamer it was ? " asked No. 1 of his informant as to the other particulars.

" Oh, yes ! " was the reply; " she belonged to Belfast ; had been a yacht once, but was now let out for hire, and used for picnics and such like. She was one of the fastest steamers on the coast, but such a bad sea-boat they did not dare push her, except in very smooth water."

That the Prime Minister had been kidnapped and sent off somewhere—probably, much against his will, to Belfast—was now clear enough to No. 1, but with what object was not so easy to understand.    The man was a mere puppet who imagined he was governing a country over which he had no sort of power, and the leader of a House of Commons who were always talking, but when it came to acting, were simply nowhere.    For what purpose, then, had Terence O'Grady taken the trouble to carry off such a man?    (For that it was the Orange leader who had caused it to be done, No. 1 never for one moment doubted.)    And though he thought the matter over again and again, he confessed himself completely puzzled; and it was in hopes of finding some solution to this enigma that he had come secretly down to the House that evening, and thus found himself close beside the man who had been the chief performer in the abduction of the Prime Minister, and could have at once told him all he wanted to know.

# CHAPTER XXIII.

## "ONE MOMENT, GENTLEMEN."

TIRED at last of waiting so long, the business of the House began, the Home Secretary assuming the leadership, and undertaking to answer questions, except such as related to the battle which had been fought in the North, about which he said the Prime Minister, who might at any moment enter the House, would be in a much better position to speak than he was, as except for the same tidings which no doubt every member present had heard as well as himself, he knew no more than they did.

As soon as it thus became evident that no further information was at present to be had on the one subject engrossing the minds of all, the House was on the point of adjourning, when Mr. O'Shaughnessy rose, and begged to call the attention of the House to the case of

Mrs. Kelly, who had been condemned to death
—really, it was hard to say exactly for what
—and was to be hung the next morning. He
really thought it was a case which the House
might take into its favourable—— Not
another word of what he said could be heard,
his voice being literally drowned in loud cries
of "No! no! no!" from every part of the
building, the Major, who had sprung to his
feet, shouting the most vociferously of all.

When the tumult subsided, and Mr.
O'Shaughnessy, convinced of the uselessness of
saying another word, had sat down, the Major,
who was in such a passion that for several
minutes he could not articulate, at last said,—

"Mr. Speaker, I am so utterly astonished—I
may say amazed—that a member of this House
—one, too, for whom I, as well as, I think I may
say, the whole House, have a strong personal
regard—should have had the—the—the—I was
going to say impudence, and I *will* say impudence—the damned impudence—to mention
the name of that infernal old hag, Mrs. Kelly,
with whom I thought we had done altogether,
—and not only to bring her case before this
House, but actually to propose that the House

should favourably consider the same ; in other words, remit the sentence so properly passed on her by the highest legal tribunal in the land. Words fail me to express my horror at this most monstrous behaviour, and I am only too glad to observe how the whole House at once marked its sense of the enormity by literally refusing to listen to the honourable member, and forcing him to resume his seat."

The Major had proceeded thus far, when members who had begun to depart, even before O'Shaughnessy rose, and had many of them only waited to listen for a few moments to the Major, who was often so funny as to make every one laugh, now again began to troop out of the House; but before any great number had reached the door, Cassidy, pushing and elbowing his way to the centre of the House, said in a loud voice,—

"One moment, gentlemen, before you go, if you please."

Every one stood still, wondering what was coming. The silence, except one or two whispers,—"Who is he ? Who is he ?"—was intense, as Cassidy continued :—

"The case of Mrs. Kelly has been mentioned

to-night in this House, and I was really sorry to observe the thirst (I can use no other word) for her blood that seemed to pervade every one present. Perhaps, gentlemen, if you will allow me to say a few words, I may place the matter before you in an altogether different light."

"Who are you?" the Major now yelled out at the top of his voice, "and what the devil brings you here? Damn your impudence, daring to interrupt me in the middle of my speech!" And the honourable member, who had remained standing, but who had only just recovered his voice, having been struck dumb at the audacity of any stranger attempting to interfere while he was speaking, now stamped his foot on the floor, as he went on,—

"Do you hear what I say? Who are you?"

" The accredited agent of Terence O'Grady, the Orange leader in the North," replied Cassidy, in the most nonchalant manner possible, and looking calmly round the House.

If a bomb had burst in their midst, members could hardly have shown greater astonishment, though perhaps consternation would be a more appropriate word; for several members who had been arrested in their egress from the House, and now found themselves close to Cassidy, backed away from him as if he had just told them he was suffering from small-pox or the plague, and thus in a moment he stood alone, the centre figure of a small circle formed round him.

"And what in hell's name brings you here?" shouted the Major, who was the first to recover his voice.

"To inform this House that it is my master's pleasure that 'the infernal old hag,' as you are pleased to call Mrs. Kelly, shall *not* die, but be set at liberty at once," exclaimed Cassidy, determined to show those there assembled that he would stand no bullying.

"Ha! ha! ha!" roared the Major; "and suppose we dare to treat the orders of your master, as you are pleased to call him, with the contempt they deserve—what then?" asked the Major, adding in an audible aside: "The man is mad! must be stark staring mad!"

The way this was said was so comical, the whole House could not resist smiling.

"What then?" echoed Cassidy, who found it difficult to restrain his laughter; "why, within an hour of the poor old woman's having breathed

her last, as sure as there is a God in heaven,
the Prime Minister of this House shall swing
from the yard-arm of a steamer in Belfast Lough.
That is the message I was sent here to give to
the House by my master, and to ask was there
any answer;" and Cassidy took a vacant seat on
the front bench close beside him, and smiled as
he observed the effect his words had produced
on the House.

Probably for the first time for many a long
day the Major was not equal to the occasion,
and resumed his seat without uttering another
syllable; nor at first did any other member
quite appear to know what to say or do; but it
was observed that all those who were on their
way out of the House quickly resumed their
seats, and many who had already left, came
hurrying back.

In the meantime, the ministers who were
present held a hurried consultation, and the
Home Secretary, addressing Cassidy, asked
curtly, " Your name ? "

For a moment it seemed as if the stranger
would not answer the question; then, apparently
changing his mind, he replied, " John Cassidy."

" Irish ? " was the next question.

"No, thank God! Australian," was the reply.

"How are we to know you are speaking the truth, and that the Prime Minister is really in the power of the traitor whom you call the Orange leader?"

"If not, where is he? and why not in his place here to-night?"

The question was rather a poser, but the Home Secretary replied,—

"The fact that I am not aware of his movements is no proof that he has been sent captive to Belfast. Perhaps you can give us some particulars as to how he left Dublin, and what means were taken to persuade him to go North."

"He left Dublin in his own carriage after this House rose last night, and drove in the direction of Blackrock. His coachman, who was drunk, fell off the box, and a man who happened to be passing stopped the horses, and then, taking the reins, drove on to Kingstown, where the steamer *Witch* was lying with her steam up. The Prime Minister went at once on board, and the steamer started instantly for the North."

"Do you mean that he went on board of his own free-will?"

" I saw no resistance," replied Cassidy.

There was again a whispered consultation among ministers, when the Home Secretary said,—

" Before making any reply to the message which the traitor to his country, who calls himself Terence O'Grady, has sent to us, it is absolutely necessary that we should have time to make a few inquiries. We propose, therefore, to defer till to-morrow night giving our answer, which can either be sent to you wherever you may be, or direct to Mr. O'Grady."

" Meanwhile, Mrs. Kelly is to be hung to-morrow morning at eight o'clock, and the Prime Minister at nine. It seems to me that under these circumstances no answer will be requisite," Cassidy coolly remarked.

Again there was a consultation among ministers, several of whom glanced over in the direction of the Major, who was listening with the most rapt attention to every word that passed. Then the Home Secretary said,—

" It is really impossible for me to say more than I have already done on this subject. In the first place, because I am by no means sure how far in the absence of the Prime Minister I have the power to delay the execution when once the death-warrant has been signed ; and, secondly, because neither I nor my colleagues can believe that Mr. O'Grady, who has the reputation of being a kind and humane man, can commit so cruel and cold-blooded a murder as to hang the Prime Minister of Ireland, untried and unheard, for no fault whatever, merely as an act of reprisal, because we allow the law to take its course. For this woman has, as doubtless you know, had a fair trial, and would certainly not have been convicted and sentenced unless she had been guilty. No! I do not believe that so iniquitous an act as this *would* be, *could* be really done in these enlightened days, unless by a fiend ; and if reports speak true, Mr. O'Grady is not that."

Cassidy shrugged his shoulders as he said, "You may believe what you like; but Mr. O'Grady's own words were, 'As sure as there is a God in heaven, if they hang the old woman, I'll serve their great minister the same.'" But Cassidy's remark fell on listless ears: the sitting was over, and members were now fast hurrying away.

And where was No. 1 ? He had waited,
an amused spectator of Mr. O'Shaughnessy's
appeal in favour of Mrs. Kelly, and also
heard the Major's impassioned denunciation
of any mercy being shown to her ; then he
had witnessed Cassidy's declaration as to who
he was, and heard the message he had delivered from Terence O'Grady. He understood *now* why the Prime Minister had been
carried off, which, as already stated, had puzzled
him much, and so at once left the House, telling
two of his own people who were waiting for
him outside not to lose sight of Cassidy, but to
let him know where he was to be found.

He turned his steps towards his own house,
when suddenly the fancy seized him to go himself and see this Mrs. Kelly about whom so
much fuss was made ; and accordingly, hailing
a car, he ordered the driver to take him to the
prison. It was half-past nine when he arrived ;
but the governor, who had obtained his situation through the influence of No. 1, on hearing
who he was, not only gave orders he should be
instantly admitted, but when he heard that the
object of his coming at so late an hour was to
see Mrs. Kelly, he himself led the way towards

the condemned cell in which the old lady was confined.

"Is it to see her only, or to have an interview with her, that your Excellency wishes?" asked the governor as they traversed the long corridors.

"Why do you ask?" said No. 1.

"Because there is a young lady with her at present, who came here with an order from the Prime Minister, and whose half-hour will not have expired for another fifteen minutes."

"Really!" was the reply; "and what is her name?"

"I have the order here," said the governor, taking it from his pocket and handing it to No. 1, who read the pass signed the previous evening by the Prime Minister for Miss Lucy O'Connor.

"She came late, eh?" remarked No. 1, as he handed back the paper.

"She said she had been very ill all day," answered the governor, "and we are not generally very particular the *last* night. Poor old woman! she bears up well."

No more was said, as at that moment they entered a small cell in which was seated a warder intent on looking through a hole in the wall. He appeared not to hear the new-comers; at any rate, he did not heed them, so the governor, touching the man's foot with his own, signed to him to be gone—an order which he evidently by no means relished, as the broad grin which had apparently been caused by what he saw or heard at his peep-hole instantly vanished, and he went off looking surly and discontented. "I will send for you when I want you," said the governor, as the man left them.

No. 1 at once took the warder's place, and found he could both see and hear all that passed in the adjoining cell, which was that occupied by Mrs. Kelly. The old lady, who appeared to have been preparing for bed when Lucy arrived, had her dress off, her neck, shoulders, and arms being bare. She was seated on the raised platform which served for condemned prisoners to sleep on, but her back was towards No. 1, who thus could not see her face, but only Lucy's, who stood opposite to Mrs. Kelly, holding one of her hands. No. 1 had said nothing after perusing Lucy's permit, but he had formed a shrewd guess as to who she was, and as he now saw her beautiful little face and enchanting figure, felt sure that he was right, though what motive could possibly have brought her to see Mrs. Kelly he could not for a moment guess.

"You see it was absolutely necessary to interest him," Lucy was saying. "He only laughed at me when first I began, said you might go to hell for all he cared, and wanted to know why I need mind what became of you one way or the other. I could not of course say it was Terence O'Grady who had asked me to intercede for you ; so then he got angry, and declared that if you were my own mother, I could not make more bother. 'Perhaps you are nearer right than you think,' I exclaimed, instantly catching at the suggestion which he had himself offered me. That is exactly how it came about."

Mrs. Kelly, who had been sitting with her head bent down, now raised it slightly as she replied, in a tone so low and so sad that it made Lucy almost cry to listen to it, while the effect of that voice on No. 1 was almost magical. He made a spring as if to jump from his seat, his face at the same time assuming an almost womanly softness; but it passed as quickly as it came, and as he settled himself down again to listen, his expression was more that of a fiend than of a human being.

"The one word 'mother,' which you addressed to me on entering," Mrs. Kelly was saying, "awoke in me thoughts of a past which I hoped and trusted I had been able to banish altogether from my mind for ever. But, alas! alas! it appears that it is not so, since the whole incident, even the smallest detail, comes back to me as clearly and as vividly as if it had only occurred yesterday, instead of more than thirty long years ago. It is the old story, and not worth the telling. It—has—happened—so—often—before. I was little more than a child, hardly sixteen, brought up in a convent, and kept *very* strict. *He* was almost the first man I ever spoke to, and he *made* me love him : how he did it, I do not know. I have often since thought that it was not love, but was worship, adoration. I obeyed him like a slave. I would have gone to the end of the world, I believe I would even have died cheerfully, had he told me to do so; but still there was one thing I would *not* give him. The principles instilled into me in the convent had taken such

root that I would sooner have parted with life
itself than honour ; and so he soon found, for
try how he would, it was useless. It was a
terrible time : twice he went away swearing
never to come near me again unless I agreed
to be his mistress. I fretted and pined, for to
live without him seemed impossible ; but before
I got really ill, he always reappeared. Lord
bless you, he could not remain away, for he was
determined to get possession of me, and often
boasted that once he had made up his mind to
a thing, no one had ever been able to say him
nay. A month passed, and then we were
married. Oh, how happy I was ! Never have
I forgotten it ; but though the recollection has
lasted, the reality did not. In fourteen days he
began to tire of me, and to show himself in his
true colours. In a month he was gone—where,
I never knew. He just hired a car, and drove
away, promising to write, but never did. In
due course my child was born, and almost
immediately afterwards my father and mother
died, and I was left in sole charge of the farm.
I was very young, but had long helped my
father, so got on well enough. My uncle and
aunt came to live with me. I thought only of

my boy, and worked hard for him. Thus matters continued till my son was six years old. I had numerous offers of marriage, for I was supposed to be a widow; but I never believed my husband was dead, though he made no sign.

"Then I met Mr. Kelly, or rather, he saved my life, and in return asked me to marry him. I told him the truth, and though I declined to marry him, as I feared to commit bigamy, I agreed that we should go away, put a notice in the newspaper of our marriage, and on our return, live together as man and wife.

"We were only to be away three weeks, and a neighbour joyfully agreed to take charge of the child, for he was a dear little fellow, and every one loved him.

"Imagine my feelings when, on my return, I was told he had disappeared the day before; and though the canal was dragged, and the police made every inquiry, from that day to this he has never been heard of. There is little more to tell. Mr. Kelly and I lived together very happily, till two years ago, when he died, soon after which my troubles began, and you know the rest."

" Did you never hear more of the child ?" asked Lucy.

" No!" answered Mrs. Kelly, sorrowfully, " never ; but I have often thought since that my husband either came or sent for him. I have always had a firm conviction also that he and I would meet again ; but I suppose now there is not much chance of it. It was for this alone I wished to live a little longer."

" Do you still love him, then ?" asked Lucy.

" I hardly know," replied Mrs. Kelly; "sometimes I think I do, and long to see him, and at others I fancy I loathe him, and dread a meeting beyond what words can express."

" What sort of man was he ?" Lucy next asked. " Tall and handsome ?"

" By no means," was the reply; "very ordinary looking, but he had a way with him which no one could resist : he seemed, as it were, to command obedience from all with whom he came in contact."

" What was his name ?" But before Mrs. Kelly could reply, the key turned in the lock, and the door was thrown open, as a warder, entering, said,—

" Now, miss, if you please."

Lucy, who was seated beside Mrs. Kelly, instantly rose, and throwing her arms round the old lady's neck, kissed her affectionately, as she said, " Good-bye, dear mother. Come straight to my house when they let you out ; you have the address."

"Good-bye, my child," replied Mrs. Kelly, returning the caress. So they parted, Lucy pausing as she reached the door to take a last look at Mrs. Kelly, whose story had interested her more than she cared to confess.

# CHAPTER XXIV.

## "YOU DARE!"

AS the warder was in the act of closing the
door behind her, Lucy suddenly observed
a well-dressed man standing in the corridor
as if waiting, and who, after making a sign to
the warder to reopen the door, entered the
cell which she had just quitted. There was
a something in the manner in which he had,
as it were, forced the warder to reopen the
cell door, that at once reminded Lucy of the
description given by Mrs. Kelly of the man
who had so cruelly treated her. Could it be
he? and had the old lady been correct, after
all, in her conviction that she and her husband
were fated to meet again? Most anxious to
be a witness of what would happen, and accustomed as she was to indulge every freak
and fancy, she slipped a handful of notes into
the warder's hand, explaining to him at the
same time her wishes. He pointed to the

355

door of the small cell which No. 1 had just quitted, saying, as he did so, "In there! but if the governor comes round, which is hardly likely, don't peach." He turned and walked away in the opposite direction, while Lucy lost not a moment in availing herself of the chance offered her, and was soon an invisible witness of the interview between No. 1 and Mrs. Kelly, in the same manner as the former had just been of her own visit to the same lady.

"So that's another of your brood, eh?" were the first words Lucy heard. "Be me sowl, she is a neat one; the man is lucky who has the handling of her. By all accounts she's not so mighty particular as her old dame was, and yet she is quite as luscious. Damme, if I don't think her figure's better than ever yours was, even when at last I humbugged you into these arms. What an awful lot of bother you did give me, to be sure! but I was determined to succeed. Whether the game was worth the candle, was another matter; and yet it was nice—awfully nice: forbidden fruit always is; and you were a fetchy little devil too—enough to make a saint's mouth water; very different to what you are now, eh? Ha, ha, ha!"

These coarse and vulgar words were uttered in a brutal, jesting way; the laugh, a cruel one, was evidently meant to irritate, and certainly succeeded in its object. Mrs. Kelly, who had risen at his entrance, stood facing him, but the light was not sufficiently strong for Lucy to see her face.

" So it's you, is it, and I was right after all," she said, in a low voice; " it *was* fated we should meet once more."

" By the merest chance," replied No. 1. " Curiosity alone brought me here. I never expected to find *you*—thought *you* had died in the gutter long ago. Ha, ha, ha!" and again he laughed in the same hard, irritating manner. Lucy could have struck him, that laugh jarred so on her whole system.

" The wish was father to the thought, I suppose," said Mrs. Kelly; " so long as you were free, you cared not what became of me."

" Free!" exclaimed No. 1. " What do you mean ?"

" Free to go through the same ceremony of marriage with some other wretched girl, whom, having once dishonoured and ruined, you would leave to her fate as you did me."

"I need not have waited for your death to do that," No. 1 said, laughing.

Mrs. Kelly shook her head as she replied, "You are too great a coward to commit bigamy; you would be afraid of being tried and punished for it."

No. 1 laughed louder than ever at this remark; then he said, jeeringly,—

"And has the old woman been really supposing all these years that we were ever really married? You poor devil! it was perhaps hardly worth while to undeceive you when you had only a few hours to live."

Mrs. Kelly advanced close to him, and shaking her fist in his face, exclaimed,—

"You dare to say that the marriage was a mock ceremony, when you know perfectly well it's a lie which you are telling, and nothing else. Did not his Rivirence himself perform the ceremony in the chapel, and did we not both sign the register book? It is cruel to deceive a poor old woman, and she so near her end too."

"Ah, bah! what a bother about nothing! What the devil does it signify whether it was a marriage or not? But if you think you will

die any the easier, I will allow it was as good
and binding as law and Church could make it.
Will that satisfy you ?" and again he laughed
in that fiendish manner which nearly froze the
blood in Lucy's veins.

"Do you suppose it does not signify to me,
who have lived all my life believing myself
your wife, to be told now at the last moment
that I am not ?   How often have I refused
to listen to the offers of good men and true,
who would have been only too glad to make
an honest woman of me !   Dare you say it
does not matter to our child whether he was
born in lawful wedlock or is the son of a—
of a——" She hesitated a moment, when he
supplied the word, using one too coarse to be
written.

Hardly had it passed his lips than, advancing
a step nearer, she swung round her arm and
struck him sharply across the mouth with the
back of her right hand.   When he had known
her before, she had been but a weak child,
whom he could tease to his heart's content; but
since that time, as she grew to be older, she had
become endowed with an amount of strength
which was very rare in a woman, and of which

she had given repeated proofs in the life she had been living lately. No. 1, however, of course, knew nothing of this, or he would probably not have goaded her as he had been doing; for though he could hardly be called a coward at heart, yet there was nothing he loved better than to torment a defenceless man or woman, when he believed he could do it with impunity.

"You dare!" he cried, confronting her as the blood spouted from his lips, where they had been cut against his teeth. "No man has yet struck me without smarting for it. You are the first woman that ever attempted it."

"Apply none of your coarse epithets to me, then," she replied, "or by Heaven *you* shall smart for it. You have a very different woman to deal with now to what you had formerly, as you will find to your cost, if you don't take care. Now tell me—if it is possible for you to speak the truth, scheming villain that you are—was our marriage a good one or not?"

"It was not," he replied surlily, stanching the blood with his handkerchief over his mouth.

"Why?" she next asked; "in what way was it bad?"

"The name was an assumed one," he replied.

"Stop your blarney," she cried; "you know as well as I do that if either party acts in ignorance, a false name is not sufficient to invalidate a marriage."

"I was already married," he hastened to add.

"Is that true?" she asked, as she looked him full in the face.

"As gospel," he replied; "divil a doubt of it."

"And is the unhappy creature still alive?"

"She is," he replied.

"And does she live with you here in Dublin?"

"She does."

The answers were given without the slightest hesitation, and certainly had all the appearance of truth; nor could Lucy help being much amused at the manner in which the tables had been turned, as Mrs. Kelly was now not only asking, but insisting on receiving answers to her questions.

"My boy," Mrs. Kelly next said, "what has become of him?"

"I do not know," was the reply.

"Why did you take him away from me?" she asked. "If our marriage was not good, you had no right to interfere with him."

"I did not do so," he answered ; but the reply was not given in the same straightforward manner as before, nor had it the same ring of truth.

"It's a lie!" Mrs. Kelly said at once. "Clever as you think yourself, your voice betrays you. I ask you again, where is my son?"

"Dead! He was tried and hung for murder two years ago."

"Another falsehood!" Mrs. Kelly again exclaimed, "villain and liar that you are! I will give you one more chance: for the third time I ask, where is the boy you stole from me thirty years ago?"

"Hoity-toity!" he cried, apparently beginning to recover his insolent manner, "and suppose I decline to answer—what then?"

"Beware!" she said slowly and solemnly, "short as is the time left to me to live, maybe yours will be shorter still. Five minutes ago I was prepared to welcome death, but now I know that I have a mission first to accomplish, and as you and I were joined together in life, so must we be in death. Listen, then, to the woman who was, who is, and who must ever be your lawfully wedded wife, when with almost her last breath she warns you that as sure as there is a God above us, in Whose presence she will stand before another sun has set, YOUR HOUR HAS COME."

He was watching her every movement now, and as she made a step towards him he placed his right hand in the breast pocket of his coat, exclaiming at the same time, "Stand back, or——" The remainder of the sentence was never uttered, for the transformation which he saw coming over her literally appalled him. Suddenly her face, which had been ruddy, became livid, her hair stood up like bristles from her head, while her eyes, which seemed starting from their sockets, were riveted on the small window of the cell, towards which also her right arm was extended, as step by step she slowly retreated backwards till stopped by the wall behind her.

"The Banshee! the Banshee!" she muttered. "See! see! she is beckoning to—us—*both*."

No sooner did No. 1 hear these words, than, superstitious like all his countrymen, his whole body seemed to shake from head to foot, large drops of perspiration oozing from his forehead began to pour down his face, while his gaze was fixed on the window as if he evidently expected the dreaded Banshee would appear to him also.

It was for this moment Mrs. Kelly had waited. Believing that he had forgotten her very existence, she crept up behind him like a cat, and, passing her arm over his shoulder, before he was the least aware of her intention had plunged her hand into his breast pocket, out of which she was now in the act of drawing a long two-edged dagger.

But by this time No. 1 was fully aroused, and recognising that were she once allowed to possess herself of such a weapon, his life would not be worth a minute's purchase, he instantly seized her by the wrist. A struggle ensued, which so frightened Lucy, that she looked round hoping to see some one whom she could summon to the old woman's assistance. Before, however, she could do this, there was a heavy fall; and when Lucy again glanced fearfully into the cell, Mrs. Kelly was lying dead, pierced to the heart, at the feet of No. 1.

Thus much Lucy saw; then she fell from her seat on to the ground in a swoon.

"You old hellhound!" said No. 1, apostro-

phizing the dead body as he withdrew the
weapon, and wiped it carefully in her skirt
before returning it to its sheath; "you have no
one but yourself to thank—not but what it is
better so. 'Dead men tell no tales,' nor women
either, I guess," with a hideous grin. "You
cannot lie there," he continued, as, taking hold of
her under the arms, he dragged her to the bed,
on which he managed to lift her, and throwing
the clothes over her, made it appear as if she
was asleep.

Hearing a step outside, he hammered at the
door, which was at once opened by the governor, who was finishing his last rounds, and who
now accompanied No. 1 to the outside gate,
saying as they parted,—

"Is it true there is a chance of a reprieve
for the old woman?"

"The question was mooted in the House to-
night," was the reply, "but there were not half
a dozen members in favour of letting her off."

"I am sorry to hear it," said the governor.
"It is bad enough to be obliged to hang a man;
but a woman!—the very idea upsets me."

"You need not worry yourself," replied No. 1
carelessly; "you will find she will not give you

much more trouble. Good-night!" And before the governor could even ask him what he meant, he was gone.

He hailed the first car and was driven to his own house, where, instead of going at once to bed, he changed his clothes, made those he had just worn into a bundle, which he carried to O'Connell Bridge and dropped into the Liffey. Again returning to his house, he learnt that Cassidy had been traced to the Imperial Hotel, and having determined to see him in the morning, he undressed and went to bed; nor was his head a moment on his pillow, ere he fell asleep, so callous was he to the cruel deed which he had just committed.

Lucy, in the meantime, had been found an hour later by a warder who happened to enter the small cell where she was lying. She was still quite unconscious. Having called another warder, who was also on night duty, they together carried her outside the prison, where the fresh air partially revived her. With some difficulty they procured a car, on which they placed her, and in due course she reached home, where the terrible sight which she had witnessed had such an effect on her nervous system, that she became seriously ill, and for the whole of the next day her life was in danger.

While these events were passing in Kilmainham jail, others of a no less serious character were being enacted in another part of the city.

It will be remembered that when the House was adjourned on that same evening, Cassidy was still inside, but he at once joined the crowd of other members, and followed them into College Green, whence he turned to the left into Westmoreland Street, and proceeded as far as O'Connell Bridge, where he suddenly stopped and looked back. He at once observed two men about twenty yards off do the same; so again proceeding, he crossed the bridge, and once more halted, when the same two men, now about half-way over the bridge, immediately turned and stood looking over the parapet into the river. Cassidy knew now that he was being followed, and so walked quickly on up Sackville Street, to his own hotel, which he entered, and making his way to the coffee-room, ordered a good supper to be prepared as quickly as possible. Ascending the stairs to his room, he dressed himself in a riding cos-

tume of breeches and boots, putting over the
latter a pair of indiarubber goloshes.    He
packed all his other things in his portmanteau,
which he locked, and returning to the coffee-
room, found his supper just ready, to which he
did ample justice.    He next called for and paid
his bill, and having given orders that his portmanteau should be taken care of, as he should
no longer require his bedroom, put on his hat
and passed out into the street.

As he expected, there was only one man
there, the other having doubtless gone off to
his employer to report progress.

The watcher seemed greatly surprised to see
Cassidy, who he had evidently made up his mind
was housed for the night, nor, to judge by the
man's face, was he by any means too well pleased
when he observed Cassidy turn to his right
and start up Sackville Street at that long,
steady stride which betokened that it was no
visit to a house in the neighbourhood he was
going to make, but probably a good stretch into
the open country.

Past Rutland Square, along Cavendish Row,
Frederick Street, so into Dorset Street, till he
entered the Circular Road, where, turning to the

left, he strode on till he came to the bridge over the Royal Canal, which he crossed, and then stopped. As he observed the man, who had been steadily following him, come up the incline of the bridge on the far side, he turned and went quickly back to meet him. The man was smoking, and, not having heard the footfall, owing to the goloshes, had no idea Cassidy was so near him.

" Give us a light, mate ; I've left my matches behind me," said Cassidy, as taking a cigar from his pocket he placed it between his teeth.

The man handed him his short pipe, which Cassidy, after having lighted his cigar, was in the act of returning, when catching the man by the throat, he tripped him up, and threw him heavily to the ground, his head striking the stone parapet of the bridge. He was quite unconscious; whether dead or not, Cassidy never stopped to inquire. At first Cassidy attempted to raise his inanimate body and throw it over the parapet, but finding that to do this was beyond his strength, he drew him by the heels down the incline on to the towing path, and there rolled him into the canal, leaving his own goloshes to keep him company, as he feared that, should there be any attempt made to trace him, the peculiar print made by the indiarubber sole would be a sure guide to his whereabouts. Instead of again crossing the bridge, Cassidy now followed the canal back towards the city, and thus arrived at Constitution Hill, where he soon found the abode of his friend Toby, who he was informed, though hourly expected, had not yet arrived in town.

Finding he could have a room, as any friend of Toby's was always welcome, here Cassidy determined to spend the night; and though for form's sake he threw himself on the bed, it was little sleep he would, he knew, get that night. The remembrance of the deed he had just committed was not to be shaken off so easily; and though he believed that his own self-preservation, which was one of the first laws of nature, demanded that the man should be made away with, still, few indeed are the individuals who can take a man's life in cold blood and not feel the effects of the deed, not only for many hours, but even for years afterwards.

# CHAPTER XXV.

## " POOR DEVIL ! "

IT will be necessary to return for a few moments to Terence O'Grady, who, it will be remembered, had, when last heard of, just been successful in defeating the Catholics who had collected on the hill above Newry. When his men, who had, as they believed, the cruel wrongs of many years to avenge, at last stayed their hands from the slaughter, it was near mid-day. It was a rare opportunity for which they had long waited, and if little mercy was shown, it would be difficult to blame them, nor did Terence attempt to influence them one way or another, but left them free to do exactly as they liked as regarded the men ; but as to women and children, he declared that the first man who injured either he would shoot him with his own hands. The fact that the other side acted as barbarians was no excuse for his men, who were Christian human beings, and as long as he had any influence with them, must act as such; but if they behaved as savages, they must choose another leader, for he would have nothing more to do with them.

He was thus able to avert the sacking of the town of Newry, which was at first contemplated, and which contained little else than women and children, the men having, with scarcely an exception, joined one side or other of those who had been fighting on the hill over the town. Tired and hungry, for they had been marching and fighting for seventeen hours almost without intermission, the Orangemen lay down on the ground, too fatigued even to prepare themselves some food; but luckily more men had been arriving all the morning by the trains, to some of whom Terence had given instructions to dig large pits for the dead, whilst others had soon started a camp kitchen whence cooked food could be served out to the tired fighters.

Amongst the earliest arrivals by the train that morning on the battle-field came Mrs. Cassidy, bringing with her between two and three hundred women, many of whom were trained nurses.    Never was an arrival more welcome, and as Terence rode up to meet them while they were descending from the cars (to use an American term), he could not resist a cheer, which, being caught up by some of the men about, was repeated again and again as the women hurried forward to their mission among the many wounded who were sadly needing their help.    As Mrs. Cassidy met Terence, they shook hands; while she, looking him full in the face, pronounced the single word, " John."

Mr. O'Grady could read the anxiety depicted on her face; even her very lips were white as she awaited his answer.

" He is not here," was the reply; "he left yesterday for Dublin."

" For Dublin ? " she repeated.    " Oh, Mr. O'Grady, he will be taken prisoner; and when they hear the news of this glorious victory, they will perhaps shoot him."

" I hope not," Mr. O'Grady answered.    " I know no one better able to take care of himself; and being an Australian and a perfect stranger there, the chances are a hundred to one he is not molested.    I am certain to hear of or from

him before night, when I will immediately let
you know." She thanked him and passed on.

It was between one and two in the afternoon, while Mr. O'Grady was himself enjoying
an *al fresco* repast, that Peter arrived; his face
was radiant with delight, though he pretended
to be angry not to have participated in the
fight.

"Well?" asked Mr. O'Grady as he appeared.

"All right," was the reply; "nothing could
have been more satisfactory. Mr. Cassidy saw
the young lady, and she promised to do her
best, and he went accordingly to our house to
hear what passed; but there was something
wrong, and he could hear nothing, so we
thought it safer to bring him away."

"And how did you manage it?" asked Mr.
O'Grady, interested to hear what had taken
place.

"Nothing easier," was the reply. "Made
his coachman drunk, and then I drove, took
the letter, which came into our possession three
months ago, to the house, and gave it to his
Excellency," Peter continued with a laugh.
"He never looked at the date, I suppose,

though he did keep us waiting a whole hour, while he and missy were—were—you know," with a wink and a broad grin. "Well, out he came at last, quite unsuspicious, and in he gets into the carriage. When we got to the gate, which was shut, the horses were that fidgetty I could not get down to open it, so he had to get out. The men were close by, who seizing him at once, bundled him into the carriage, and away we went to Kingstown, stopped close to the quay, where the *Witch* was lying, had him on board in a moment, and with a warp fast to the buoy and the steam winch, hauled out at once, and away we went. There was not much wind, but a nasty sea, and she is a terrible boat to pitch and tumble. Poor devil! how sick he was! and so was nearly every one. Even I, who was never ill in my life, was not comfortable."

"And where is he now?" asked Mr. O'Grady.

"His Excellency, do you mean?" replied Peter. "Oh, enjoying himself immensely, I fancy. I told them to lie off and on well out in the lough while I came to get instructions from you. He won't give much trouble if you like to leave him there, as it is terribly rough."

"I am going to Belfast in an hour, and will see to it.  What about Cassidy?"

"He was to drive the carriage back to Dublin, and would sleep at the hotel, he said. I was to tell you that he'd take care of himself, and not to be uneasy about him."

"Try and find his wife and tell her about him," said Mr. O'Grady.  "I promised her the latest news.  Then you can stay here to-night, and to-morrow make your way back towards Dublin, and let me know what is going on there, especially about Mrs. Kelly."

"Yes, sir," replied Peter, as he went off to find Mrs. Cassidy, while Mr. O'Grady, mounting an engine which was waiting for him, started for Belfast.

Apprised by telegram of his coming, the heads of the Orange lodges, together with an immense concourse of people, were assembled at the station to receive him, and as he stepped on to the platform, the cheers which rent the air were deafening.  Totally unprepared for anything of the sort, Mr. O'Grady was much affected as he shook hands with those near him, who one and all congratulated him warmly, several of them declaring he was the saviour of Ireland.

They informed him that the effect of the victory had been crushing, and that they had had no difficulty in securing possession of the town, the Catholics having lost heart altogether. From the latest accounts, Londonderry, and the other large towns in the North, were also one after another falling into the hands of the Orangemen, who might be said to be already masters of the whole North. Under these circumstances, Mr. O'Grady gave orders that the steamer *Witch* should enter the harbour; that the gentleman on board, who had come in her from Dublin, should be taken to an hotel and every attention paid to him, but he must be strictly guarded, and on no account allowed to escape. Mr. O'Grady would call himself to see him in the morning, when he was rested and recovered from the voyage, by which time Mr. O'Grady hoped and trusted to have heard from Cassidy as to Mrs. Kelly's fate.

# CHAPTER XXVI.

## THE DINNER PARTY.

IT wanted still a quarter to seven the following morning when the servant entered the room in which No. 1 slept, and opened the shutters. "What time is it?" mumbled that individual, only half awake.

"A quarter to seven, sir," was the reply.

"Then what the hell——" began No. 1; but the servant, interrupting, said, "Please, sir, I was to tell you there are several large steamers, flying the American flag, just entering the river, and you gave orders that you——"

"That will do," replied No. 1, springing out of bed, and beginning to dress with the utmost speed.

He was ready in a few minutes, and as, leaving his own house, he turned to the left, and almost immediately entered Grafton Street, he at once became aware of the stream of people all going in the one direction.

At O'Connell Bridge the crowd was already immense, but No. 1 could still force himself a passage, as well as along Eden Quay, till he reached the Custom House, where the block was so great, it seemed hopeless to proceed farther. He could now, for the first time, hear the distant cheering, which was gradually getting nearer and nearer as the vessels steamed up the stream. With some difficulty having procured a boat at the Custom House, No. 1 dropped down the river, and had soon the satisfaction of seeing the first steamer coming slowly up in charge of the pilot. Arrived opposite the North Wall, the steamer stopped, and No. 1 seizing the opportunity to go alongside, ascended the gangway, and was soon on deck. Nearly every one was on the bridge, except the men who were watching the shore, evidently greatly amused at their enthusiastic reception, which was precisely the reverse of what they had expected, some of them having been even doubtful whether their landing might not be disputed.

With difficulty making his way to the bridge, which was crowded with persons, all of whom seemed in the best of spirits, No. 1 soon

found O'Donovan Rossa and several other
leaders, with whom he was personally acquainted, and whom he welcomed to the
"ould country," expressing his unbounded
delight, as well as that of all Ireland, at their
most opportune arrival.   Not a soul on board
had spoken a word, but, so far as was possible
in the midst of such vociferous cheering, had
listened to what was said, which must have
seemed to them intensely amusing, as no sooner
had No. 1 ceased speaking, than, after exchang-
ing significant looks, there was a general laugh.
Hawsers having in the meantime been made
fast fore and aft, the vessel was hauled alongside the quay, while the enthusiasm of the
people, assembled literally in thousands on the
shore, exceeded all belief.

"Whatever does it all mean?" shouted one
of those on the bridge to No. 1.   "There must
be some cause, I guess, for their delight at
seeing us."

"Yes!" was the reply.   "There has been a
fight with the Orangemen in the North, in which
our people got the worst of it, and they believe
that with your help, not only will the defeat be
avenged, but the Orangemen be soon hunted

out of Ireland." Again significant looks were exchanged among the few who could hear the reply that had been made, and there was another laugh.

The noise, however, was so deafening it was impossible to say more ; and while the eyes of all on board were directed to the shore, those of No. 1 scanned the steamer, her crew, and passengers. The vessel was a very fine one of between three and four thousand tons ; but as to those on board, though accustomed as No. 1 was to come into contact with men of all sorts and kinds, more especially of what might be termed the greatest ruffians to be found in Ireland, never in his whole life did he remember to have seen brought together such a set of villains, to judge by their countenances, as those whom he now beheld from the bridge on which he was standing.

Looking down the river seaward, No. 1 now observed there were altogether four steamers, all of which were flying the Irish flag from the foremast and the stars and stripes at the main. They were all hauling in to the quays, and as each came alongside and a bridge was made to the land, the people, who were literally packed on the shore like herrings in a barrel, poured on board, all vieing with each other who should show hospitality to the strangers.

In an incredibly short space of time the decks were cleared, the Americans being only too anxious to reach *terra firma*, after having been for twelve days cooped up in close quarters on board. In considerably less than an hour from the time the steamers were made fast alongside the quay, the crowd had dispersed, taking with it the whole of the new arrivals, and the steamers were left in charge of their own crews.

No. 1 having apologised for not having a single spare room to offer any one, asked O'Donovan Rossa and his immediate followers both to breakfast and dinner; but, they being anxious to get settled in their hotel, declined the former, but accepted the latter invitation ; and, as the quay was now clear, cars were procured, and the luggage sent on shore, several custom-house officers who attempted to interfere being coolly told to go to hell and mind their own business, while one, who was more officious than the rest, received a quietus in the shape of a blow on the back of the head, which laid him flat on his face in the mud. They drove to Jury's Hotel in College Green, where, after some trouble, the whole twelve found accommodation, and having ordered breakfast, they parted with No. 1, telling him to expect them at six o'clock, that being the hour they always dined. As he strolled home, he could not resist a smile as he thought of the cool manner they had fixed their own dinner hour; but, apart from this, there was a something he did not like in their off-hand manner of proceeding. He remembered how they had themselves settled with the custom-house officers, instead of asking his assistance; and when he further thought of the men whom they had brought over with them, he felt far from comfortable as to the future.

The day passed as usual. No. 1 saw nothing more of the new arrivals, nor would any one walking or driving through the city be the least aware that fifteen hundred Americans had been let loose in it that morning.

A few minutes before six, O'Donovan Rossa and his crew arrived in Nassau Street. They were in exactly the same dress as when they had parted from him in the morning, not even having taken the trouble to wash their hands, some of which were literally ground in dirt. Dinner was announced in a few minutes, and they sat down to table, the conversation turning chiefly on the voyage from America, concerning which they related many amusing, if not very refined, anecdotes. The dinner was what was considered in Dublin a really good one, no expense having been spared to make it first-rate; but, to No. 1's utter disgust, not one of his visitors ate anything. They just tasted the soup, and no more; of fish they did eat a few mouthfuls; but the *entrées* they would not even touch, nor did the roast meat fare much better.

"Our breakfast was bad enough, I guess," said one of them, addressing the others; "but I'm darned if this dinner isn't worse. I'm that hungry, I could eat the soles off my shoes; but as for such stuff as this"—turning over with his knife some slices of meat on his plate,— "I'm of opinion that the beggars in New York city might nibble at it before throwing it to the pigs, but as to swallowing it, it wouldn't be no sort of manner of use, for stay down it *wouldn't*; for even if they sewed their mouths up as they do the ferrets, it would come out of their noses

or ears. It's bound to part company somehow."
All laughed at this sally, except No. 1, who
stared in astonishment at such an impertinent
speech, and was for a moment so taken aback
that he could not open his lips.

"What could you expect?" continued another,
speaking in a mixture of the Irish brogue and
American twang. "Sure, the people are nothing
but a set of savages, who have never been out
of their darned country, and know no better.
The best thing we can do is to wire to New
York city for a couple of cooks, and the gentleman who was kind enough to ask us here
to-night will, I daresay, send the message for
us after dinner, for you see there is no time to
lose, or we shall be all that weak from starvation, that when the cooks arrive we shan't be
able to swallow."

There was another laugh at this remark,
when No. 1, who by this time had recovered
his speech, exclaimed angrily, "What is the
*matter* with the food, gentlemen? that is what
I should like to know. There is not better
meat to be had in Dublin, and it is a perfectly
well-known fact that the meat in this city is as
fine as any in the world."

"Nobody said it wasn't," replied the last speaker; "the meat itself, I reckon, may be good enough, but it's the way it is cooked that is so abominably bad."

"There is not a better cook in Ireland, and very few in England," No. 1 persisted.

"Nobody denies that," was the reply; "but that does not make 'em any the better, and is the more reason why the telegram should be sent with the least possible delay."

The first course having been cleared away, the second began with a *mayonnaise* of lobster, of which there were two dishes, one for each side of the table. The first to whom it was handed, before helping himself, took a piece of the salad in his fingers and tasted it. Evidently approving, he took the dish from the servant and held it at an acute angle over his plate, on to which, by the help of his own fork and an occasional shake, he caused quite half the contents to slide, and immediately began with both knife and fork to shovel it into his mouth. His proceedings, having been observed, were at once followed, and the second man on each side finished the dish; the *mayonnaise* being thus divided among four, the remaining

eight guests were left without. In little more
than a minute, the individual who had first
helped himself, having finished his plateful,
raised his eyes for the first time, when, looking
round and observing that some of his companions were not eating, he at once exclaimed,—

"Well, I'm darned, if you chaps don't eat
that, I tell you you are wrong, for it's good—
darned good. Here, waiter, bring me some
more." But the waiter, going to his side,
began to whisper something in his ear, when
the stranger, passing his hand up quickly over
his shoulder, hit the man with the back of it in
the face, exclaiming, "Don't! please don't blow
into my ear—it gives me a headache ; and if
you have anything to say, speak up, and don't
be ashamed ; these gentlemen will be as glad
to hear it as I shall. No more crawfish, did
you say ? Then dinner's over, and I'll have
a smoke. Bring me a light." And turning his
chair sideways to the table, he pulled over
another, on which he put his legs, and taking
a huge cigar from his pocket, sat waiting for
the light.

The servant, however, who had observed his
master give a slight shake of the head, went

on with his work, ignoring the order altogether, which the Yankee observing, he rose from his seat, and crossing the room to where he saw a newspaper, he deftly rolled a long spill of paper, and was thus enabled to obtain the desired light from one of the two duplex lamps suspended over the table.   But if the Americans objected to the food, such was by no means the case with the liquors.   Using tumblers for the champagne, bottle after bottle disappeared with marvellous celerity : sherry, port, claret, and, lastly, whisky followed suit, till No. 1 literally stared at the consumption.   He had the good sense, however, to say nothing.   He felt that if he spoke he could not command his temper; his only chance, therefore, of averting a row was to look on in silence, and allow his guests to do exactly as they liked.   Soon the whole twelve were smoking and filling the room, so that it was impossible to see across it; but what made matters almost unbearable was the expectoration which they each shot out from between their teeth all over the Turkey carpet.

At first No. 1 thought of adjourning to another room, but changed his mind, as he considered that one carpet having been already pretty well spoilt, it was better to stay where they were. At eight o'clock they began to make inquiries about "the House," to which No. 1, to his great delight, heard they were bound; but O'Donovan and another, who had ensconced themselves in comfortable armchairs on each side of the hearthrug, declared they would not be wanted, so they would enjoy a doze, as there were quite enough without them. There was a loud wrangle, of course; but eventually seven of them started at twenty minutes to nine; while No. 1, uncertain whether to leave his house at the mercy of the five who remained, or to accompany the other seven, finally decided on the latter course, impelled by his curiosity to see what would happen. He determined, however, to keep in the background, and take no active part in the proceedings. The one who had been the first to commence smoking at the dinner, whose name was Finerty, and who evidently knew the city well, led the way. The distance was short, and as they walked fast, in two minutes they were at the door of the House. Here they were stopped, and informed that unless introduced by a member they could not enter.

Though not even the least screwed, still, they
had had enough wine to make them inclined
to be facetious, and accordingly they began to
chaff the door-keeper most unmercifully, one
asking him to take the green out of his eye,
another if his mother knew he was out; and
while thus laughing and joking, they altogether
ignored what he said, and continued their way
into the inner room where the members were
sitting.   They entered in a compact body, and
though again warned there was no admittance,
it was only too clear that they were not men
to be meddled with, but best left alone.

# CHAPTER XXVII.

### "OH, DON'T! PLEASE, DON'T!"

THE Home Secretary was speaking when they entered, and was informing the House how that now help had arrived from the other side of the Atlantic, they would soon avenge their late defeat, and teach the Orangemen a lesson they would not in a hurry forget; in fact, he trusted before many days had elapsed the larger portion of those troublesome people would have left the country for ever. Guessing that the speech had reference to themselves, for a moment the strangers stood together and listened; then Mr. Finerty, who, while still in the street outside, had lighted another of his enormous cigars, strolled up the centre of the House, and observing the seat usually occupied by the Prime Minister vacant, coolly took it, and, lolling back, stretched out his long legs and sent the smoke in a cloud up to the ceiling.

Astonishment at his effrontery kept those near him silent for a moment; then two members, one on each side, leaning towards him, whispered something in his ear. As he had done at dinner, so now, withdrawing both hands from his pockets, he threw them up, as if to drive away the flies, exclaiming,—

"Oh, don't! please, don't! it gives me a headache. Speak up; don't be ashamed. *I* have no secrets, and don't want to hear any."

This was said in so loud a tone of voice that it attracted the attention of all present, and there was a profound silence. Seizing the opportunity, Mr. Finerty drew in his legs and rose, still, however, keeping his cigar between his lips.

"We are very much obliged," he began, looking round the House, "at the reception you have given to us on our arrival to-day. It was tarnation kind of you, and that's a fact, more especially as it's not what we expected, nor what is usually given, I calculate, to those who come as we do, on what may be called a disagreeable job; in other words, to dun for money which is due to us, and which we mean to have before we go back, and that's a fact. Now, gentlemen," he went on, " I am not going to spin a long yarn, as that is not at all in my line. We have our Currans and our Grattans in Ameriky, but I am not one of them. Deeds, not *words*, for me; still, it is necessary to say a few *words*, and so I must do it. The five millions we claim as being due to us are not an almighty big sum to ask from a rich country like this, which received more than two hundred and fifty millions from the Britishers only the other day; but though we have written again and again for the money, not a shilling have we ever received, so here we are, and, of course, now there will be our expenses over to pay as well. Well, gentlemen, we want to know what you intend to do; but if you will allow me to make a suggestion, I would advise that you should give us the money without any more bother, and let us go home—first, because every day we stay here the expenses are increasing enormously, and, secondly, because some of those who came with us—though gentle and quiet as lambs, if in good humour—are apt to be nasty if they don't get their own way; and as none of them have a penny in their pockets, their ideas as to the exact meaning of the two

pronouns, *meum* and *tuum*, may not altogether
accord with those generally taught in this old-
fashioned country."

There was a dead pause as Mr. Finerty
let himself drop again on to his seat, no one
seeming to know exactly what to say or do.
At last the Home Secretary rose and said,—

"In the absence of the Prime Minister, it is
impossible for the House to give any reply as
to the extraordinary request which has just
been made ; nor have I—and I think I am
correct in saying any other member of this
House—ever had the least idea that any such
outrageous sum as five millions sterling had
ever been seriously demanded from this country
by our American brothers. But perhaps I am
in error, and it is five million *dollars* which we
are thus called on to pay at a moment's notice.
In either case, time will be necessary in order
to see what can be done. It is no secret, and
I see no reason why I should shirk mentioning
the fact, that our exchequer is at present very
low, nor is it likely to be increased to any
appreciable extent until the Orangemen are
brought to their senses, and made to understand that this Parliament governs Ireland, and

the laws and taxes which are made here must be obeyed and paid by them as well as elsewhere. Unfortunately, such at present is not the case; they have not only refused to acknowledge our authority, but have risen into open rebellion, and attacked and defeated a small force sent against them. We hoped that our American brothers who have so opportunely arrived in our city would have helped us to bring these refractory subjects to listen to reason; and even now I cannot help feeling that when our visitors hear how we are situated, and that certainly the easiest, if not the only way in which this money can be procured, is from these very Orangemen, that they will aid us in proving to these stubborn, obstinate people that the taxes *must* be paid."

Mr. Finerty, however, shook his head, as, without rising, he replied, "I reckon you altogether misunderstand the situation. We come here as creditors, who, after having again and again applied for the money which is due to us, have now crossed the water in order to get it by fair means if you will allow us, but if not, by foul, for *have it we must;* but as to interfering in any way with the government of

the country, or helping to put down any rebellion, it would be too absurd to ask us to do
anything of the sort, unless," he added, after a
moment's pause, "after you have settled with
us as to our five millions and expenses, you
like to add one or two millions more. We
might then entertain the idea of doing a little
throat-cutting before we go back, by way of
a divarsion."

Had a bomb exploded in their midst, there
could not have been greater consternation
visible than appeared in the faces of those who
had listened to Mr. Finerty's last speech ; and
though it may be said that the Irish never
altogether despair, still, it was with very sad
forebodings as to the future that the Home
Secretary replied :—

"We are to understand, then, that our American brothers, whose arrival this morning filled
us all with such joy, and whom we welcomed
so enthusiastically as the saviours of Ireland,
now decline to help us in our sore need, and,
instead of being a godsend, must be looked on
as our despoilers."

"If you mean by 'declining to help,' that we
object to fight your battles unless you make it

worth our while, I guess you are right there, stranger; and as to 'despoilers,' if that is the name you give to those who ask to be paid back the money which they have lent, you are right again, I reckon."

" But suppose we have not got the money you are demanding, and further declare we find it quite impossible to procure it—what then ?" asked the Home Secretary, apparently plucking up courage.

" Why, then," replied Mr. Finerty, with a contemptuous smile, and speaking very slowly, with the longest American drawl conceivable—"then we should have to help ourselves ; but for the honour of the ould country, which *must* have the money, as fifty times the amount was so lately paid by the Britishers, we guess it will hesitate to declare itself smashed up."

" We will see what can be done," said the Home Secretary; "but must have time, of course, as we must communicate with the Prime Minister.  So give us forty-eight hours, and you shall have an answer."

" Very good ! " was the reply ; " but I guess you are making a mistake.  Better to have paid us off slick, and get rid of us, and so I reckon you will find to your cost."

He rose as he finished speaking, and sauntered off out of the House, followed by his companions, who all went straight home to Jury's, not twenty yards distant.

And in the meantime, what had been passing in the city during this eventful day? Received by the citizens with open arms, all of whom vied with each other who should take the strangers in, the Americans had been fêted and made much of, treated to the best of everything, and supplied with any amount of liquor, which they imbibed in such a manner as to astonish even the Pats, themselves no mean performers in that line. Towards evening, tired of staying at home, they paraded the streets in parties, and whatever they saw in any of the shops which they fancied, they immediately declared they must have, and walking coolly in, at once took possession of, utterly ignoring the question of payment.

Of course before long the battle in the North was discussed, and opinions joyfully expressed as to how the tables would be turned, and what spoil they would get when the Orangemen were driven clean out of the country, as the Government had quite determined should be done.

" But have you no Orangemen here in Dublin ? " asked one of the strangers.

" No! " replied one ; "they are not such fools as to stay here. It would be rather too hot for them."

" But there are plenty of Protestants," cried another, "and they are all the same."

Thus it came about that the idea was started that the Protestants in Dublin should be punished for the victory of their co-religionists in the North. With so many heretics close by, the Yankees declared it would be folly to go away from Dublin, and so in a few minutes it was settled that a raid should be made that very night on the dwellings of the peaceful Protestants of Dublin ; and while Mr. Finerty was coolly asking Parliament to pay over the five millions and let them go back to America, the whole city was in an uproar, as the Americans and Irish Catholics were banded together visiting house after house of the Protestant middle and lower classes, taking

possession of everything of value, turning the
men into the streets, but subjecting the women
to treatment too brutal to describe.

Luckily many of these latter had been in-
duced to listen to the advice of Terence
O'Grady and his agents, and not a few of the
young women had been sent away, some to the
North, others to England. Thus the number
of women on whom these hell-hounds could lay
their hands was comparatively small, and they
were greatly enraged in consequence. As the
devilish work proceeded, the crowd that collected was enormous; and so great was the
exultation at the Protestants being thus served,
that numbers of young Catholic women, both
married and single, anxious to have a finger
in every pie, were foremost in pointing out
the houses which belonged to the Protestants.
It happened that four houses one after the
other had been searched, and not a woman,
young or old, found in one of them, when a
huge, villainous-looking Yankee, coming down
the stairs, saw standing at the door of the
house a sweetly pretty woman who had been
married only a couple of weeks before to a
carpenter who was now close beside her.

Catching her by the arm, the ruffian drew her inside the house and into a room, on the ground floor of which he shut and locked the door so suddenly that no one had time to interfere; but as the woman kept scream-ing to her husband to come to her assist-ance, the carpenter, armed with his hammer, attacked the window and soon effected an entrance. The woman was lying on the floor where she had been thrown; the man, with one foot on her chest to prevent her rising, stood waiting for his antagonist, a diabolical gleam in his bloodshot eyes which should have made any one but a madman pause before approaching him.

"Let that woman go! she is my wife, and as good a Catholic, bedad, as there is in all Oire-land," the carpenter exclaimed, as he stooped as if to raise her from the floor. But before he could touch her, the American, with the quick-ness of lightning, drew one of those terrible knives, such as were used in the Phœnix Park murders, and stabbed the wretched man to the heart, catching him at the same time by the shoulder, and hurling him back towards the window to prevent him falling on his wife.

Observing that others were following the carpenter into the room, the brute caught up the woman in his arms, and kicking open the door, quickly ascended the stairs, calling at the same time to some of his mates to keep back the mob and settle any who were troublesome.

Thus it came about that the whole city was soon at the mercy of fifteen hundred of the greatest blackguards that the slums of New York and other large American cities could produce. They took what plunder came in their way, but it was women they wanted, both young and pretty, and such they very soon showed they would have; nor did they trouble themselves to ask questions as to what their religion might be. They visited house after house, and when a girl or young woman caught a man's fancy, he took possession of her at once, and kept her against all comers. Of course both fathers and husbands interfered, and tried to save their unhappy daughters and wives; but the result was invariably the same—the natives were no match for their "American brothers." Thus the night wore on, and before morning came, more than two thousand young and pretty women, who the evening before had been virtuous, happy, and unsuspecting, had been ill-treated and ruined at the hands of their merciless visitors, while over a thousand natives had been assassinated for daring to interfere and come to the rescue of the victims.

# CHAPTER XXVIII.

## "THE SOONER, THE BETTER."

WHEN, the following morning at nine o'clock, Mr. O'Shaughnessy came down to breakfast, his astonishment may be better imagined than described when he found John Cassidy seated in the dining-room waiting for him.

" Delighted to see you, John," he said; " but is this wise or prudent? You have openly declared yourself a friend of Terence O'Grady, the man whom they call a traitor to his country, and is it not more than probable they will make you suffer for some of O'Grady's sins?"

" And who sent me to Mr. French," asked Cassidy, laughing, " and actually gave me a letter to him, may I ask? However, joking apart, as I was taking a stroll round by the canal the night before last, an individual did follow me, and so I left him in the canal, and since then have not been molested. People's

heads are too full of the Yankees to trouble
themselves about an Australian.    What do you
think, Shaugh, of your visitors ? "

" A more ill-conditioned set I never set eyes
on," replied Mr. O'Shaughnessy.    " Did you
hear that some of them came down to the
House last night and coolly demanded payment of five millions sterling, which they
asserted they had advanced to enable Ireland
to get her freedom, and as they declared the
' Britishers ' had paid us two hundred and fifty
millions, so we could well afford to hand them
five ; and what's more, they seemed inclined to
insist on getting the money *there and then*, as
the sooner they were off back again, the better
for us, they said, as if we could possibly pay
even five hundred pounds down in a moment
like that, let alone five millions."

" And what was done about it ? " asked
Cassidy.

" You have carried off our Prime Minister,"
said Mr. O'Shaughnessy, smiling, " so we had
a good excuse to ask for time, and it was
settled an answer was to be given in forty-
eight hours."

" Then God help poor Ireland, for no one

else can," said Cassidy, as he rose to shake hands with the two ladies who then entered the room, the younger one looking sweetly fresh and pretty.

"What do you mean?" said Mr. O'Shaughnessy. "Never fear, we shall get the money somewhere; and in the meantime, I suppose the Americans will favour us with their company for a week or two."

"If they do, before that there will not be a virtuous woman in Ireland, let alone Dublin." [All three stared at Cassidy, evidently totally at a loss to understand his meaning.] "While you have been sleeping quietly in your beds," Cassidy continued, "you are not, of course, aware what has been going on in other parts of the city. You do not know that these American fiends—for they are nothing else—the vilest scum of such cities as Chicago and New York, have been spending the night in sacking the city, stealing everything they could lay their hands on, murdering any men who dared to interfere with them while they ravished the unhappy women before their husbands' and fathers' very eyes. Oh! it has been a fearful night; and some of the scenes, of which I was an eye-witness, I shall never forget. Last night they attacked only the lower and middle classes ; but how long they will confine themselves to such, who can say ? " and he glanced meaningly at the two ladies listening breathlessly to every word he was uttering. As for Mr. O'Shaughnessy, he was struck literally dumb with horror and consternation, not for himself—for he was, like all true Irishmen, constitutionally brave—but for his two sisters, the younger of whom he loved very dearly.

" This is indeed awful ! and to think that we knew nothing of it," he said at last. " But where are these devils now ? Can nothing be done to drive them out of the city ? What do you advise, John ? "

" If we could only trust the people, it ought not to be so difficult to get together enough men to account for these fellows ; but they are so demoralized at the thrashing O'Grady gave them the other day at Newry, that I fear there is no dependence to be placed on them—at any rate, it would be madness to attempt anything of the sort as long as there are any women for whose safety one is responsible."

" Flight, then, is the only alternative," exclaimed Mr. O'Shaughnessy. "There is not a moment to lose. Come, ladies, get what few things you require together, and let us get a car and be off. You will come with us, John?"

"Where to? Where are you going?"

"Anywhere so long as we get out of this. To the North, I suppose, will be safest."

"Of course it would, if you could only get there; but how to do so is the question."

Mr. O'Shaughnessy stared. "Why not by train?" he asked.

"They have taken possession of every station, and not a soul is allowed to leave the city," replied Cassidy. "Every road also is watched. Oh! they know what they are about, and no mistake."

Mr. O'Shaughnessy wrung his hands as he exclaimed, "Can you suggest nothing, John? Is there really no hope of saving my poor sisters from these infernal barbarians?"

"I sent off a man on horseback about midnight when I saw how things were going on, and instructed him to make the best of his way to Malahide, and thence wire O'Grady to send the *Witch* to Kingstown as fast as possible. If he is at Belfast—but which is, I fear, very doubtful—she may be there this evening; but the great difficulty will be to get on board, and at present I confess I hardly see how it is to be managed."

" But what is to be done in the meantime ?" asked Mr. O'Shaughnessy; " between now and to-night God alone knows what might happen."

Cassidy looked at the ladies : both were *very* pale, but otherwise showed no sign of fear.

" My advice would be to disguise yourselves as two old women," he said, addressing the ladies, " but on no account to leave the house, nor show yourselves at the window, no matter what you may hear, and of course keep as much as possible in the back rooms, putting your trust in that Higher Power Who alone can save you in this hour of trouble and terrible necessity." Hardly had Cassidy finished speaking, when all started from their seats, as two piercing shrieks from the street outside rang through the whole house. The impulse of every one was to rush to the window; but Cassidy, catching the younger Miss O'Shaughnessy by the arm, hurried her away, followed by Shaugh with the other sister. They ascended the stairs to a bedroom at the back of the house, where

Cassidy left them, warning them to lose no time
in assuming their disguise, and promising to
return again in the afternoon should there be
any news of the steamer. Again and again
the ladies implored him not to forsake them;
but he told them that there were others more
helpless than they, who required his assistance
quite as much as, if not more than, they did.

As soon as he was out of the house, Cassidy
made the best of his way towards the Westland
Row station, hoping to catch a train; but there
was no sign of anything of the sort—only
several Americans standing as sentries at the
door. He looked round for a car, but could
see none; so entering a livery stable, he, with
some difficulty, persuaded the proprietor to let
him have the use of a carriage as long as he
wanted it for five sovereigns—three paid down in
advance. Telling the coachman he was a doctor
going his rounds, he started, and though stopped
twice on his way, eventually arrived at his destination—the house of Miss Lucy O'Connor at
Blackrock. He was told, however, on ringing
the bell, that that young lady was ill in bed, and
it was impossible he could see her. Ridiculing
all remonstrances, and with the judicious gift of

five shillings to the servant, he persuaded her
to take up his name, and to say that he *must*
see Lucy without a moment's delay on a matter
of life and death.   Admitted at last, he found
her upstairs lying on a sofa, looking very ill, but
sweetly pretty, and at once proceeded to explain what was the cause of his visit.   He had
been greatly struck with the young girl on the
evening of his first visit, when he had asked her
to advocate the cause of Mrs. Kelly ; and her
ready promise to try and save the old woman's
life had so won his heart, that as he, Cassidy,
had been the one to carry off her protector, so
he now felt himself bound to take her under his
charge, and endeavour to save her from the
brutal treatment she would experience at the
hands of the blackguards who at present were
in possession of Dublin.   She held out her
hand to him when he appeared, saying, " It is
kind of you to come and see me.   I have been,
and may say I am still, very ill, and can with
difficulty move even from my bed to the sofa."

" That is unfortunate," Cassidy replied, " as
you must make an effort and try and leave
this to-day."

At first she declared it to be impossible ; but

when Cassidy had informed her of what was going on in Dublin, and that it was only too certain that Kingstown, Monkstown, and Blackrock, would soon be visited, and the inhabitants subjected to the same treatment, then she quite recognised the situation, and admitted that she must make an effort, not only on her own account, but on that of another.

" To whom do you allude ? " asked Cassidy.

" A young girl whom her dying mother asked me to befriend and protect. I call her my sister, and had she really been so, there could not be more true love and affection between us."

" Does she live here with you ? " asked Cassidy.

" She does. I will send for her ; but she is as innocent as a child, and "—hesitating and getting very red—" neither knows nor suspects anything."

" All right," said Cassidy, as, in answer to a hand-bell which Lucy rang, the door opened, and one of the prettiest little creatures Cassidy ever remembered to have set eyes on entered the room. Though in reality eighteen years old, she looked little more than fifteen, and all her actions were so graceful and so youthful, that she won every heart directly. As she came over to Lucy's side, glancing shyly at Cassidy, and sank down on the carpet beside the sofa, she looked so awfully jolly that Cassidy felt tempted to take her up in his arms and kiss her, as you would a child of six; and then, as he remembered the treatment to which the little darling might be subjected ere twenty-four hours had elapsed (for would she not be a rare prize for one of those villains from America to get hold of?), he then and there swore to himself that sooner than such should happen, he would shoot her with his own hand.

"Miss Lucy," Cassidy now said, "I have a favour to beg of you, which you will not, I hope, refuse, notwithstanding the fact that I am, I know, taking a great liberty in asking it. I mentioned just now that it is absolutely necessary you and this young lady should leave here to-day. Mr. O'Grady is sending a steamer to fetch you, as well as any others who may be able to get on board, amongst whom are some friends of his and mine of the name of O'Shaughnessy. There are two sisters and a brother, the latter a Member of Parliament. It is, of course, quite uncertain when the steamer will reach Kingstown; but if you would allow me to invite those two young ladies and their brother to come here this afternoon and remain till the steamer comes, it would simplify matters much, as by this means there would be only one party to get on board instead of two."

Lucy had made a *very* wry face as she had heard she was to go to sea, for, being one of the worst sailors imaginable, the very idea of a steamer made her ill. As, however, she observed Rose, as her friend was called, clap her hands with delight, and then thought of what remaining there would mean for her darling, she said nothing, but, in reply to Mr. Cassidy's question, gave him a look as if to ask how much his friends *knew.* He shook his head in reply, and Lucy then said, "Any friends of yours, Mr. Cassidy, are welcome to such shelter and accommodation as this house affords, and Rosy will do her best to make them comfortable. When are we to expect them?"

"The sooner, the better," said Cassidy. "I will go at once to Dublin, and if by any means possible, bring them here within a couple of hours."

# CHAPTER XXIX.

### "BARNEY, I WANT YOU."

MR. CASSIDY rose as he finished speaking, and having bowed to the two ladies, left them and rejoined his carriage. There was a something about Lucy that attracted him strangely; while as to Rose, her image haunted him all the way to Dublin. He stopped his carriage outside the city, and entering on foot, he passed unmolested, and safely reached his friend O'Shaughnessy's house, where he was welcomed most enthusiastically, as if he had already achieved their escape, instead of having, in fact, only suggested how perhaps it might be managed. The ladies, however, he was glad to observe, were already disguised very effectually, and the experiment must be made as to how far they would pass muster.

Cassidy now explained that a lady friend of his, and also of Terence O'Grady's, had commissioned him to say that she hoped they would make her house their home while waiting for the steamer, as by this means they could all go on board together, which would be much easier to accomplish than if in separate parties. The ladies accepted at once, their one sole idea apparently being to get out of Dublin as quickly as possible, and their spirits rose instantly in proportion ; but both Cassidy and O'Shaughnessy knew better the risks that had to be run, and felt very nervous as to the result. They made no plans, thinking it better to be governed by circumstances. The state of the streets was not yet very bad—at least, not in the part of the town which they would have to traverse—but there was a man lying dead in College Green whom they must pass, and Cassidy again and again urged the ladies rather to keep their eyes shut, and allow themselves to be led, than show by any means either disgust or horror at whatever they might see or hear.

They left their house in Dame Street about three o'clock, and turning to the left, walked towards College Green, O'Shaughnessy and his elder sister leading the way—Cassidy, with the younger, following. The gait of the first lady was admirable, but that of the other, too springy and elastic to suit her disguise, and she seemed quite unable to improve it. They met with no molestation as they passed in front of the House of Parliament and Trinity College, close to the entrance to which the dead man was lying. In order to avoid him as much as possible, they kept to the left, intending to pass by College Street into Great Brunswick Street. At the corner of Westmoreland Street a woman was sitting, crying bitterly, and wailing and moaning as the Irish so often do at wakes. As O'Shaughnessy's party approached, she got up, and planting herself right in front of them, appealed in the most piteous tones for help, declaring herself to be a poor widow woman, whose only daughter had been taken from her and carried off, she knew not where; and would not the two gentlemen help her to find the poor child, who was only seventeen, and as innocent and good as she was pretty? Sure, they were not " jintlemen " at all if they allowed a poor " crittur " like that to be ruined and destroyed without making an attempt to save her.

What was to be done? To push past her without a word as she stood in the middle of the narrow pavement seemed brutal, and yet there was no help for it. Before, however, this could be done, wild shrieks were heard from the direction of the river, and the next moment two young girls came running at the top of their speed up Westmoreland Street, straight to where O'Shaughnessy and Cassidy were standing, followed by three or four of the American crew, who were laughing heartily, evidently enjoying the fun, while behind them were several elderly females who were shriek- ing for help. That the two girls intended to apply to O'Shaughnessy and his party for pro- tection there could scarcely be a doubt, and the situation was, to say the least of it, most grave, when one of the fugitives, looking over her shoulder to see if her pursuers were gaining, stumbled, and then, in the hope of saving herself from falling, caught hold of her sister, with the usual result of bringing her also down in the middle of the muddy road.

The Americans laughed louder than ever at the sight; while O'Shaughnessy, with a true Irishman's warmth of heart and impetuosity, actually let go of his sister, and seemed about to fly to the rescue. Cassidy, however, having, luckily for them, a much cooler head on his shoulders, seized his lady companion by the arm, and dragging her past the woman, who was also engaged watching the others in Westmoreland Street, called to O'Shaughnessy to follow, and so they continued their way into Great Brunswick Street, along which they hurried towards Westland Row, their object being to see whether trains were running, and, if possible, take advantage of one to get away; but if not, they must only make their way to the carriage which Cassidy had left outside the city.

They had arrived safely within twenty yards of the turning to Westland Row station, when five unmistakable Yankees emerging from Lombard Street (as that portion of Westland Row is named which runs between Great Brunswick Street and the Liffey), stood grouped together at the corner, evidently undecided which way to go. They must, of course, have seen Cassidy and his party, but, without apparently noticing them, crossed the road and placed themselves at the corner of Westland Row. What was to be done? The hearts of both O'Shaughnessy and Cassidy sank, as, quit-

ting the pavement, and walking in the muddy
slush of the road, they approached the five men,
who were now intently watching them. To
say that it was an anxious moment conveys
no sort of an idea of the situation; for though
there had been no preconcerted action between
O'Shaughnessy and Cassidy, both intuitively
felt that death to the two ladies was infinitely
preferable to falling into the clutches of such vile
gaol-birds as the ruffians standing now within
a few yards of them; and Cassidy set his teeth
hard as he clutched his revolver, determined
that one of the five shots which it contained
should be reserved for the poor girl by his
side, should such a terrible necessity arise.

As the four passed—O'Shaughnessy and his
elder sister now again in front—Cassidy, whose
eyes never for one moment quitted the faces of
the Americans, could see that the acting of the
elder sister had defied detection, and that the
Yankees fully believed her to be an old woman;
but when he observed a grim smile stealing
over the diabolical faces of two of the ruffians,
he knew at once that his own companion had
not been so fortunate.

"It ain't no sort of earthly use to try and

catch an old bird with chaff," exclaimed one
of the five; "the get-up is first-rate, and might
do to deceive a Britisher, or maybe a Pat, but
Jonathan Barney warn't born yesterday, and I
guess the gal's not born *yet* who could gammon
him as to her age when he sees her walking. So
let's have a look at your face, Missy. I'll wager
it's a pretty one." Cassidy and O'Shaughnessy
instantly turned and faced the ruffians, standing side by side, and placing the ladies behind
them.

"Now, look ye here, young men," went on
Jonathan Barney, a huge, burly man, considerably over six foot and stout in proportion,
"just you go your way, and don't ye interfere
in this here business. You'll only get into
trouble, and come to grief yourselves, without
doing any good; for when Jonathan Barney
says a thing, he means it, and I tell you now
I *must* see that young woman's face, and if
she pleases me, I'll take her with me down to
where I am lodging, near the water yonder.
That is what Jonathan Barney intends to do,
and if you try to stop him, you will have
to hook it, I reckon, to the place where all
good niggers and bad Pats go; for, by the

Almighty Creator of the univarse, that young woman shall be mine, even though heaven combine with hell to try and stop it;" and he advanced with outstretched arm, apparently intending to push Cassidy to one side and seize Miss O'Shaughnessy. It was a risky thing to do, as Cassidy was so close to him, he could, if armed, have shot the man dead on the spot; but whether it was bravery, or, as is more probable, only his inordinate conceit, he seemed to have no fear of personal harm. Before Jonathan Barney could touch Miss O'Shaughnessy, Cassidy sprang back, and the Americans, mistaking the action for cowardice, laughed derisively. The next moment they were undeceived, however, as Cassidy, putting his arm round Miss O'Shaughnessy's waist, half carried, half dragged her into the middle of the road, and placing his revolver to her head, exclaimed, "Dead, yes! alive, *never!* Take another step, and I fire!" Jonathan Barney's face was not a pleasant one to look upon as he stood still at the order, and even Cassidy, with all his experience of Australia, thought he had never seen anything so diabolical. It seemed to be an understood thing amongst the other four that the two should be left to fight the matter out; and so long as O'Shaughnessy did not interfere, they would not do so either. Cassidy, whose eye was never for one moment taken off the huge ruffian, observing him now plunge his hand into his pocket, instantly exclaimed, " Move hand or foot, she dies !"

For the first time almost since he could remember, Barney found himself checkmated, and that, too, in the presence of four of his most intense admirers, whom he had taught to believe him a sort of deity, who could, by sheer force of will, accomplish almost any task, no matter how difficult. This time, however, Barney's arrogance and vanity were at a discount, and he was forced to temporize, for he saw that in Cassidy's face which told him plainly that what he said he would surely carry out; and though Barney did not care one pin whether the young lady was shot or not *ultimately*, still, at the present moment this did not suit him, as he required her for another purpose.

" Now look ye here, stranger," he began, in the long American drawl, " as I take it, you're neither this young ooman's husband or brother."

" How do you know that ?" interrupted

Cassidy curtly, anxious to take down the man's conceit, and also to gain time, hoping something might happen.

For a moment the ruffian again looked disconcerted ; but recovering himself, continued, but in a much milder key,—

" I guess, stranger, you don't understand our lingo.   The young ooman is not, I reckin, your wife nor your sister, and therefore it is altogether onreasonable for you  to have the imperence to take on yourself to decide for her whether she would not much prefer to pass a couple of hours in the company of Jonathan Barney to being shot like a dog in the streets.   Let her speak for herself, and say if she don't prefer a good, honest cove like Jonathan  Barney, to a roll in the  mud  with a  piece of  cold  lead in  her brain."

Before Miss O'Shaughnessy, who may be said to have been rather lying supported by Cassidy's arm than standing on her own feet, could reply, a voice was heard calling,—

" Barney ! Barney ! come here ; " and at the entrance of the station close by, on the top of the steps, stood  a gentleman whom Mr. O'Shaughnessy at once recognised as Mr. Finerty.

Barney turned at once, but with a very bad grace, to obey the summons; the other Americans followed, and so also did Mr. O'Shaughnessy, his two sisters, and Cassidy, who remarked in a low voice to O'Shaughnessy,—

" While there is life, there is hope. We have a reprieve, at any rate."

As Cassidy ascended the steps, Barney was saying in a sulky voice,—

" By all the laws of the Brotherhood, the lass is mine if I choose to claim her. Is she not, mates ? "

" Damn your Brotherhood!" replied Mr. Finerty, who was leaning his long figure against the door-post, both hands in his pockets, as usual, and a huge cigar in his mouth. " When I agreed to bring you with us, Master Jonathan, I did so on certain conditions, which I'll take very good care are strictly adhered to ; so don't let me hear any more about Brotherhoods, nor do you attempt to give me any of your cheek, for I'll not stand it, I guess, either from you or any one else. Enough!" he concluded, holding up his hand, as he saw Barney about to reply ; and he spoke with that air of deter-

mination and authority which, as it were, compelled obedience.

As O'Shaughnessy mounted the steps, Mr.
Finerty looked at him hard. "I've seen you
somewhere before," he muttered, half to himself.
"I wonder where?   I know," he said, answering
himself; "you are a member of Congress, or
Parliament as you call it, and sat just in front
of me last night, when I was there.   And who
are these?   Your wife the young 'un, eh?"

"No," said O'Shaughnessy—"mother and
sister."

"And where are you going?" Mr. Finerty
continued; "ladies are better at home than in
the streets to-day."

"To visit another sister, who is dangerously
ill at Blackrock," answered Cassidy.

"And who the hell are you, that have the
impudence to answer questions that are not addressed to you?" inquired Mr. Finerty, turning
sharp on Cassidy; "engaged to the young lady,
perhaps, and would sooner see her lying dead
on the road than take her second-hand after
my friend Barney had had the first of her; and
upon my soul I am not sure but what you
are about right."

Cassidy shook his head, as he replied,—

"I am the doctor attending the sister at Blackrock, and came to fetch her relatives to see her before she dies—which will probably be the case before morning. I am a married man."

"Irish or English?" asked Mr. Finerty, whose quick ear detected a difference in the accent.

"Neither," was the reply; "I am Australian."

Mr. Finerty gave a low whistle, as he next asked,—

"Long since you left?"

"A few weeks only."

"What part—Melbourne?"

"Yes," assented Cassidy; "that is my home."

"What part of the city? What street?"

Cassidy told him exactly where he lived.

"The corner house, did you say? That is the office of the large firm of Butterworth & Co. No one lives there."

"I am a partner in that firm."

"Just now you told me you were a doctor," said Mr. Finerty. "You can hardly be both."

"Why not?" asked Cassidy coolly; "brought

up as a surgeon, could get nothing to do at home, so emigrated to Australia—was lucky enough to do a good turn to one of the firm, who offered to take me into the office. I was, of course, only too glad to accept, and in time became a partner."

"What brought you home?"

"To get married. I was engaged before I went out."

"And your wife—where is she?"

"In the North, staying with a friend."

"A very pretty story if true. Can you prove it?—that you are a member of the firm, I mean."

Cassidy put his hand into his pocket and took out several letters. He selected one, which he opened and showed to Mr. Finerty; it had the printed heading of the firm at the top, and was marked—"Private and confidential."

"Turn it over," said Mr. Finerty; and as he read the address, "John Cassidy, Esq.," he paused to consider, and then said, "I have certainly heard the name somewhere. I suppose it must have been in Melbourne."

At this moment the shrill whistle of an engine sounded.

"There is a train starting, if you would like to take advantage of it, as far as Blackrock. Come," continued Mr. Finerty, politely.

"Governor," cried Barney, as they were moving away inside the station, "the lass is mine, and you daren't deny it, and what is more, I intend to have her, unless——"

He stopped short, for there passed a look over Mr. Finerty's face at the insolent remark that literally appalled even *him*.

"You—intend—to—have—her, do you?" He repeated each word slowly, as if to make sure he had heard aright. "You are a brave man, Jonathan, and the first, I reckon, that ever made use of such words to me, and lived to boast of it. You said 'unless.' I am curious to know what more you have to say. Go on—unless what?"

"Unless you choose to pay me for her," continued Barney, though by no means in a very confident tone, but rather as if feeling how far he dare go.

Mr. Finerty burst into a loud laugh, as, withdrawing his hands, he, in so doing, turned his trousers pockets inside out, and showed them to be perfectly empty.

Cassidy, however, who had heard the remark, now took a bundle of notes from his pocket, which he proffered to the ruffian, who shook his head, saying,—

" None of your darned paper for me. 'Tain't no sort of good in Ameriky, I reckon, and shan't spend none here. Gold, good honest gold, is what I want, and nothing else."

Cassidy felt in his pocket and produced two sovereigns, which he handed to Barney, saying,—

" It is all I have ; no one carries gold here."

The ruffian's eyes sparkled at the sight as he took possession of them, and then dropping his bullying Yankee tone, he assumed the wheedling manner and brogue of the low Irishman, as, taking off his hat, and holding it in his hand, he said,—

" Is it two sovereigns, your honour, and for a fine, upstanding young woman like that ! Why, it is not half what your honour would pay for a young sow ! "

What more he said was drowned in the shout of laughter which greeted his admirable mimicry of an Irishman's manner and brogue ; and as the engine now again whistled, Mr. Finerty and Cassidy hurried away, the former calling out,—

"Come to Jury's Hotel at six, Barney. I want you."

# CHAPTER XXX.

### "WHERE IS PETER ?"

IT did not take many minutes to reach Black-rock, but during the journey Mr. Finerty never addressed either O'Shaughnessy or the ladies, but talked incessantly to Cassidy about Melbourne, asking innumerable questions about people and places, many of which Cassidy was totally unable to answer. As the train slowed at Blackrock station, Cassidy held out his hand, saying, "We shall, I trust, meet again—if not here, then in Melbourne, as, should you return there, be sure you find me out, and give me an opportunity of proving my gratitude for what you have done for us to-day." Mr. Finerty laughed as he took Cassidy's offered hand, and, the train having by this time come to a stand-still, the four descended, and were moving along the platform, when they were again joined by Mr. Finerty, who remarked that he might as

well come with them, as the walk on to Kingstown would do him good.

There was, of course, nothing to be said, so
the two ladies walked behind with their brother;
Cassidy, who alone knew the way, going in
front with Mr. Finerty. The distance was so
short that in less than five minutes they arrived
at the gate leading into the drive up to the hall
door, when it struck Cassidy for the first time
that he had not warned Lucy to be sure and
keep Rose out of sight.

For the second time Cassidy shook hands
with Mr. Finerty, and, pointing out the way to
Kingstown, showed as plainly as he dared that
he, Mr. Finerty, was not wanted at the house;
but, of course, this only made that gentleman
the more determined to remain, and so the
five arrived at the hall door of Lucy's abode.
Cassidy rang the bell. They were evidently
expected, as the door was opened instantly,
and there, standing in the hall, was the one
person whom Cassidy dreaded to see—namely,
little Rosy. She made a step forward to
welcome, as she expected, two young ladies,
but being instead now called on to receive two
old ones, she paused, uncertain what to do, and,

as Cassidy advanced to introduce the new-
comers, he thought that in his life he had never
seen such a bewitching little darling as Rose
now looked.   Opening the drawing-room door,
he signed to Rose to enter, which she did,
followed by Mr. O'Shaughnessy and his two
sisters, Cassidy rejoining Mr. Finerty.    A
single glance told Cassidy the effect produced
by the sight of Rosy on the American, and
inwardly he cursed his own folly bitterly for not
having warned Lucy.   It was too late, however, now ; the harm, if any, was already done.

"Who was that pretty little girl ?" asked
Mr. Finerty casually, as Cassidy and he walked
back to the high road.   "Hardly a relation, as
they seemed strangers."

"A young orphan girl whom Mrs. O'Connor
has just engaged as a sort of companion, and
who, now she is ill, is, of course, most useful to
her."

No more was said, and they parted at the
gate, Cassidy returning to the house, and Mr.
Finerty starting to walk to Kingstown.   Why
the latter stood looking back after hearing the
hall door close, and why he seemed to be taking
his bearings (as sailors say), as if anxious to be

able to find the house again, might not be too difficult to guess, more especially if any one had heard the remark which he made to himself as he resumed his walk : " What a rare little filly ! A job for Barney ; but if he dare to lay a finger on her, I'll——" He clenched his teeth, and shook his fist in the air—an action which demonstrated his meaning far better than any words.

Cassidy, in the meantime, had found the house in the greatest confusion, for the younger Miss O'Shaughnessy, who had with the utmost difficulty been able to bear up in the train, now that she found herself in comparative security, gave up altogether, and fainted away, and it was some little time before she could be brought to herself. She then felt so unwell that she implored Cassidy to let her go to bed, but which that gentleman, though permitting her for a time to lie down, would on no account allow, as they must, he said, all be ready to be off at a moment's notice the instant the steamer appeared, and he was then going to see if she had been sighted.

As he (Cassidy), however, had eaten nothing since morning, he was easily persuaded by Rose to wait for dinner, which was just ready, and consequently it was past seven before he started. There were only the four at table—Miss O'Shaughnessy and her brother, Rose and Cassidy; nor could the latter fail to be struck with the barrister's most marked attentions to Rose, which that young lady accepted with evident pleasure, but it struck Cassidy more because not accustomed to such homage, than with any idea of their meaning. That it was love at first sight with Mr. O'Shaughnessy was true; but that Rose would ever return his affection, time alone would tell.

It was eight o'clock when Cassidy arrived at the end of Kingstown jetty, and looked seaward along the land to the North. There was not a vessel in sight, either sailing or steam; but Cassidy fancied he could detect something like black smoke coming out from under Howth. The sun was setting to the left far away over Dublin, and it was sinking into a nasty, angry-looking bank of clouds, which by no means prognosticated fine weather.

"We shall have a rough night, your honour," said a voice at Cassidy's elbow, as an old weather-beaten fisherman, coming up from the

rocks below with his long rod in his hand,
scanned the heavens knowingly.

" Why do you think so ? " asked Cassidy.

" The sun has set in a heavy bank, and all
along the sea to the northwards and eastwards
the scud is rising fast. It is bound to blow
hard before morning."

"Which way do you think ? "

" North-east—sartain to be."

" Damnation ! " cried Cassidy, between his
teeth. " Do you see anything under Howth ? "
he asked.

The old boy shaded his eyes with his hand,
and stood a moment watching. " There is a
steamer in there under the land," he said ; " but
I can't make her out, she's keeping so close
in."

No more was said, and the old fellow, wishing Cassidy good-night, toddled homewards.

Cassidy seated himself to watch. It was getting very dark, but in less than fifteen minutes
he could see the mast-head and also the red
and green lights of a steamer coming straight
towards him. She seemed to be flying through
the water; and as her hull shortly loomed out,
Cassidy had little doubt it was the *Witch.*

He had a long way to go in order to **reach** the spot where only a few nights before **the** same steamer had embarked the Irish Prime Minister, and, as there was not a moment to lose, Cassidy started at once, half running, half walking, along the pier.   In a few minutes he could distinctly hear the thumping of the steamer's engines, and before he was at **the** head of the harbour, the *Witch* was already fast to the buoy, and warping into the quay.

Running at his utmost speed, Cassidy **was** the first on board as the vessel came alongside, and, as he set foot on the deck, he found his arm seized, and, turning, recognised, even in the intense darkness, Terence O'Grady.

"You here!" he exclaimed, as their hands met.   "Oh! how glad I am to see you, but how very, very foolish."

"Come below," said O'Grady, as he descended the stairs.   Cassidy followed.   They entered the saloon, in which burnt a miserable oil lamp, and seated themselves at the table.

"What is the report I hear?" asked O'Grady, as soon as the door was closed.

"About the Americans, I suppose," interrupted Cassidy.   "They have asked for five

millions of money, and as they have not been
paid, are sacking Dublin, murdering the men,
violating the women."

"This is true, you are sure ?" O'Grady
asked. "We heard some reports which were
too awful to be probable, and so I doubted the
truth of the story altogether."

"No report, however horrible, can come near
the truth. The wildest imagination can picture
nothing so fearful as the scenes that are being
enacted in that unfortunate city at this moment,"
Cassidy replied.

A groan came out of the obscurity at the end
of the saloon.

"What is that?" asked Cassidy ; but before
O'Grady could reply, a gentleman rose to his
feet and came towards the table, and Cassidy
recognised the Prime Minister. He had been,
as usual, dreadfully sea-sick, and looked very
pale and ill. It was with difficulty he could
walk.

"You will allow me to go ashore at once and
see what can be done," he said, addressing
O'Grady.

"Of course," replied that gentleman, "if
you think you can do any good ; but I fail

myself to see how you can, and think you had much better stay here."

"I might be able to raise the money," he said, as he made his way towards the door, which he opened in order to ascend the stairs. Cassidy and O'Grady shrugged their shoulders, and could hardly repress a smile.

"We cannot lie here, sir," the skipper of the steamer called down. "It promises to blow hard, and the sea is coming right in. We had better haul out to the buoy at once."

"Wait till we are on shore," said Cassidy, springing from his seat and going at once on deck, followed by O'Grady.

"Where is Peter?" asked O'Grady of Cassidy, as he came on deck.

"I have not seen him since last night," began Cassidy, when a voice out of the darkness cried, "Here, sir," and the little old man came bustling up.

"Now, gentlemen," cried the skipper, "it is time we were moving." Both Cassidy and O'Grady examined the heavens, and were forced to confess the weather looked as dirty as it well could.

"Have you any men with you?" asked Cas-

sidy of O'Grady; "the decks seem crowded.
Who are all these people?"

"Twenty-five," replied O'Grady. "They
insisted on my having an escort. This skipper
and his men are not to be trusted."

"What luck, to be sure!" exclaimed Cassidy.
"Let us land a dozen, and be off at once to
fetch the ladies. We can leave Peter in charge
of the steamer."

"Ladies!" exclaimed O'Grady in astonishment; "what are you talking about?"

"The two Miss O'Shaughnessys, Lucy
O'Connor, and a friend who is staying with
her, all of whom I have promised to take with
us; so the sooner they are on board, the better."

"But if the steamer hauls out to the buoy,
how will they get on board, your honour?" said
Peter, who had heard Cassidy's remark.
"Make him haul in on the other side of the
harbour," whispered Peter to Cassidy.

"We shall leave you in charge while we are
away, when you can do as you like," replied
Cassidy.

Peter turned to one of his own people, and
whispered something to him, when the man
sprang ashore and disappeared. Cassidy,

O'Grady, and twelve of the men who had come in the steamer having by this time also landed, marched off towards Blackrock, and the skipper immediately gave orders to cast off the hawsers from the shore, and haul the steamer out.

Peter, however, who had been warned by some of his own people that there was some devilment on foot, though they could not make out exactly what, now interfered, and at once declared that, having been left in charge, he would allow nothing of the sort; and though the skipper stormed and swore lustily, yet he could do nothing, as he had only six men on board, and Peter and his party were double that number. In a few minutes the man whom Peter had sent on shore returned with a pilot, who at once declared it was madness to have come in at all without dropping an anchor; and who, having hauled out sufficiently to do this, then slacked out enough cable to enable the vessel to lie near the shore, but not close enough to touch the quay.

# CHAPTER XXXI.

### " ALL RIGHT, GOVERNOR ! "

AT ten o'clock that same night a carriage was standing in front of Jury's Hotel in College Green. As the clock struck, Mr. Finerty and Jonathan Barney left the hotel and seated themselves inside, while two other Yankees mounting to the box, they started immediately, taking the road towards Kingstown; but on arriving at Blackrock, the carriage stopped within a few yards of the gate leading to Miss Lucy O'Connor's house, and Barney and the two others alighted, when Mr. Finerty, who remained seated in the carriage, said,—

" Bring the little 'un here, Barney, and do what you like with the rest. I reckon you know *me* pretty well by this time, Barney; so let's have none of your tricks."

" All right, governor," was the reply.

With bare feet and quietly as mice the three approached the house. They tried the hall

443

door : it was not even locked, no one having been near it since Cassidy left. There was a lamp burning in the drawing-room; but though they listened intently, they could hear nothing. Very cautiously one of the men peeped in. O'Shaughnessy and his sister were alone—the former in an armchair, the latter on a sofa, both fast asleep. They closed the door and locked it, and Barney ascended the stairs. There were two doors—one to the right, which, as he heard voices inside, he approached, and putting his eye to the keyhole, saw a lady as he supposed preparing for bed, and the " little 'un," as he called her to himself, assisting her. Approaching now the other door, he again tried the keyhole; but not being able to see anything, turned the handle noiselessly, pushed open the door, and entered. At first he thought the room was empty, but as there was a candle left burning on the table, this seemed hardly likely. Advancing a couple of steps, so as to see the bed which was on the far side of the room, he then observed a lady lying half dressed, and the next moment he recognised her as being the same whom he had vowed that very afternoon should be his.

But what a change had come over her! Her disguise was all gone now, and though pale and ill, still Barney thought he had never seen a more lovely creature, as, with one beautiful arm encircling her head, her neck and bosom bare and of an almost dazzling whiteness, she lay fast asleep, quite unconscious of the villain's presence.

How long he stood there, lost to all external sounds, he knew not, feasting his eyes on the poor girl whose whole future life he was about to blast for his own sensual gratification; and when he remembered how he had told Cassidy that very day that the young woman should be his, though heaven combined with hell to stop it, he rubbed his hands softly together, and his eyes sparkled in a manner that made his face positively revolting to behold. Altogether forgetful of Mr. Finerty and his orders, he approached the bed very gently, and lowering his head, pressed his lips on hers, smothering her almost with his brutal kisses. Thus suddenly aroused from sleep in a strange place, and only half recovered from her swoon, she for a moment thought it was some dreadful nightmare which had come over her; but as she found herself encircled with a man's strong arms, who was thus holding her down in bed while he still continued to shower kisses over her whole face and neck, she struggled violently to get free, and before he could stop her gave one long, ringing shriek.

"It is useless," he cried; "there is no one to hear you.   You are mine, my darling, my *very own*," and again his lips were pressed to hers. She turned her head on the pillow quickly away from him, and made at the same time a frantic effort to get up; but she was a mere baby in his powerful grasp, and she sank back exhausted, while tears rolled down her cheeks.

"Useless, I tell you," the ruffian exclaimed; "what Jonathan once says he will do is sure to come to pass, as I said to-day, though heaven combine with hell to stop it."

"Help! help! Oh, save me, save me!" cried the unhappy girl, as she fancied she saw the door which had been left ajar pushed open; "death itself were ten thousand times preferable to this."   Barney laughed, but the next instant he found himself seized by the hair of his head and hurled to the floor, where he was at once secured, a sack passed over his head and made fast round his waist, thus tying his arms to his sides.

"It appears I was only just in time," said Cassidy coolly. "Come, Miss O'Shaughnessy, we have not a moment to lose. We will move this brute downstairs, and wait for you there. Get up," he continued, giving Barney a kick, but the big beast never stirred. One of the men who had bound him, stooping, quickly however produced more effect, and Jonathan Barney was soon downstairs, where Mr. O'Shaughnessy and his other sister, Lucy, Rose, and Terence O'Grady, were all assembled.

"Come," said O'Grady, who seemed very fidgetty, "we are all here now; let us be off."

"No!" said Cassidy; "there is another lady. She will be down directly."

"Let some one go and hurry her," said O'Grady, "or we must leave her behind. That man we allowed to escape, let alone the carriage which went off at a gallop, will bring some of these Yankee devils about our ears, and before long too."

The elder Miss O'Shaughnessy ascended the stairs, returning a moment after with her sister, when the whole party started, twenty-two in all, for Lucy asked leave to bring her servant, who had been with her some years, and could hardly be left behind.

The weather about this time was about as bad as it could possibly be, the wind coming in gusts so strong that at times both Lucy and Rose thought they would be blown off their feet, and clung to Mr. O'Grady, one on each side, for protection. It was so dark that it was impossible to see a yard ahead; and when the showers of hail beat in their faces, they were nearly blinded. They had accomplished about half the distance, when the whole party suddenly came to a halt; even above the roar of the storm there was a concussion of the air, and at the same time a trembling of the ground under their feet, which caused them all not only to stand still, but, brave men though most of them were, to hold their breath for a moment. On such a night and in such intense darkness, what, they asked themselves, could have happened?

"Come on! come on!" rang out the loud voice of John Cassidy, as, half dragging Miss O'Shaughnessy, he pushed forward in the direction of Kingstown. "Anything, even being swallowed up by an earthquake, would be preferable to falling into the clutches of those damned Yankees," he continued, half to his companion, half in a soliloquy to himself, "and we have no time to lose; they will be here soon enough. We ought to be on board even now." In another quarter of an hour they were all assembled on the quay, and the work of embarkation commenced. Jonathan Barney and his companions were sent first, and had a very narrow escape of falling between the steamer and the quay into the sea; the ladies one at a time went next, and then the men, Cassidy and O'Grady being the last. It was nearly half an hour before they were all safely on board, and then came the question as to what was to be done: to remain where they were would be madness, as they would to a certainty fall into the hands of the Yankees, who would soon arrive in force, if only to rescue their comrades.

But both the skipper and Peter's friend the pilot looked very glum at the idea of going to sea in such a notoriously bad sea-boat, to meet the whole force of the gale, and with such a heavy sea right in their teeth. Still, Mr. O'Grady proposed to start.

"A thousand times better to be drowned than be taken prisoners by the Yankees. We men can only die once; but for the ladies, there are worse evils than death, so let us risk it," he said.

Hardly had the words passed his lips ere a terrific squall struck the little vessel, throwing her nearly on her beam ends. It only lasted a moment, and then there was a lull, when a second time the squall struck her. Another lull and then a third squall, the fiercest of the three, seemed as if it would tear her in pieces. A minute more and the gale recommenced in all its fury; but the wind had changed to the West, and was coming off the land. Accustomed, of course, to the harbour, the pilot had slacked off the haw- . sers fast to the shore and also his cable, letting the vessel lie almost entirely to the long hawser fast to the buoy in the centre of the harbour. At the same time the screw was kept going to ease the strain. Just as the pilot expected, a huge sea driven by the squalls came roaring into the harbour, and had the vessel met it, held and pressed down by her own anchor and cable, she would probably have gone down where she lay, as, even with all the precautions taken, the water came over her bows in tons, and for a moment it seemed doubtful if she had buoyancy enough to throw it off. All, however, went well. Very soon the heavy sea was beaten down by the contrary wind, and an hour later the little *Witch* was flying away towards Howth, and following the coast kept close to the shore, where the water was as smooth as a millpond. She averaged over sixteen knots the whole way to Belfast, where she arrived at seven the next morning.

During their walk from Blackrock to Kingstown, Mr. O'Grady had, as already stated, Lucy on one side and Rose on the other, and when they all seemed for a moment paralyzed by the shock, the two ladies both clung to him in their extreme terror; and Cassidy, who had watched curiously the effect that Rose would have on O'Grady, wondering whether he, like every one else, would feel the charm of her presence, at first thought that such was the case. When, however, he observed that Rose, who did not suffer the least from sea-sickness, though it was the first time she had been to sea, was on deck nearly the whole night, and that Mr. O'Grady, moody and silent, never once approached her, he altered his mind, and believed that Terence O'Grady had not yet met his fate. A short time before they arrived, however, Cassidy, who happened to be standing close to O'Grady, heard him say, apparently to himself, as if his mind was made up,—" There seems to be no help for it, so I suppose it must be done ;" he then seated himself beside Rose, and for half an hour chatted and laughed with her most agreeably.

As they arrived at Belfast, Mr. O'Grady left his seat, and shaking hands with Rose, said, " I will try and see you again this afternoon ; but I have a very busy day before me. Peter will take you to an hotel. Cassidy, come with me." The two sprang ashore, and hurried away in order to get some breakfast before attending a meeting of the Masters of the Orange lodges at ten that morning.

# CHAPTER XXXII.

## "POOR, DEAR, DIRTY DUBLIN."

BEFORE proceeding to narrate further the incidents of that day, it will be necessary to pause for a moment to describe the events which had been passing in Dublin since Cassidy and his party had left it on the previous afternoon.

The Americans, anxious to find some place which they could occupy and make a sort of head-quarters, had taken possession of the Royal Barracks, in which about a thousand at once located themselves, the other five hundred being scattered about the city—some at the railway-stations, some in the public buildings, and a few in private dwellings.

The Irish inhabitants, who had been so thoroughly surprised on the previous night as to be totally unable to organize any resistance, had, during the following day, recovered from their panic, and congregated in large numbers

453

in the neighbourhood of the Royal Barracks,
determined to oppose, by every means in their
power, the entry of the Yankees into the city,
and, if possible, shut them up in the barracks.
As has been invariably the case, the Irishmen
were not true to themselves, and traitors were
not wanting who at once informed the Yankees
of the plot which was being organized against
them. Though thoroughly despising their op-
ponents, still they at once took steps to render
abortive any attempt to shut them into barracks,
as such a proceeding would not at all suit their
purpose.

Thus matters remained till near ten o'clock
at night, when a body of about one hundred
and fifty Americans attempted to force a passage along the quay. As soon as they made
their appearance, they were furiously attacked
by the Irishmen, who seemed literally to swarm
out of the houses and by-streets in the neighbourhood. Thus a regular fight began, the
Americans, who were quickly reinforced, and
who fought as if they were devils, not men,
gradually gaining ground till they arrived at
Barrack Bridge, where, large numbers pouring
from the other side of the river to the assist-

ance of the Irish, the advance of the Yankees
was checked, and slowly at first, but soon much
more rapidly, they began to fall back. Cheering lustily, and urged on by the women, many
of whom fought side by side with, and quite as
gallantly as, the men, the Irish pressed on, till
in a few minutes the Yankees turned, and taking to their heels, ran as fast as ever they could
towards the barracks, the gate of which was
instantly closed. Hardly had this been done
ere a terrific explosion occurred, the sortie
in reality having been only undertaken to
enable the Americans to place their dynamite,
and then retreat as quickly as possible to save
themselves. The slaughter was simply awful,
the unhappy Irish, both men, women, and children, who were assembled in thousands, being
blown in every direction.

Half an hour later, when the barrack gate
was again opened and the Americans made
their way to the river, they were themselves
literally astounded at the havoc which had been
wrought. A large portion of the wall which
shut the Liffey into its channel had been blown
away, while the enormous mass of ruins from
the fallen houses blocked the quay, and forced

the Yankees to ascend the river as far as King's Bridge before they could cross and make their way into the city. The events of that night can be better imagined than described. One thousand of the greatest blackguards and cut-throats to be found in the whole world, exasperated by the attempt to interfere with their "amusements," flushed with the success of the trap they had laid, were not likely to be very particular as to how they spent the night, the consequences being that when daylight appeared next morning, the city presented such a sight as no pen could adequately describe. There was not a single street in which old men and young, as well as old women, by hundreds did not lie murdered in every imaginable attitude. Little children were toddling about crying piteously in search of some one to own and befriend them; while the shrieks, cries, and piteous moans of the younger women were so dreadful to hear, that if the whole civilized world had before cried shame, shame at the blackguard immorality of the Union, and by its pressure forced England to dissolve it, surely this latter state was ten thousand times worse than the first, and demanded much more imperiously that an end should be put to such hideous atrocities, which, though at present confined to the capital, would doubtless in a few days be extended to the whole country.

The clocks were striking ten in the city of Belfast when, on the morning after this fearful night, Terence O'Grady entered the room where were assembled the Masters of the Orange lodges to receive him; and having read them a telegram detailing some of the events of the previous night, he called on Cassidy to relate what he himself had witnessed, and then, in the dead silence which prevailed after Cassidy had concluded, O'Grady himself addressed them.

"Gentlemen," he began, in a voice that shook with emotion, "it has, I know, been decided long ago amongst us that we should content ourselves with acting on the defensive, and holding the North, leaving the capital and other parts of Ireland alone so long as the other side in no way interfered or molested us. This was my own proposition, and it was agreed to and accepted by you all. The Almighty has been graciously pleased to so far crown our efforts with success, that the whole North of Ireland is quiet and peaceful, and, though necessarily in such times as these held with an iron hand, still I have endeavoured to use the velvet glove as much as possible, and I do not conscientiously think that those whom for the time being we are forced to hold in subjection have any just cause of complaint as to the way in which it is done. Such being the case, gentlemen, I appeal to you as *men*, altogether independent of the position you hold—married men most of you, with happy homes, wives, and children,—and I put it to you, one and all, what would your feelings be if you heard there was a chance of those homes being ruthlessly destroyed, yourselves murdered, your wives and daughters violated perhaps before your very eyes? and I ask you, would you not look round on all sides for help to put an end to such barbarity, and would you not be the first to cry shame on any one, whether friend or foe, who having the power to stop such a state of things, would not put out so much as a little finger to do so? I know we have many and great grievances to complain of at the hands of the so-called Government of the day. I am quite aware they have done their utmost to ruin us and drive us out of this country ; but, gentlemen, if we are strong, and have hitherto been able to laugh at their futile efforts to harm us, let us show that we are also generous, that in their hour of sore need and necessity we can forget and forgive, and have not lost a moment in hurrying to their assistance to free the capital (for, after all, it is the capital of our own country) from the villainous horde of blackguards and cut-throats which are now let loose upon it. Gentlemen, I ask only your permission, and if you consider you owe me anything for my humble efforts in your behalf, I will ask it as a personal favour to myself, that you sanction the expenditure of the necessary funds to enable me to advance instantly with ten thousand men, take possession of Dublin, and hold it till these fiends incarnate are got rid of and some sort of stable government established."

As he ceased speaking, a short discussion ensued. A very large majority of those present were in favour of O'Grady's proposal, but three or four were entirely against it, declaring they could see no reason whatever for interference, nor for spending their money in aid of those who had always treated them with the greatest contumely. "As they have made their bed, so let them lie on it," they said. Those, however, who held these opinions were in a very small minority, and in a few minutes it was decided that Mr. O'Grady should be allowed full powers to advance and at once occupy the capital, should he think fit to do so. He paused yet another moment to state that there were three American prisoners whom he had brought with him in the *Witch* from Kingstown, and he would be glad to know what was to be done with them.

Surprised to hear that he had been himself at Kingstown, they condemned in the very strongest terms his rashness, and then decided that the Americans should be sent to prison, and there remain for the present.

That Mr. O'Grady and Cassidy, acting as his *aide-de-camp*, had a busy day of it goes without saying; yet, notwithstanding the amount of work which devolved on his shoulders, Terence O'Grady found time before leaving Belfast to pay a short visit to Rose and Lucy at their hotel, and, having informed them of his departure for Dublin, he had, at their earnest solicitation, promised to telegraph to them as soon as ever it was by any means possible for them to return home.

"We are perfectly miserable here," Rose declared, looking up at Mr. O'Grady so sadly, "and are counting the minutes to get back; and when *you* are gone, we shall not know a soul in the place. Whatever shall we do with ourselves? If you do not send soon, Mr. O'Grady, I will never forgive you." With another promise that not a moment should be lost in sending for them as soon as it was by any means possible, he tore himself away, Rose looking after him with such wistful eyes, that they seemed to haunt him for hours afterwards.

Before dark that afternoon, the same steamers as before, together with two extra ones for commissariat purposes, were chartered and ready for sea. During the whole night the work of embarking stores, ammunition, and arms was pushed on with the utmost despatch, so that before daylight the five thousand men were all on board, and the vessels fast disappearing as they steamed out of the lough.

The railway also was put into requisition, and train after train despatched with men and

stores, as fast as they could be got ready—
the Catholics, as soon as they knew that the
object of the expedition was to drive the
Yankees out of Dublin, vieing with the
Orangemen in pushing forward the work with
the utmost despatch. Thus it came about that
the following evening—that is, within thirty-six
hours of the time when it was decided that
the enterprise should be undertaken—Terence
O'Grady found himself established on the Hill
of Howth in command of ten thousand Orangemen, five thousand of whom had come by sea,
the others by land.

By this time also a regular system of trains
had been organized, so that every half-hour
more men, stores, arms, and ammunition
arrived regularly without any delay or hin-
drance, every van, the moment it was unloaded,
being attached to trains of " empties," and sent
off to the different stations where it was needed.
Mr. O'Grady had been in great hopes at first
that he would have been able to enter the city
before sunset that afternoon, but there had
been unexpected and unforeseen delays, and
though he did not anticipate any severe fighting, still he had reluctantly decided to wait for

morning, when, by starting from their present camping ground an hour before sunrise, they hoped to enter Dublin about eight o'clock.

Both he and Cassidy had had a hard day's work, and having been round to many of the encampments the last thing, to make sure that the orders for the following morning were clearly understood, were returning just before midnight to the house which Mr. O'Grady had made his headquarters, when the sound of horses' hoofs was heard coming quickly along the road, and in another minute Peter, who had been sent to report what was going on in Dublin, arrived with the astounding intelligence that the English had about sunset landed a force of nearly five thousand men; and so the city, which was being patrolled by the red-jackets, was now quiet and orderly, the Americans, who had altogether disappeared, being supposed to be sneaking off by twos and threes to their own steamers still lying in the river. Almost immediately after, it was reported to Mr. O'Grady that three or four large steam vessels were lying off Ireland's Eye, but what they were it was impossible in the darkness to make out.

To decide at that late hour what was to be done was out of the question, so, ordering Peter to take a short rest and then return as quickly as possible to Dublin, Mr. O'Grady was in the act of throwing himself, dressed as he was, on his bed, when he suddenly remembered his promise to Rose. Recalling Peter, who was as yet only a few yards off, he took a telegraph form and wrote, " Come as soon as you like," and having addressed it to Miss O'Connor, told the old man to see that it was sent at once, and five minutes after was fast asleep.

# CHAPTER XXXIII.

## " AY, AY, SIR ! "

THE sun was just rising the following morning, when Mr. O'Grady was aroused by Cassidy, who informed him that heavy guns were distinctly audible out at sea, and proposed that they should not lose a moment in ascending the hill, in order to ascertain by whom they were being fired. They had not far to go, before a view of the whole of Dublin Bay was obtained, and they could then see that the four steamers, flying the American flag, which had, at daylight, evidently dropped down the Liffey, had stood out to sea, believing the coast clear, not a vessel of any sort being in sight. The Yankees had, however, soon found out their mistake; for hardly had they emerged from the bay, before three English ironclads, which had been lying hidden behind Howth, opened fire. Thinking it better to avoid Cork, in which neighbourhood English cruisers were generally to be found, the Yankees had decided to stand to the North, and thus found themselves close to the ironclads before they had any idea of their presence. ·With such heavy guns and at such close range, two of the Yankees were very quickly disabled; but the other two, being much faster vessels, were enabled to make good their escape, and though much damaged, soon disappeared in the distance, followed by two of the ironclads, the third remaining in charge of the two disabled steamers, at which, as they had not yet hauled down their flags, she still continued to fire. Watching the Yankees with his field-glass, Mr. O'Grady could discern several small dark objects in the water near them, and at once guessed that the Americans were dropping quietly into the water, and attempting to swim ashore. He was in the act of sending orders down to the beach, ordering a party of his own men to be on the look-out, and secure at once any who might land, when Peter again came running up the hill to where Mr. O'Grady was standing, stating that the English troops were marching out of Dublin, and coming in the direction of Howth, that they had both cavalry and artillery, but the infantry were mostly the merest boys, two or three regiments being volunteers, none of whom, Peter declared, were able to contend for a moment with their own men. Mr. O'Grady said nothing, but at once returned to his house, which he had hardly reached before a young officer in staff uniform rode up, escorted by a few dragoons. As he commenced hammering at the door with the butt-end of his whip, Cassidy went out to see what he wanted.

Putting his glass into his eye, he surveyed Cassidy from head to foot, as he said in the most contemptuous manner,—

"You are, I presume, the individual who call yourself the commander of the rabble I see scattered over the hill; if so ——" But Cassidy at once interrupted him, saying curtly,—

"You have been misinformed; I am *not* that person."

"Send for him, then, at once," exclaimed the officer imperiously; "I bring him a message from the commander-in-chief."

Cassidy was at first inclined to be angry, and resent such cool impudence; but when he observed the youth of the officer, he changed his mind and burst out laughing, which made the officer so angry, that, losing his temper, he exclaimed,—

"What the devil are you laughing at, you giggling baboon! Will you do what I told you, or by God I'll soon make you!" and touching his horse with the spur, he brought the animal close up to where Cassidy stood.

Still laughing, Cassidy also advanced a step, and before the officer had the least idea of his intention, he seized his leg, and whipping the stirrup from under his foot by a dodge he had learnt in Australia, in a moment deposited the young man on the road at his feet. Even the escort could not resist laughing; but the officer sprang up in a fury, and in another moment would have struck Cassidy with his riding-whip, when he was arrested by the sudden appearance of Mr. O'Grady, who, in the quietest and most cool manner, said,—

"You bring me a message from the officer commanding Her Majesty's troops;" and Mr. O'Grady, who had come to the door of the house, lifted his hat as he pronounced the Queen's name.

"I do," replied the officer, but in a much milder tone of voice and manner than before. "My orders are to inform you that he is now on his way here, and that on his arrival the men under your orders will at once deliver up their arms and ammunition, when they will be allowed to return peaceably to their own homes."

"And suppose we refuse?" said O'Grady, with a quiet smile.

"In such a contingency, which was considered to be so remote as hardly worthy of consideration, I was to tell you that you must be prepared to take the consequences."

The way the last words were pronounced, Cassidy declared afterwards to have been simply delicious : it reminded him of a bantam cock strutting up to a game-cock, and crowing under his very nose.

"Young man," replied Mr. O'Grady, "you can return to the officer who sent you, and inform him that on his arrival here I shall be prepared to give him an answer;" and so saying, both he and Cassidy entered the house and shut the door.

Feeling very small, and with the conceit taken considerably out of him, the officer remounted his horse and rode off.

Cassidy and O'Grady sat down to breakfast,

but there was little conversation ; both felt the situation was too grave.  Half an hour later they left the house, and took up a position on the side of the hill, whence they could watch the English troops ; nor could a more beautiful sight be imagined than the view which, on that lovely morning, met O'Grady's and Cassidy's gaze, enlivened as it was by the red-coats, as they appeared occasionally through the trees, the sun reflected from their accoutrements, while both the cavalry and artillery could be observed some distance in front, and very soon almost beneath where the pair stood.

Presently a group of mounted officers caught the quick eye of O'Grady, and the cocked hat and plumes of the one riding in front of the others told him what he had already guessed— that it was no other than the commander-in-chief of the little army, who was himself ascending the hill, and evidently going towards the house where his *aide-de-camp* had met O'Grady that morning.  As the Orange leader looked at that brilliant and gay *cortége*, and then at his own half-dozen grey frieze-coated men behind him, he could not resist a smile, the contrast was so great.

Despatching one of his men to intercept the general on his way to the house, Terence O'Grady waited, seated on a small cob pony, for the arrival of the great man. Not many minutes elapsed ere he appeared—a very fine, handsome officer, apparently about sixty years of age, and as good a specimen of an English general as could be found in the world. A thorough gentleman, as a rule most courteous and affable, he was, nevertheless, a great stickler for military etiquette, and the respect which he considered due to his position,—consequently, was by no means in the best of humours at O'Grady's not even having come a single yard to meet him; but after the manner in which the *aide-de-camp* had behaved that morning, O'Grady had quite determined to remain passive, as any advance he made would most probably be misunderstood, and only subject him to a snub.

Cassidy, who had fallen in rear of O'Grady, so that there might be no mistake as to who was the Orange leader, watched with much amusement the advance of the general,—and as that officer rode brusquely up on his splendid charger, Cassidy thought at first that neither would salute; but whether it was owing to innate high breeding, or to any effect O'Grady himself may have had, the commander-in-chief lifted his cocked hat, as he checked his horse when about five yards from where O'Grady had placed himself.

" Mr. O'Grady, I presume," he said.

O'Grady bowed.

" I sent you one of my *aides-de-camp* with a message this morning," the general continued, " who informed me that you declined to give an answer to any one but myself. Anxious to avoid any unpleasant consequences, though many would consider my action derogatory to the position I hold, I am here to receive your answer."

" On certain conditions I am willing to disband the men; but as to laying down our arms, I would ask by what authority you make such a demand ? "

" My instructions are to disarm the whole country, as the only way to restore law and order out of such chaos."

" And you begin with the only loyal people in all Ireland," said O'Grady. " I am sorry to be obliged to refuse, but *under no circumstances whatever* will I allow a single man to give up his arms."

"You know the alternative," exclaimed the general, who was fast working himself up into a passion.

" I care not what the consequences may be," replied O'Grady; "you have heard my irrevocable determination, and *nothing* can or will alter it."

Removing his cocked hat from his head, and with a low bow, the general turned his horse's head and rode off down the hill, followed by his staff.

Cassidy rejoined O'Grady, asking as he did so,—

"What will he do ?"

"We shall see; but I can hardly believe he will butcher us in cold blood."

As soon as the general and his staff reached the foot of the hill, O'Grady observed an officer leave his *cortége* and start at a gallop in the direction of the two batteries of artillery posted on the right. He rode straight as an arrow across country, and both Cassidy and O'Grady could observe how he took the few intervening fences, and finally arriving at his destination, conversed for a few minutes with the officer in command of the batteries, and then started to return to his chief.

With breathless excitement the two gentlemen then saw how one of the two batteries was ordered to advance till it reached some open ground close to the bottom of the hill, and terribly near the spot where between three and four thousand of the Orangemen were stationed. These latter had received no orders to " fall in," so were either sitting or standing about, or lying stretched on the ground in all sorts of positions, their arms piled in their rear. They were watching the artillery, and noted their advance, and how the guns were unlimbered and run into position. They could not imagine what it meant; but when they saw the men actually proceeding to load their guns, though still not believing they could really be going to fire, yet, by the advice of the old hands, they all stretched themselves flat on the ground.

All was now ready; the gunners, though clearly very unwillingly, had obeyed their orders to the letter, but the officer commanding, not supposing it possible that it was anything more than a pretence, gave no order to fire. A second time a mounted officer left the general and galloped up to the battery. " What are you waiting for ? " he cried, as soon as he was within speaking distance. " Why do you not fire ? " and when the Orangemen heard what was said, brave though they were, they shuddered.

The officer in command of the battery, whose name was Parsons, stared at the *aide-de-camp* in astonishment, and then, as the latter rode up, said to him in a low voice,—

"Surely you are not in earnest, Ridley ! you cannot mean me to fire at those poor wretches on the hillside ! Why, it would be simply murder—neither more nor less."

Instead of answering him, the *aide-de-camp* turned to the gunners. " Is all ready ? " he asked.

" Ay, ay, sir," answered a sergeant.

" Then fire," he cried ; but instead of obeying, the men stood as if turned into stone.

" Do you not hear me ? " he now asked. " It is the general's order that you should fire. Will you or will you not obey orders ? " Not a man moved, not a word was spoken.

Wheeling his horse round, the *aide-de-camp* was about to return to his chief, when he observed the general and his whole staff riding towards him.

"Major Parsons!" the chief said, as he approached, "what is the meaning of this behaviour? Will you or will you not obey orders?"

"I have not refused to obey orders, sir," was the reply. "I am in no way responsible for the men's declining to fire at the command of your *aide-de-camp*, though I will not attempt to deny that such conduct on their part meets with my full approval."

"Are you aware, sir," cried the general, "of the full purport of what you are saying? Do you know that such conduct on your part is mutinous, the punishment for which is death?"

"So be it," replied Major Parsons; "one can only die once, and I would sooner ten thousand times it should be now, than live with the knowledge that I have been guilty of an action which not only my own conscience but every officer in the whole service would condemn." He unbuckled his sword as he finished speaking, and handed it to one of the officers of the staff; while the gunners, without waiting for an order, proceeded to limber up their guns and retreat towards the other battery.

" What does this mean ? " asked the general, turning to his staff with a face on which astonishment was so plainly visible as to be almost absurd.

" It means," said the young officer who had been sent to O'Grady early that morning, "that the whole army is in a state of mutiny, and that an example must be made to bring both men and officers to their senses, or the service will go to the devil."

" Say, rather," remarked an old and grizzled warrior who was acting as chief of the staff, "that, like everything else, discipline is not what it used to be; the days of blind, unquestioning obedience of orders have disappeared. The British soldier is no longer a machine, but a man who thinks and reasons like other human beings, and who does not therefore now consider himself called upon to obey an order which is manifestly unjust."

" Which is only another way of asserting that you approve of the action of both men and officers which we have just witnessed," said the general.

There was no reply, so the general continued, "Speak up, Colvin; I always like a
man who has the courage of his opinions; besides, after what you have said already, you are
bound to say more."

Colonel Colvin was not a man to shrink from
speaking the truth; it had, in fact, been his misfortune during life to be too outspoken, and he
had thus made for himself many enemies and
marred his chances of promotion, for he was
an older officer than even the general, on whose
staff he was now serving.

" Had a single shot been fired," he now said,
very determinedly, " I, for one, should most
certainly have at once thrown up my appointment and returned to Dublin."

The general bit his lips to keep down his
temper, which was again fast rising, and forced
himself to reply with studied politeness,—

"Will Colonel Colvin have the kindness to
state the reasons which could ever induce him
to so far forget himself as to show such a lamentable example to both men and officers;
they must, I conclude, be very strong ones."

The sneer with which this was said set loose
the colonel's tongue at once.

" Had I remained here, even as an unwilling spectator," he replied haughtily, as if not caring what he said now, " I consider I should have made myself a party to an act of cold-blooded, deliberate murder, such as has few parallels in history."

" You forget, Colonel Colvin," said the general, by an almost superhuman effort still remaining calm, " that I have received orders to disarm these men; and if, on being sum- moned to give up their arms, they decline to do so, I have, it seems to me, no alternative but to make them."

If the general kept his temper admirably, it is more than can be said of Colonel Colvin, who now replied very excitedly,—

" Such a summons never ought to have been made. It is contrary to all usages of war. By what right do you presume to peremptorily demand an army of twenty thousand men, with another hundred thousand behind them, to lay down their arms at your command? *You* must have forgotten that they are not subjects of the Queen, that Ireland is now a free and independent country, and that the mere fact of taking possession of the capital to save it from being any longer sacked by barbarians can confer no sort of right to rule over a people whom you have not conquered. What have these men done that you should interfere with them in any way? Nothing! absolutely nothing! for they have far more right here than we have. They are at home in their own land, and on their way to the capital of their country; whereas we are in a foreign land, which, though once ours, we of our own free will gave up, and until some act of union is again signed, we have no right whatever to assume any act of authority over any one in the whole island. I have now stated my view of the situation. I may be wrong or I may be right; but one thing is certain, and that is, that holding these opinions, and having presumed to state them so openly, my position here is no longer tenable, and I therefore, with all due submission and most unfeigned sorrow, beg to tender my resignation of my appointment."

"Not so fast, Colvin!" said the general; "not so fast! Upon my soul I am not at all sure but what you are right, after all. This country is, as you say, no longer ours, and perhaps I was too hasty in so peremptorily ordering these

men to give up their arms, which, not having ill-
used them, they certainly had a right to keep in
their own country; and besides, suppose, instead
of passive resistance, they had assumed the
offensive and attacked us—twenty thousand
men you say, and we have little more than
three, and half of them volunteers—why, they
must have driven us into the sea, by God they
would!

"Here, give that fellow Parsons his sword,
and let him return to his duty. March the
men back to Dublin at once, while I see that
Flaherty, or whatever he calls himself, and
find out on what conditions he will take his
men home, for that they cannot stay here is
quite certain."

So saying, he put spurs to his horse, and
again ascended the hill accompanied by his
staff. Mr. O'Grady was still seated on his
pony in the same spot as before, but Rose and
Lucy O'Connor, who had left Belfast the moment they received the telegram, were now
standing one on each side of him.

They distinctly saw the general coming, but
Mr. O'Grady, who from his position had been
an eye-witness of all that had occurred below,

and correctly guessed what had happened, fully
expected the general would be quite unable to
command his temper, and looked forward with
by no means pleasurable anticipations to the interview.  He was agreeably surprised, therefore,
when the general, with a low bow, rode up at
once close to him, saying,—

"Mrs. O'Grady, I presume?"

"No," replied O'Grady, "my foster-sister
Miss O'Connor, and her friend."

The general bowed again, as each lady on
being named did the same, while his eyes
seemed loth to withdraw themselves from
Rose's charming face.

"Mr. O'Grady," he said presently, "I have
made it a rule during my life, when I have
discovered myself to be in error, to openly
confess such to be the case, and, if possible,
make any reparation in my power.  This morning I am quite willing to own that I was wrong
in demanding that your men should lay down
their arms, and I——"

"Say no more about it, general," interrupted
O'Grady, holding out his hand; "the least said,
the soonest mended."

"But what do you propose to do?" asked

the general, as he took the offered hand: "You cannot stay here; and with the city in the military occupation of our men, do you think it would be quite wise to advance? I mean, do you not think there would be a chance of a collision?"

"Not the slightest," replied O'Grady, "judging by what I see going on at present; and as to stopping my men entering Dublin, some of them are more than half-way there already."

Turning in his saddle, the general gazed in the direction indicated by O'Grady, and at once observed how the troops and Orangemen were fraternizing together, the latter, as regiment after regiment moved off, accompanying them on their march back to Dublin.

"Unless I misunderstood you, you stated this morning that on certain conditions you would march your men home," persisted the general. "Am I not correct?"

"Yes," said O'Grady—"quite right; and what I said, I will do."

"And the conditions?" asked the general; "they are——"

"The immediate reincorporation of the whole North of Ireland with England, to be again under the rule of Her Gracious Majesty the Queen," O'Grady said, uncovering his head as he pronounced her name ; "and when the act of union has been signed, permission for my men to return to their homes free and un-molested."

The general shook his head as he replied,—

" It is altogether out of my power to grant such terms. I know no more of the intentions of the English Government than you do. I was sent off at a moment's notice, with what troops could be got together, to save Dublin and its inhabitants from annihilation."

"I do not want an immediate answer," said O'Grady ; "you can either write or wire to London, stating the conditions I ask, and let me know the reply in a day or two. But on one point we Orangemen are quite decided ; and that is, if the English troops are to be withdrawn, and the whole of Ireland left again to govern herself, the Orange Lodges intend to hold Dublin till some firm and strong Government, capable of maintaining law and order, is established."

" And you remain here pending the decision of the Government ? " asked the general.

"Some of us will; but our service being voluntary, many will doubtless go home, holding themselves in readiness to return if wanted. I shall leave them to do pretty much as they like."

"And if any unhappy disturbance should occur between our men and yours, — what is to be done then?"

"There is, I assure you, not the least likelihood of anything of the sort; but if by chance any misunderstanding should arise, leave me to deal with it, and I will answer for the result."

There was no more to be said, so the general was forced to be satisfied, and, with a bow to the ladies, rode off on his way back to Dublin.

# CHAPTER XXXIV.

## "A VERY PRETTY STORY!"

LATER in the day, Mr. O'Grady followed in a carriage, with Lucy O'Connor and Rose. They drove straight to Blackrock, where Lucy found her house had not been touched, and, needless to say, was truly glad to be once more at home. Mr. O'Grady spent the evening with them, sleeping at his own house close by. That he was much smitten with Rose was only too evident; and if a brightening of the whole face as he appeared, a lowering of the eyes as he addressed her, and an only too marked expectancy when *he* was absent, had any signification, Rose also was a victim of the winged god.

Early the next morning Mr. O'Grady started for Dublin, where his first visit was to the Prime Minister. As might be supposed, he found that gentleman in by no means high spirits. He had been taught a lesson which it

was not likely he would forget, and had learnt
from bitter experience that to agitate in the
British House of Commons, to be cute enough
to take every advantage of party disputes, and
cleverly to turn them to the gaining of his
own ends, was one thing; but to be able to
organize and effectively carry out the government of such a country as Ireland was altogether another; and though he had put on his
coat in token of success in the former, his failure
in the latter had been most lamentable.   Nor
could he forget that he had been cognisant of the
intention of the Americans to come to Dublin,
and, if not actually aiding and abetting them in
so doing, had certainly made no objections; consequently, was it not a fact, he asked himself,
that he was thus, to a great extent, responsible
for all the iniquities that had been perpetrated ?
Such he himself, at any rate, felt to be the case,
and certainly did not spare himself when alluding to the subject in his conversation with Mr.
O'Grady.   It was not, however, in reference
to any public matters that Mr. O'Grady had
called, and so that gentleman very soon gave
him to understand, but with regard to his
*liaison* with Lucy O'Connor; and so well did

he argue the point, that when he got up to take leave, he had been given a solemn promise by the Prime Minister, that before that day month Lucy should be his wife.

That same afternoon, Mr. O'Grady intended to return to the Hill of Howth, where Lucy and Rose promised to pay him a visit, dine, and spend the night, as Mrs. Cassidy would, by that time, have arrived to do the honours. Before starting, Mr. O'Grady had a long interview with Peter, who, as he was leaving, said,—

"It had better be to-night; he is a shifty customer to deal with."

"Very well," was Mr. O'Grady's reply ; but it was only too evident that he acceded most unwillingly to Peter's proposal. "At what time am I to expect you?"

"Between nine and ten," Peter answered.

It was a lovely evening, and both Lucy and Rose enjoyed the drive out immensely, and looked forward to a most agreeable evening ; but Mr. O'Grady was not in force—he seemed sad and preoccupied, and the little party was, in consequence, a failure, even though Lucy was in great spirits, and Rose showed more and more that she was hopelessly in love. It was about ten o'clock that Mr. O'Grady, who for the last half-hour had been walking restlessly about the room in which they were sitting, stopped to listen, and Rose's quick ears caught the words, " Coming at last ! "

He went at once to the hall door, and, opening it, stood listening attentively. He could hear the distant rumbling of wheels, the loud cracking of whips, and the sound as if of many horses galloping. At the rapid pace at which the cavalcade was advancing, he had not long to wait ; in less than five minutes a large open break drew up in front of the house, and a number of grey-coated men, both from inside as well as from the box, quickly alighted, while the half-dozen horsemen who had accompanied it at once dismounted. They were now joined by other men, who seemed to spring out of the earth, so suddenly did they appear. As they all gathered round the carriage, a large, heavy body was lifted out of it, and carried by a dozen strong arms into the house. The whole party entered the dining-room, going to the far end of the room, where, by Peter's orders, the burden was deposited on the floor, between the end of the table and the wall.

As Mr. O'Grady, who had been joined by
Cassidy, followed them into the room, there
could not be less than twenty-five men present,
half of whom had drawn bayonets in their
hands.

Mr. O'Grady advanced to the end of the
table nearest the door, close beside which he
stood, resting his hand on it, Cassidy placing
himself on his right.   Mr. O'Grady made a
sign to Peter, and instantly half a dozen men
knelt down and busied themselves untying
divers strongly knotted cords.   Not a word
had been spoken, but as Peter stood by, a
quick ear might have caught the words, "wild
beast," muttered under his breath.

In a few minutes a sack was removed, and
then a man could be seen seated on the floor,
the expression of whose countenance was so
truly diabolical, that several of those nearest to
him instinctively stepped back, as he glared at
them with a ferocity impossible to describe.

"Get up," said Peter, advancing and touching
the man with his foot.

For a moment more he moved his head only,
which he slowly turned round and round; even
yet his eyes were hardly accustomed to the

bright light; then, as Peter was again about to repeat the injunction, he sprang to his feet, made a dash at one of the bayonets held by a man close beside him, which he attempted to wrest from the Orangeman's grasp, but finding this more difficult than he expected, he caught one of the man's hands in his teeth, and bit it cruelly to the bone. The ferocity and suddenness of the attack had taken every one by surprise, from which even Peter had not recovered, when Cassidy, rushing to the rescue, struck the brute, while his teeth were still fastened in the man's hand, with his closed fist on the side of the head, close to the eye. It was a fearful blow straight from the shoulder, and sent the wretch reeling against the wall at the end of the room.

"Quick, quick!" cried Cassidy, following up his advantage, "bear a hand some of you; where's the sack? We do not want any bloodshed here;" and in less time than it takes to tell, the sack had again been slipped over the inhuman wretch's head, while he himself had been lifted and seated on the table, his two legs tied together, to each of which, by the same rope, one of his arms was tightly fastened.

When he had been thus secured to Cassidy's satisfaction, the sack was again removed.

And thus, for the first and last time, those two met—No. 1, the redoubted head of the League, for he it was, and Mr. O'Grady, the Orange leader, the two who alone, during the several years that had elapsed since the repeal of the Union, had been able to exercise any real power in Ireland—the one for his country's good, the other in furtherance of his own base and selfish ends for what terrible woe.

"What is the meaning of this? Who has dared to bring me here, and for what purpose?" asked No. 1, defiantly.

"I have," replied Mr. O'Grady very quietly, but with a tone of sadness in his voice, at which Peter and the others with him marvelled.

"And who are you," asked No. 1, still more rudely, "who have the damned impertinence to seize a quiet and unoffending citizen, and carry him off against his will? I will appeal to the English general to-morrow morning against such treatment."

"My name is Terence O'Grady, and I command the twenty thousand Orangemen in whose midst you now are, and any one of whom would, even without my bidding, be only too ready to rid Ireland of the greatest curse that ever infested her."

" That an Orangeman should, on all and every occasion, be only too ready to commit an act of cool and deliberate murder, goes without saying ; but that a gentleman of so deservedly high a character and reputation as Mr. O'Grady should *permit* such an act to be committed, does indeed surprise me. I appeal to the commander-in-chief of the English troops for a fair and impartial trial by a jury of my own countrymen, and I feel certain I shall not appeal in vain."

" The English general has already decided that as Ireland is no longer a portion of the United Kingdom, he has no jurisdiction whatever, even in Dublin, except over his own soldiers. Nevertheless, you are right in saying that I would never allow an act of deliberate murder to be committed, nor will I. Anything you have to urge in your defence shall be carefully and impartially considered ; of that I give you my word of honour."

" Of what am I accused ? " inquired No. 1, still preserving a bold front.

"The charge brought against you, Mr.——
(but no, I will not be the one to bring a slur on
a good and honourable name by letting it be
known that one who bore it had been guilty of
every crime of which the world is cognisant),—
the charge, I say, of which I accuse you, is that
you were the organizer of the so-called National League ; and, as its present head, are not
only responsible, but in nearly every case the
instigator of the numberless murders and other
hideous atrocities committed by its members."

No. 1 smiled as he replied, "It is very easy
to make so vague an accusation, but to try and
hold me responsible for the deeds of the League
is as absurd as it is impossible.  Every man
must be considered innocent till he is proved
guilty, and I defy you or any one else to spe-
cify any 'murder or other atrocity,' as you call
it, and produce the slightest proof that I have
been guilty of it.  When you have done that, I
will gladly submit to whatever sentence may
be passed on me by a competent tribunal."

"What about that poor old woman, Mrs.
Kelly ?" asked O'Grady.

"Mrs. Kelly !" repeated No. 1, as if trying to
recollect who was the person referred to.  "Do

you mean the old woman who was attacked and defeated by the coastguardmen sent down by the Government for that purpose? Surely you are not going to pretend I am in any way responsible for that!"

"I refer," said Mr. O'Grady, "to the visit you paid her in the prison the night before she was to have been hung."

"I!" exclaimed No. 1 indignantly, and with such well-assumed innocence that it staggered nearly all his hearers. "I take the trouble to go and see an old hag who had been sentenced after a trial of her own countrymen to be hung! Who could have told you such a ridiculous story? Consider for one moment, Mr. O'Grady; is it likely that——"

"Enough! enough!" exclaimed O'Grady interrupting. "*That you did go to the prison on the evening before Mrs. Kelly was to have been hung is certain.* What your reasons may have been is no concern of mine."

"But I say that I did NOT go near the prison on that night," exclaimed No. 1 excitedly; "whoever informed you that I was there told a wicked and shameful lie, doubtless for the purpose of injuring me. I could, if the opportunity were only allowed me, prove how every hour of that evening was spent."

"Peter," said Mr. O'Grady, "state in as few words as possible what the warders told you. Was this person in the prison that night, or was he not?"

"Sure, and he was, your honour," replied Peter, "and visited the old woman in her cell too, where——"

"Enough!" said O'Grady; "you are quite certain as to what you are stating?"

"Would I be telling it to your honour if I was not? Sure, four of the warders told me the same story, and were all of them willing to swear to it, if necessary."

"And suppose I *was* at the prison on that evening," now said No. 1, "what then?"

"Sure, wasn't the old woman found dead, stabbed to the heart after you went away, and no one else to do the cruel, cowardly deed but just yourself?" exclaimed Peter.

"And might not the hag have preferred suicide to being hung, which she well knew was certain to be her fate the very next morning? I never laid a finger on her, I most positively swear, so help me——"

" Hush! oh, hush!" cried Mr. O'Grady, interrupting, and with a pathos in his voice impossible to render; "pause, wretched man, for Heaven's sake pause; do not dare to invoke the Almighty—before whom in one short hour you will surely stand—as a witness of one of the most infamous lies that ever sullied human lips. For, as the poor old woman told you, almost with her dying breath, so now I this night repeat to you, 'as sure as there is a God above us, YOUR HOUR HAS COME.'"

" But she was wrong," replied No. 1, laughing derisively, "and so maybe will you be too. Nothing has been, nor ever can be, proved against me, and therefore I appeal to your word of honour, not only to release me from my present position, which is fast becoming most painful to me, but also, in the absence of any evidence against me, to let me go free and unmolested back to Dublin."

" Had you not acted more like a wild beast than a human being, you would not have been bound at all," said Mr. O'Grady; "however," he continued, addressing Peter, "untie those cords, and take him off the table;" then, as Cassidy whispered something to him, Mr.

O'Grady went on, " Yes, put on the handcuffs ; we cannot trust him."

While this was being done, Mr. O'Grady, addressing one of the men at the door, said : " Ask Miss O'Connor to come here ; she is in the room opposite."

The next minute Lucy entered, followed by Rose and Mrs. Cassidy.

" I am sorry, Lucy," Mr. O'Grady said, " to be obliged to recur to a subject which is, I know, most painful to you.   Look well at that person now standing beside Peter, and tell me, have you ever seen him before ?"

Lucy did as she was told, but no sooner had she caught sight of the man than she started, turned pale, even to her very lips ; and had not Mrs. Cassidy offered her a chair, it is probable she would have fallen.

Covering her face with her hands, she began to sob violently.  She appeared to see the whole dreadful scene re-enacted before her, and would in a few minutes have become hysterical if Mrs. Cassidy had not administered a glass of brandy, and then, taking her by the hand, led her for a few moments into the open air.

" A pretty child, and acts well," said No. 1,

nonchalantly, as, kicking over a chair, he coolly seated himself beside the table. In a few moments Lucy returned, and, standing between Mr. and Mrs. Cassidy, said,—

"Once only before to-night have I really seen that man; but it is difficult to believe that I have not known him for years, so terribly does his image haunt me, associated as it is with the fearful deed I may almost say I saw him commit."

"Where and when did you see him?" asked Mr. O'Grady.

"In Kilmainham prison the night before Mrs. Kelly was sentenced to be hung," was the reply.

"At what time?" was the next question.

"As near as I can guess, between ten and eleven o'clock at night."

"And what took you to the prison at such an hour?"

"I had an order from the Government to admit me, and intended to have gone in the morning, but I was not well enough. In the evening, feeling better, and knowing if I wished to see Mrs. Kelly alive there was no time to lose, I presented my pass, and was admitted."

"Go on," said Mr. O'Grady, observing that she paused; "describe what happened in your own words."

"After my interview with Mrs. Kelly was over, the warder, who opened the door to announce that the half-hour was expired, at the same time admitted the man sitting there. Prompted, I believe, more by curiosity than anything else, I gave the warder a present to allow me to be an unseen spectator of the interview about to take place. He showed me into a small cell adjoining, and I could thus see and hear all that passed."

"I know how painful it must be to you," said Mr. O'Grady; "still, it is absolutely necessary that you should describe to us, as exactly as possible, what occurred in the cell that night."

"They—that is, Mrs. Kelly and that man— appeared to have been very intimate together when very young," Lucy went on hesitatingly and in a low voice, "and she seemed to be under the impression that he had married her; but he in the most brutal manner undeceived her, declared the marriage to be only a sham, and goaded her into such a fit of desperation that she at last, hardly knowing, I believe, what

she was about, flew at him like a tigress. A
terrible struggle ensued. I would have called
for assistance, but could see no one about.
Then there was a heavy fall, and when I again
looked into the cell, Mrs. Kelly lay at that
wretch's feet, stabbed to the heart. Oh! it was
too horrible! I see her now, as if lying there
before me. The poor old lady was only half
dressed; her neck and shoulders were bare,
and when I saw the handle of that fiend's knife
protruding from her bosom, the—the blood, and
the dreadful expression of her upturned face,
I tried to shut my eyes; but no, I couldn't. I
was fascinated. Some power stronger than my
own will held me spellbound, and I could no
more withdraw my eyes than I could fly, until
I suppose I swooned, for I remember nothing
more, until I found myself outside the prison,
supported by two warders."

"A very pretty story, and very nicely told,"
coolly remarked No. 1; "but even if for the
sake of argument we allow it to be true, it is
conclusively proved that I merely acted in
self-defence when attacked by this old hag,
who knowing she was doomed to die herself,
would, in her fury, I believe, have torn me

limb from limb before she let me leave the
cell."

"You have all heard," began Mr. O'Grady,
ignoring the last remark made by No. 1, and
addressing those there assembled, "that the
warders declare that when, on the night before
she was to be hung, the man sitting there entered Mrs. Kelly's cell, she was alive and well;
further, that no one else could have had access
to her during the night, and yet the next morning she is found murdered. You have heard
the account given by Miss O'Connor, who,
having been an eye-witness of what passed, has
now in a few words related to you how the
poor old woman came by her death; how the
ruffian, who had ruined the whole life of his
victim, and actually seemed to glory and revel
in his iniquitous acts, purposely worked her up
to such a state of desperation, that, excited
almost to madness, she flew at her destroyer;
then this villain, who doubtless only wanted an
excuse to make away with his victim, seized
the opportunity for which he was waiting, and
having drawn his long knife and stabbed her
to the heart, is now mean and cowardly enough
to ask us to believe that he only acted in self-

defence. I now ask you whether you credit this story, or do you not? Speak out, and do not be afraid to answer, for I want the opinion of all of you here present as to whether you consider this man to be guilty or not guilty of the death of Mrs. Kelly."

Without a moment's hesitation, every one there uttered the single word "*Guilty*," and No. 1, who seemed now for the first time to realize the position in which he was placed, sprang from his seat; but before he could speak, Mr. O'Grady continued, still addressing those there assembled: "Having unanimously pronounced this man guilty, what sentence, in your opinion, should be passed upon him?"

"*Death!*" was the reply; and the word was uttered in that firm, determined tone indicating that in the mind of the speaker the decision was irrevocable.

"You have had as fair and impartial a trial as in the present state of this unhappy country is possible," Mr. O'Grady now said, turning to No. 1, who however only shook his head, exclaiming, "No, no!"

"I am quite aware," Mr. O'Grady went on, "that if law and order were established in

Ireland, there are proper tribunals appointed to try cases of this sort, before whom you ought to be arraigned; but in the present state of things, it would be the merest farce to attempt to get any jury to convict the head of the National League of any crime whatever, more especially as witnesses literally by hundreds or by thousands, if necessary, would be only too proud to come forward and swear that on the night in question they had met you, and spoken to you too, in the Broadway of New York. You told us here just now that if, after a fair trial, you were found guilty of any crime, you would only too willingly submit to any punishment to which you might be condemned. You firmly believed when you uttered those words, you had been so cute that, though morally guilty of the murder of thousands of your wretched victims, the terror of the League was so great, not a living soul would dare give evidence against you. *You* may perhaps have some idea—no one else has or ever will have—of the real number of unhappy human beings who, for some trivial disobedience of your orders, have been sent into the presence of their Maker, unheard and unprepared—ay, and without a

minute's warning. I believe I should be quite
justified in doing unto you as you have done
unto them ; but no one shall ever accuse Terence O'Grady of being inhuman, and therefore
I am quite willing to listen to anything and
everything you may have to urge in mitigation
of the sentence, which, as commander-in-chief
of the Orangemen here assembled, I feel it to
be my sad duty to pronounce against you."

As Mr. O'Grady finished speaking, the most
intense silence reigned throughout the room ;
the unhappy prisoner, who still remained standing, was clasping the back of his chair, while
his face had become livid, as little by little
he recognised that the death to which he had
so often and so cruelly condemned others was
now staring him in the face.

" I—I—I—appeal—to—to—the—English,"
he gasped out ; but Mr. O'Grady interrupted
him, saying,—

" I ask you, have you anything to urge in
extenuation of the sentence I am about to pass
on you ?  If so, I am willing to hear it."

As, raising his head, the miserable man looked
from one to the other of those present, he read
his doom only too plainly in the stern coun-

tenances of all, Lucy, Rose, and Mrs. Cassidy
having already left the room ; then letting himself fall on his knees, he held up his hands
to Mr. O'Grady, as he exclaimed in the most
piteous, whining tones, " Oh, mercy ! mercy ! "

Mr. O'Grady shook his head as he said,—

"The same mercy which you showed to Mrs.
Kelly in prison, and to the hundreds of other
poor women who have been made widows and
childless at your command, will I now mete out
to you.   It is, *I* feel and know, an awful thing
that I should take on myself to say the word
which will hurry an erring and sinful man into
the presence of his Maker, and in any other
case than this I almost doubt if I dare arrogate
to myself such a fearful responsibility ; but as
I am satisfied that as long as you are permitted
to live, there is no hope of any rest, peace,
or quietness for our unhappy country, so, in
Ireland's name and for her sake, I do not hesitate to tell you to prepare for death, for in one
short hour from this present time you will have
left this world for ever, and have gone to meet
that God whom, during your whole life, you
have dared to openly outrage and defy."

# CHAPTER XXXV.

## " GOD ALONE KNOWS."

THREE years have passed. Ireland has again been incorporated with the United Kingdom, and peace and quietness have reigned throughout the land. English capital, which alone can help Ireland to prosperity, has begun slowly to flow into the country; and if such a state of things could only continue, there might be some hope for the future, more especially as America has altogether ceased to supply the needful. The lesson she received in the loss of the four steamers, with the whole of their vile crew, effectually cured her of any further desire to interfere in Irish affairs; for so justly exasperated was the population of Dublin at the cruelties to which it had been subjected, that the inhabitants insisted on the heaviest penalty the law could inflict being meted out to the few who had been successful in swim-

ming ashore when the steamers were disabled;
while the English ironclad never approached
within a mile of either vessel, so fearful was
her captain of a trap being laid for him, and
that he and all his men would be blown to
pieces by some infernal dynamite bomb, which,
as likely as not, would be thrown on board;
for, as he himself justly remarked to his commander, it would be a sin to risk the lives of
good honest sailors to aid such utter ruffians
and blackguards as were those on board the
American vessels, one of which blew up
within an hour of her engines stopping work—
whether from dynamite or her boilers bursting
no one knew, while the other foundered, many
of her crew being saved in the boats; but *to*
the last they kept the American flag flying,
whether from sheer dogged determination not
to give in, or from forgetfulness, who shall say?

Of the other two, nothing was ever heard.
They got clear away from the English ironclads who chased them; but as they never
arrived in America, it is supposed they must
have foundered in mid-ocean; and considering
the little inquiry that was ever made as to
their fate, it seems probable that no one much

regretted their loss, but were glad to be so easily and quickly rid of so worthless and troublesome a gang.

As time, the healer of all wounds, passed, the Irish began to forget the miserable fiasco they had made a few years before in trying to govern themselves, and once more the League seemed likely to spring into life again. But as it happened, the English Government of the day was a strong one, and put its foot down at once on the agitation ; so for some time longer all was peace and tranquillity ; but the Irish have always known how to wait, and the instant the opportunity came, to take advantage of it. A general election was imminent ; quietly but surely the electors were tampered with, and persuaded that the English were treating them as a conquered race, and oppressing them mightily. Grievances were invented where none existed, the consequences being that the elections returned to the old groove, and members were returned pledged to obstruct the Government, and once more clamour for Repeal.

Such was the news brought by the newspapers received by the last English mail in

Melbourne, and which was being discussed by Terence O'Grady (or, as he was now always called, Mr. French) and John Cassidy, at the hospitable board of the latter, with whom Mr. French had been now staying for the last four months. Immediately on his marriage with Rose, which took place three months after the English once more resumed possession of Ireland, Mr. French determined to fulfil the darling wish of his heart and see the world. They started on the evening of the day on which they were married, and had been absent for nearly three years, having come to Australia, *via* Ceylon and India, and were now on the eve of returning *via* San Francisco and New York.

"The old agitation is evidently again beginning in our ill-fated country," remarked Mr. French to Cassidy, as he laid down *The Times*, which he had been reading for the last half-hour. "God help our unhappy Ireland, for no one else can. It is really too sad and too unfortunate that these elections should have gone so terribly against the Government, for so sure as there is a change, the other side will never cease till they have persuaded the people to agitate, and so undo the little good which has certainly been effected, and the result of which was already apparent in the fact that a few English capitalists were, to my certain knowledge, beginning to invest money in the country ; but now, of course, all such luck is at an end, and our last chance gone, for, as you know, I have always affirmed, and shall never change my opinion, that the sole hope for Ireland is precisely that very introduction of capital which is always coming, but somehow never comes."

"When crossing the Channel, the day before I had the misfortune to meet a certain Terence O'Grady," Cassidy replied, laughing, " I made the acquaintance on board the steamer of a queer fish (who, by the bye, declared you were a great friend of his, Terence), who went by the name of 'Toby,' and declared himself to be a horse-dealer by profession. It was he who first gave me some idea of the state of affairs in Ireland, which I confess I then thought he must have exaggerated, but which I found afterwards to be only too true. In the course of our conversation, he, in his odd, jerky way, asked me if I had ever read 'Froude.' I replied No, and he at once said I ought certainly to procure and study it.

"From that day to this I never thought more about the matter, till I happened to come across the book at an auction here the other day, when, acting on Toby's suggestion, I bought the copy, and am just finishing it. It is worth your while to read those few lines, and tell me how far you agree with the author in his opinion."

Taking the book which Cassidy offered to him, Mr. French read aloud as follows :—

"Be it so. Then let Ireland be free. She is miserable, because she is unruled. We might rule her, but we will not, lest our arrangements at home might be interfered with. We cannot keep a people chained to us to be perennially wretched, because it is inconvenient to us to keep order among them. In an independent Ireland, the ablest and strongest would come to the front, and the baser elements be crushed."

Mr. French paused a moment as if considering ; then he said, " ' Ablest ! ' where are they to be found ? ' strongest ! ' yes, but for evil, not for good ; nor can ' the baser elements be crushed,' for if, as I suppose, it is the people who are referred to, is it not they who must elect their governors? Have they not been taught to prefer anarchy to being governed at all? and is it then likely they will ever return any representatives who are able and strong enough to form a good firm government, which will not only make laws, but also insist on their being respected and obeyed?"

Turning again to the book, Mr. French continued: "The state of things which would ensue might not be satisfactory to us, but at least there would be no longer the inversion of the natural order which is maintained by the English connection and the compelled slavery of education and intelligence to the numerical majority. This, too, is called impossible; yet, if we will neither rule Ireland nor allow the Irish to rule themselves, nature and fact may tell us, that, whether we will or no, an experiment which has lasted for seven hundred years shall be tried no longer. Between the two impossibilities, we may be obliged to choose if Ireland is to cease to be our reproach, and the Irish race a danger and a torment to every country to which they emigrate."

Again Mr. French paused to consider, then he remarked: "There is one fact of which your friend Mr. Froude seems altogether to have lost sight, and that is, when the day comes, as come it will, when England will be again at war with three-fourths, if not the whole of Europe (for does not history invariably repeat itself?), the situation under such circumstances is utterly ignored. Endeavour, if you can, to realize the position in which England would find herself with Ireland independent, not with a firm, strong Government able to hold its own against all-comers, but poor, weak, and miserable (for without money, how could the dear ould country be anything else?), a thorn in her side, which England must, in her own self-defence, instantly seize and hold at all costs; for if she does not, France or Russia will, and then the knell of England's power will indeed have sounded, and the finest, freest, most enlightened Government the world ever saw, or ever will see, will disappear for ever."

"I should like to hear the opinion of the G. O. M. as to England's position in such an emergency," said Cassidy.

"Oh, John, John! why will you be always holding up a red rag to a bull?" asked Mr. O'Grady.

"Because I think the bull likes sometimes to be given the opportunity to show what he is made of," replied Cassidy, with a laugh.

"In other words, you want to draw me out, to hear me repeat for the hundredth time my conviction that the G. O. M.'s one ambition was that his name should be handed down to posterity as the saviour of Ireland; and had he only known how to take advantage of the opportunity offered to him, there can be no doubt such would have been the case."

"How do you account for his lamentable failure?" asked Cassidy.

"It is not very difficult to do that," was the reply; "allowing—but only for the sake of argument—that he was correct in his assertion that the tenants were babies, the dear darlings, whom it was necessary that the law should intervene to protect from the oppression of the landlords, the G. O. M. decided that, by fair means or foul, these latter must be got rid of; but as he had not the courage to do this off-hand, his subtle mind invented the system of dual ownership, knowing full well it could never work, and only end in one way—namely, sooner or later, the extinction of the unhappy landlords. Now let us suppose that, having once made up his mind that, in consequence of the manner in which, as he declared, the land-lords ill-treated the tenants, it was absolutely necessary to interfere, but before moving in the matter, as a preliminary step, he had care-fully studied the *nature* and *character* of our tenant class, he would, I cannot help thinking, have soon convinced himself that, search the world through, it would be impossible to find a race more thoroughly unfitted to raise the dear old country to that state of prosperity and that high position which we must all desire to see her occupy."

"Go on," said Cassidy, observing Mr. O'Grady pause. "What would you have him do?"

"Can you not guess? Exactly the reverse of what he did do: make it worth the tenants' while to emigrate to a country where, in a few years, they would have been, not only con-tented, but well-to-do and happy; lay the land in Ireland down in grass, and let it out in large grazing farms, and in a very few years prosperity would have appeared everywhere, the League and all such abominations would have died a natural death, and the country would have had that rest for which she panted, but which now seems farther off than ever. It was a rare chance gone, never to return; but had he only seized it, how appropriately would he have been named the G. O. M.! And a few years hence, what blessings would have been showered on his head by high and low, rich and poor, whereas now——"

"Hold!" cried Cassidy, laughing, "not another word; you forget that he is still the people's idol."

Mr. French did as he was told, but muttered something strangely like a very, VERY big D. Whatever it was, it instantly caught Rosy's quick ear, as she at that moment entered the room. Running over to her husband, she placed her pretty little hand over his mouth, saying, as she did so,—

" How dare you, Terence! You know I don't allow you to use those naughty words. Mr. Cassidy, I believe it's your fault; what were you talking about ? "

"Ireland, and the G. O. M.," replied the latter, much amused.

"Oh, in that case it's different," Rosy continued. "Terence, you have my full permission to say anything you like; it can't well be too strong; only, you must let *me* listen."

With a smile Mr. French closed the book, and handed it back to Cassidy, who, without taking it, said, "Turn back a page, Terence, and see what Froude says there." Mr. French did so, and read aloud,—

"Were England even now at this eleventh hour to say that she recognised the state of Ireland to be a disgrace to her; that she would pass no hurried measure at the dictation of incendiaries, but that deliberately and with all her energies she would examine the causes of her failure and find some remedy for it; that meanwhile she must be free from political pressure; that the constitution would be suspended, and that the three Southern provinces would for half a century be governed by the Crown, the committee of the Land League are well aware that, without a shot being fired in the field, their functions would be at an end. Quiet people would recover confidence, and the law its authority; and if in that golden period of respite a better order of things could be introduced, which would know no difference between rich and poor, but would be just to all, enterprise would take heart again and capital flow into the soil, and the shameful past would be forgotten like a black dream. The curse which has blasted Ireland is anarchy. Not the Church, not the landlords—though Church and landlords have both needed mending—but the 'Blatant Beast' which all brave men hate and all cowards tremble at."

"Amen!" exclaimed Mr. French, "and Amen! There I thoroughly agree with Mr. Froude; and to stamp out the beast, we need the iron hand and velvet glove of a Bismarck. Would to God we had one!"

"Or a Terence O'Grady," said Cassidy; but Mr. French shook his head as he replied,—

"No! even if I had the ambition—which I have not—the three Southern provinces would *never* either forget or forgive the past, nor would they ever believe that they would get either justice or fair play from a Northerner."

"I believe you are right," said Cassidy. "Then what is to be done?"

"God alone knows—I am sure I don't; but I suppose, like Mr. Micawber, we must only wait for something to turn up."

THE END.

Butler & Tanner, The Selwood Printing Works, Frome, and London.

CPSIA information can be obtained at www.ICGtesting.com
Printed in the USA
BVOW07s1332170515

400560BV00019B/349/P